M. + J. Walzer
December 1989
Princeton

Wisdom  and the Hebrew Epic

Chicago Studies in the History of Judaism
Edited by.
Jacob Neusner

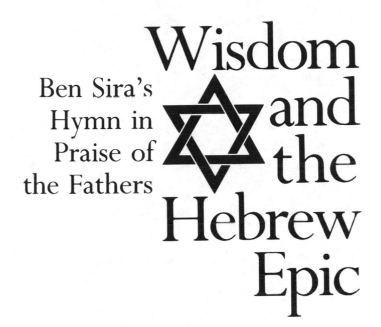

Wisdom and the Hebrew Epic

Ben Sira's
Hymn in
Praise of
the Fathers

Burton L. Mack

The University of Chicago Press
Chicago and London

BURTON L. MACK is professor of New Testament in the School of
Theology, Institute for Antiquity and Christianity, Claremont Grad-
uate School.

The University of Chicago Press, Chicago 60637
The University of Chicago Press, Ltd., London
© 1985 by The University of Chicago
All rights reserved. Published 1985
Printed in the United States of America

94 93 92 91 90 89 88 87 86 85   54321

Library of Congress Cataloging-in-Publication Data

Mack, Burton L.
    Wisdom and the Hebrew epic.

    (Chicago studies in the history of Judaism)
    Bibliography: p.
    Includes index.
    1. Bible.   O.T.   Apocrypha.   Ecclesiasticus XLIV-L–
Criticism, interpretation, etc.   I. Title.   II. Series.
BS1765.2.M32   1985   229'.406   85-8564
ISBN 0-226-50049-7

To JONATHAN Z. SMITH,
whose imaginative discourse
makes thinking about religion
possible

I will again make instruction
shine like the dawn.

Sirach 24:32

I will hide no secret from you.

Wisdom 6:22

Contents

Tables

Preface

Ben Sira's hymn landed on my desk four years ago and arrested my attention in the course of a general reading of Hellenistic-Jewish literature. I had been looking for texts to chart that intersection of cultures, Jewish and Hellenic, within which a remarkable reflection on human nature and social experience had been generated. Now I find myself astonished at the scholarly labors Ben Sira's poem has educed and sustained and at my findings. I had thought to move quickly, from this text to others, through a cultural epoch of a history of ideas. But the text did not yield until I gave it its rightful position at the center of the intersection I sought to understand. As all the other texts piled up around it on my desk, texts that I discovered formed the framework of Ben Sira's intellectual world, his hymn took its place upon another desk as well—his own.

I've imagined his study a bit more tidy than mine, but filled nonetheless with all those things befitting a scholar's workshop. That I hadn't expected. I had wanted to bridge the difference of two thousand years by studied reconstructions of what we've come to call history. But history turned to Once upon a time, Ben Sira's time. And there, working with his own texts, tracing out the lines from one to the other in quest of that sense of things he called wisdom, was a scholar I could recognize as someone like myself. I had known, of course, of his achievements as a poet—that his hymn was on my desk, having come so long a way, was proof enough. But that he was a scholar also, and that he knew himself to be one—thus I came to see the social situation of his composition—gave me courage to proceed with yet another round of readings of his text. This time the heroes of his hymn were not the only human figures in my view. It was now Ben Sira with whom I was engaged. I sought to understand how he had managed such a reading of his texts and times, with what purpose he wrote, and for whom.

I discovered something of what I think was his way with words, his inventions, and his achievement. Hence this book. I wouldn't call it a book of wisdom, to be sure, and there the difference between Ben Sira's work and mine comes clear. But it would not do to let that difference keep one from pondering the similarities. Ben Sira claimed more for his poem than I do for my study—mainly because he wrote as a scholar-the-ologian and I write merely as a scholar of human history—but both of us started with our several sets of texts and, aided by imagination, sought the intersection of their lines in some comprehensive view. Thus my study also is a scholarly in-vention, although not one Ben Sira himself might have recog-nized. That is because my reading of his poem takes it up into the imaginative discourse about history, literature, and religion appropriate to the modern academy.

It is Jonathan Z. Smith who has taught me how important it is to acknowledge the discourse of the academy as a product of the scholarly imagination. It is also Smith who has made me aware that the categories we use for understanding religious phenomena need to be tested by rigorous investigation of texts in specific social-historical contexts. This is especially so in the case of texts from other times and cultures, lest we miss the "social labor" of the peculiar form of "meditation" on a soci-ety's patterns of practice that religion is. I've tried to see Ben Sira's powerful poem, a mythic reading of his own cultural history, as such a meditation on his social system. I trust my reading has been rigorous enough, even though imaginative, and that it will enhance appreciation for Ben Sira's own kind of inventive labor as well.

That Jacob Neusner has accepted my study for publication in this series is reward indeed. His own work has exemplified time and time again the value of a critical way with texts for Jewish history. He has called regularly for an investigation of texts that will open them out upon their place in history and let us see their function within specific social settings. That he has judged my work on Sirach to be a contribution to this program is very gratifying, and I wish to express my thanks to him.

To the Institute for Antiquity and Christianity, where my studies were pursued and my work supported, I also wish to say thank you. I am indebted to David Seeley for a penetrating reading of the manuscript, and Char Matejovsky and Debbie DeGoyer, masters of the magical machines, will not be forgotten for their labors.

Introduction

This book is about a remark-
able poem written by a Jewish priest in Jerusalem in 180 B.C.E.
The poem traces the illustrious leaders of Israel's history, beginning with Noah and ending with the high priest Simon, and
it opens with the author's announcement "I will now sing
their praise." Heroes and history joined in this way set this
text apart. It is the earliest poem on record in which figures of
Israel's epic are presented as the sole subject of a literary composition expressly to be eulogized. It is found tucked away in a
most unlikely place—a book of ethical instruction in the mode
of Hebrew wisdom. Since the older traditions of Hebrew
wisdom do not betray an interest in Israel's epic history, the
context is surprising. Nor do the earlier wisdom texts prepare
us for a reading of an epic history that comes to a climax in
praise of a high priest offering sacrifice on a high holy day.
That is because, if the conventional scholarly consensus is
right, most Hebrew wisdom was either uninterested in or critical of the cult. So the poem is a most interesting text, and its
presence in a wisdom book is quite unexpected. How to account for its being there, how to read it with understanding,

and how to assess the importance of its achievement are the goals of this investigation.

The poem is known as the "Hymn in Praise of the Fathers." It has long been recognized by scholars as an important text, for it reflects a moment in Jewish history when significant cultural changes were taking place. The author wrote at the crucial moment of transition from Ptolemaic to Seleucid hegemony of Palestine, and just before the shattering events of 167 B.C.E. that unleashed the troubled history of the Maccabean revolts. Temple and Torah, high priests and kings—these were the centers around which conflicts raged. Violence attended the repeated attempts to take, defend, and exercise the powers residing in the political and religious institutions. But the battle lines shifted in keeping with ideological positions, and for these the issue was one of authority: Torah on the one hand as code, constitution, tradition, or epic history; *paideia* on the other as the spirit of Hellenic culture, values, and social organization. The suspicion has always been that Ben Sira's hymn in praise of the fathers was composed by an author fully aware of his world and sensitive to this emerging conflict.

There is, in fact, a great deal known about Ben Sira.[1] His book of wisdom is a precious document from a period that has left us little other written legacy. It has been pored over repeatedly by scholars seeking a reconstruction of this period of history. In the course of these readings, as much has been learned about Ben Sira and his book as has been learned from them about their times. The author's political preferences have been discerned, his attitude toward Second Temple institutions determined, and his activity as a schoolmaster made plausible. Most have regarded Ben Sira as a conservative, loyal to Torah and Temple, cautious about Hellenism and about Cynical views of Jewish piety and wisdom. But the picture is more complex than that, for the marks of *paideia* upon his book are also very clear. His learning was broad, and his texts were many. His intellectual and literary accomplishments reveal a man of great cosmopolitan erudition. His book is a crossroads of the cultural traditions competing for his times.

Ben Sira's poem about the fathers belongs to his turbulent

milieu, but the specific way in which it relates to it has been very difficult to understand. Even its place in its narrower literary context, its function within Ben Sira's book of wisdom, has never been accounted for. If the hymn could be shown to cohere, to sustain essential lines of contact with Ben Sira's book and its explicit concerns, a most interesting configuration of ideas would result—heroes and history; history and wisdom; wisdom and Torah; Torah and Temple; Temple and Hellenism—just that bewildering mix of ideas, traditions, and institutional ideologies that determined the times. If it would be possible to place this text amid these many "texts," to see it open out onto its complex social world, then read it as a singular moment of reflection upon and comprehension of its author's time—that would be to understand it.

It is a curiosity of the scholarly tradition that such little effort has been devoted to solving the problems of the hymn. Only one monograph, three articles, and one dissertation that have addressed the text directly are known to me.[2] Several of the recent monographs on Sirach as a whole have avoided any study of the hymn at all.[3] The reasons, perhaps, are the difficulties one encounters when approaching the text with critical questions. The literary critic is confronted with an unfamiliar genre and hardly knows how to begin. The historian sees only a hymn to the pious and finds it impossible to discern any relation to types of piety actually in evidence for the period. Clearly we have a difficult text on our hands.

The poem consists of a proem, followed by a long series of poetic units, each devoted to one of the heroes. These units are of uneven length, and they are juxtaposed, for the most part, without transitional statements. One has the impression merely of a collection of little poems, a list or catalog of Israel's leaders. The question is whether the collection as a whole shows any principle of selection or of structure at all, beyond that of a series. If history is being recast, reread, what holds it together? What might be the poem's purpose in reading that history as a series of illustrious leaders? The call to praise these heroes is explicit enough. But the very notion of singing praises to the human figures of Israel's history strikes one as strange, given the usual assumptions about Jewish reluctance to reify the human creature. Even if one were to bracket that consideration for a moment, however, the reasons for praise would be unclear. One seeks in vain the customary marks of great human achievement in these men, for instance. The only models available for comparison from Ben Sira's time are given with the Greek encomiastic literature. Scholars have always sensed some vague relationship in this regard. But the closer the reading of the hymn, the more difficult it is to determine from such a comparison exactly what it is about these men that is deemed worthy of fame and glory. It is hardly the Hellenic *aretē*.

That the last hero in line is Simon seems to provide some clues. The history is read right into Ben Sira's present, and the theme of glory seems to reach an appropriate climax there. But this said, the question of the text's intention bursts the bounds of understanding once again. Although the hymn does appear to intend some signification of Ben Sira's own religious-social setting, what that significance might be is extremely hard to tell. By whom would the hymn have been read, and on what occasions? Would it have been effective, and by what imaginative means? These are the questions raised by the text for the critical scholar. They have seldom been asked, much less resolved.

I decided to tackle this text because I thought it important. I suspected that it stood near the beginning of what was to become an intense preoccupation with the notion of the special man in all the forms of Judaism entering the Greco-Roman period. I was intrigued by the possibility that this preoccupation might have been influenced by Hellenistic anthropology and its heroic ideals. That the hymn was written by a Jewish sage, versed in the traditions of wisdom, also teased my fancy. Jewish wisdom and Greek *paideia* had long been scholarly concerns of mine. To explore a meeting of these two influential cultures in a text dated from the middle of the Hellenistic age appeared to be an attractive task. If the hymn could be explained by placement in this cultural climate, a bit of history might be better understood.

I approached the text as a scholar trained in the traditions of biblical criticism, dissatisfied, however, with the limited horizons of understanding customary to this field. It was, I thought, the inadequacy of traditional biblical criticism in general to read a text specifically in relation to its contigent, complex social context that accounted for its failure in the case of Ben Sira's hymn. What appeared to be needed was a larger frame of reference to help with the phrasing of questions. This I discovered to be in the making in recent discourse in the academy. There it has begun to be thought that in order to understand a text, it must be seen as part of a larger system of signs. The insight comes from the early scholars of structural linguistics, of course. But it now pervades studies across the range of the humanities and human sciences seeking relations among the several fields. This discourse is learning to treat religion and culture, literature and society, as complex, interrelated systems of signs. Regarding them as "texts," the scholarly endeavor is to "read" them together, "translating" from system to system, and so come to understand their "meaning." It is quite true that academic study along these lines has not succeeded in reducing the insight to a workable theory of social formation. There is no comprehensive model for the integration of, say, religion and society as semiotic systems. Nor is there an adequate general theory of the social function of literature. But the basic insight about how signs take their meaning in relation to other signs in a system of signs has effected significant advance. The goal is a more comprehensive understanding of the human cultural enterprise.

Intrigued by this discourse, I thought to test its basic insight by an exegesis of a single text. The results have been gratifying, and they are presented here. But the problems of approach, both to the reading of the text and to the writing of the study, have been horrendous. A comprehensive reading of the text could not be done in a single set of operations. Instead, a series of explorations had to be undertaken, each with a specific set of intertextual relationships in view. The text's own structure or system of signs had to be discovered. This composition then was set in relation to (1) its several Jewish precursor texts; (2)

its several Hellenistic precursor texts; (3) the systems of signs called wisdom and *paideia*, taken both separately and together, systems that shaped the hymn's intellectual texture; (4) the social structure of Second Temple Judaism that it mirrored and addressed; and (5) the text of Ben Sira's book of wisdom, which yielded the clue to the hymn's mythic rationale. Each exploration had to follow the traditional norms of responsible scholarship to begin with, and the old hermeneutical circle worked its way to constrain and correct the readings by turn. But each of the individual studies in the text's relation to other texts also demanded its own mid-course correctives to the study as a whole. So the circles of reflection were extremely difficult to control. This was so even though the several studies were centered on a single text.

My thesis is that the poem does sustain relations with all of these other "texts," and that these relations can be demonstrated. The poem takes its place creatively and intentionally, deriving its meaning in relation to its social world and its cultural milieu. That meaning is available to us also, to the extent that we become imaginative readers of those other texts as well. Specifically, the poem demonstrates marvelous mastery of patterned poetic description of the individual figures, a careful balancing of hero-types to achieve a unified structure for the whole, and a most skillful development of plot, which works with themes and hero sequences to achieve a significant and celebrative climax. The discovery of the author's study desk, of his use and abuse of precursors, and of his readers at their reading did not destroy the power and beauty of the hymn, but its rhetoricity was disclosed. It is a charter text, a mythic etiology of Second Temple Judaism centered in the covenants that undergird the priesthood. It is Ben Sira's fantasy, of course, how he wanted to see the world, with the Temple at its center, a world intended by God, actualized in Israel's history forever more. It is also a "meditation," to use a term that Jonathan Z. Smith has pressed into service for myth and ritual studies, on the incongruity Ben Sira saw between the vision of Israel given with its scriptural traditions and the actualities of its social institutions and history of his own time.

How to transcribe this study has been my subsequent dilemma. The circles of relationships hardly allow for a single point of departure. So I've chosen to ask the reader to enter in naively, beginning with some simple observations on the text. I've tried to arrange a sequence of demonstrations that follow somewhat the several studies on the text's relation to other texts. But these are perspectives, and they must pile up and be taken finally together if one wants a comprehensive view. In order to lead the reader along, I've tried to recapture the inductive mood and let the discoveries come one by one. The final chapter yields the clue that solves the mystery and makes it possible to see how it all hangs together. Reflections on the investigative process are given at the beginnings of chapters and major sections. These may serve as guides to the reader, glances at the treasure map that one should keep in mind. I hope the ruse of taking the way of discovery sustains the appropriate anticipation through to the end. I've found it to be a rewarding study, full of surprises. I share it with the reader with a set of anticipations of my own.

But before we begin, two scholarly acknowledgments are due. The first has to do with the history of scholarship on Sirach in general. I am deeply indebted to it, and assume its labors at every turn. I've not been content with any notion of mine about the text except after debate with the traditional scholarly rubrics and archives. In the course of this scholarship, many extremely helpful observations have been made about the hymn in praise of the fathers. Though most have occurred as asides within the context of other studies, I've learned from them all and found most to be helpful, many borne out by my own analyses. Thus the hymn has been seen as a novel rewriting of Israel's history that moves beyond precursor texts, emphasizes the covenants, and reflects cultic interests, on the one hand; and on the other, it has frequently been compared with the Greco-Roman genre *De viris illustribus*.[4] My own work shows these observations to be correct, and I have acknowledged specific indebtedness in notes along the way.

The other recognition appropriate here has to do with the

state of the text. Readers may be aware of the exceedingly complex problem of establishing a Hebrew text for Sirach. They may also know about its early translation into Greek by Ben Sira's grandson and the debate about the value of the Greek texts extant for reconstructing the Hebrew texts we have.[5] The manuscript traditions are messy, an indication that Sirach was frequently appropriated in the immediately subsequent centuries. The labor required to establish the texts is a cause for deep appreciation. The Greek is now available in the Göttingen Septuagint edited by Joseph Ziegler, and a most convenient edition of this text parallel with the Hebrew texts, together with the Syriac and Latin versions on the page, has been published by Francesco Vattioni. I have used Vattioni for my work. Reference to the Hebrew text, however, has been made only in exceptional cases, and then mostly in the notes in regard to certain terms. I have supplied pointing and followed the code for transliteration suggested by the Society of Biblical Literature. For the English translations appearing in the study I have followed, for the most part, that of Box and Oesterley because of its literal quality.

A bibliography of works consulted is provided. A few exegetical demonstrations thought to be tedious within the narrative discourse of the study, but important for readers who may wish to follow the course of my judgments, are given in Appendices.

Part 1

Literary Analysis: Heroes and History

The Profile of 1
the Hero

The glorious figures of Israel's history are to be praised. So begins the hymn.

> Let *me* now hymn the praises of men of *piety,*
> Of our fathers in their generations.
> No little *glory* did the Most High allot them,
> And they were great from the days of old.
> (44:1–2; emphasis mine)

Piety (*ḥesed*) and glory (*kābôd*) have been joined and are said to reside in the singular figures about to be described. These men are well known—"our fathers in their generations" whose greatness has been recognized from times immemorial until the present day. The poetry is strong, and the reader is swept up at first into the mood created by the subtle call to join the author in singing their praises.

This may be the reason for the shifts that occur in the Greek translation. Ben Sira's grandson caught the mood and phrased it for Greek ears to hear:

> Let *us* now sing the praises of *glorious* men,
> Even our fathers by generation;

11

The Lord established much glory,
  His majesty from ever.
                (emphasis mine)

The problem of praising piety is solved by erasure. But the aura of glory cannot be resisted. The translator joins in, taking his place in the first person plural and laying implicit claim to having seen and sung, read and rewritten, the powerful poem. But now the problem is the glory itself. The second distich makes it clear that the majesty in view is really the Lord's.

Troubled apparently about just these things—piety and glory, glorious men and the glory of the Lord—the translators of the New English Bible proceeded with more caution, seeking some compromise between the Hebrew and the Greek. But the notion of the hero could not be given up.

Let us now sing the praises of famous men,
  The *heroes* of our nation's history,
Through whom the Lord established *his* renown,
  And revealed his majesty in each succeeding age.
                (emphasis mine)

Hasidim, fathers, great ones, glorious ones, heroes—the designations multiply even as attempts are made to make more precise what it is about these men that one is called upon to see. What shall we call them? To ask the question is to admit that we do not know. We have no name, no definition, mainly because this special kind of hero appears in Ben Sira's hymn for the very first time. It is a new creation, imagined by a clear poetic vision and presented to the world as a study of the human face in Israel's history. This image is proposed as complement or substitute for all that's gone before—the ways in which the Jews have storied their epic figures and the ways in which the Greeks have delineated their anthropological ideals. As new configurations taking their place amid competing profiles, Ben Sira's great men have no common name. If we want to know what makes them great according to Ben Sira, we need to find a way to see them clearly, looking through his eyes. How are they like, how different, from other alternative views, either of the figures of the Hebrew epic or of the Greek ideal types? Is there a new profile of greatness? Is there a pattern of characterization that Ben Sira has employed to recast all of these figures from Israel's epic history for his hymn of praise? That is the question to be addressed in this first chapter of our study.

APPROACHING THE TEXT

The Literary Context

There are several ways one might imagine approaching our text in order to ask what it is that makes its epic figures great and worthy of praise. One way would be to read it in its literary context as the final section of Ben Sira's book of wisdom. This would have the advantage of coming to the text as the author intended his readers to do. The reader would already have been informed about piety, about the Lord's glory, and about Ben Sira's own summary of the types of great men to be praised. Immediately preceding the hymn there is a strong poem in praise of the Lord's creation. It begins with the announcement "Now I will call to mind the works of the Lord" (42:15). It ends with the affirmation "The Lord has made everything, and has given wisdom to the hasidim (43:33). Then follows the proem to the hymn (44:1–15), which continues the earlier theme of the glory of the Lord but shifts the locus of its manifestation from creation to history. Now the heroes are in view, and the proem sings about their many accomplishments, their rewards, and their glorious memory. This prepares the reader for the long poem to follow, which takes up each hero in turn by name and concludes with the festive description of Simon officiating at the temple on the Day of Atonement (44:16–50:24).

Approaching the text in this way, that is, by reading it in its literary context, it is difficult to determine exactly at what point one has entered into the sphere of the poem's influence. The notion of glory is firmly in place from 42:16 on, but it is being imagined there in the orders of the created world. The not-so-slight problem of shifting one's focus to the arena of

human history without losing sight of that glory is addressed in
44:2 ("No little glory did the Most High allot them") and
worked out in the generalizing descriptions of the proem that
follow. It is there the themes of wisdom, power, and heroic
exploits are introduced. These moves appear to be extremely
important if the reader of the roster of the illustrious ones is
not to misunderstand.

The literary linkage of the text with the preceding hymn to
creation does help with the problem of where in the world
"glory" is to be seen and how it is to be understood. Whether
in creation or in history, it is the Lord's glory that is manifest.
One might begin an investigation with this observation, to be
sure, for the pattern of depicting divine wisdom as manifest
first in creation, then in history, occurs repeatedly throughout
the book and could conceivably be brought to bear upon the
question of how wisdom and glory are to be attributed to the
great men praised in the hymn.[1] But this essentially theological
affirmation, though very important as a clue to Ben Sira's
larger vision of the order of things, is simply inadequate for
getting started. It alerts us to the need to keep track of the
moments in the descriptions of these men that are called
glorious moments, but it cannot help us understand why those
moments are called glorious to begin with. Some profile of
description is needed to give the proper perspective.

Many scholars therefore have started with the proem (44:1–
15). It is there that the author lists the kinds of illustrious men
he has in mind. But even a cursory reading of the proem in
relation to the poem that follows quickly stumbles upon certain incompatibilities between the two accounts.[2] The wisdom
of the illustrious ones, for instance, is highlighted in the proem, but it plays almost no role at all in the succeeding characterizations. The poem includes priests among the illustrious
ones and emphasizes their glory. But the proem does not mention priests at all in its roster of hero-types. If one begins with
the proem, then, the questions one is apt to ask of the poem
will be determined by discrepancies like these. The proem es-
tablishes the pattern of characterization, and one will seek to
find it reflected in the poem. Scholars who have pursued this

line of inquiry have succeeded only in demonstrating how much the two texts must be stretched in order to achieve the fit. So we need to find some other way to begin. We shall come back to the problems of glory and wisdom, creation and history, proem and poem later on.

The Midrashic Comparison

A second approach commends itself as soon as it is seen that the poem draws upon other texts. Comparison perhaps could highlight the differences between these texts, and in the differences the new could be seen. Isn't the poem a midrash on the epic history? Taking up the proem at 44:16, one senses immediately that a mode of composition is in play quite different from the wisdom poetry that precedes it. The poetry of the hymn is still strong and follows the usual style of parallelism.[3] It may even be considered stronger than much of the preceding poetry, if one marks the tensions of the heightened style and pungent description. But the overriding impression is that one is in the presence of scriptural language.[4] Another text, the text of the epic history, is being evoked purposefully even as the poem proceeds on its way, carrying the reader along by its own powerful imagery.

The sense that one is recalling biblical episodes is both illusory and real. It is real because the statements that are made about the heroes are traceable to scriptural loci. It is illusory, however, because the several individual statements used to paint the picture of a hero have been selected from various scriptural loci and frequently combine disparate textual accounts. Thus the reader is actually caught in the space between two texts, the old and the new. What is achieved is a new characterization. The procedure is a kind of proto-midrash, a midrash that anthologizes both in the sense of collecting and combining disparate descriptive details and in the sense of using the language of the scriptural accounts anthologically in the new poetic vision. The precursor text that is being evoked is quite complex and may be as vast as the entire corpus of Jewish literature available to the author. That "text" would be difficult to control in any comparative study.

Nevertheless, a kind of comparison may eventually be possible and should be attempted. Selection has taken place, and in that process, the author has revealed his interest in only certain details. Were it possible to mark that interest, arrange those details, the rationale for selection might come into view. But to be certain about it, a comparison of the texts can proceed only by degrees. We cannot be certain of the precursor text or texts until we've analyzed the poem and traced the relationships. Even then, supposing there are several texts, several Jewish histories and the suspicion of Hellenic models as well, the comparative process would have to begin precisely with the shape of the poem, and not the other way around. That Ben Sira knew the five books of Moses, the histories, and the prophets in some arrangement is clear from the commentaries and mongraphs that have cited the many parallels.[5] It has been assumed that this arrangement was already very close to the Tannach as we have it, and some very general comparative observations have been allowed to help with early judgments about the structure of the poem. But the real work of comparing the poem with its precursor texts can only come after it has been determined what it is about the poem that calls for comparison in the first place.

The Literary Structure

This leaves us alone with the text. It consists of a series of poem units, in most of which a single figure is described. The question is whether this series is more than a list, and whether the individual units betray any pattern of characterization. It would be helpful to know whether the poem was composed with any plan in mind, and whether it is possible to tell wherein the greatness of the heroes lay for the author. There are two ways to proceed.

One would be to trace out the sequences from beginning to end, looking for indications of a movement or plot within which units are interconnected, themes developed, and so forth. This approach would test the unity of the composition, its coherence, and its overall structure. Although I will argue that such a pattern does exist, it is not possible to trace it out unless the functions of the heroes are first carefully defined. This is because the main principle of continuity in the overall schema is the significance of the sequences of different types of hero. Since the poem is built upon a series of heroes, each with his own name and particular identity, plot development cannot be achieved by following one character or set of characters through the story or history that the poet wants to retell. Ben Sira worked with types of heroes or functions of heroes in history and used the devices of type recurrence, success and failure of type functions, juxtapositions, comparisons, escalations, and so forth, in order to delineate the course of "the heroic" from beginning to end in a systematic way.

It is necessary, therefore, to work out the character types of the heroes before proceeding to the overall pattern of history achieved. To do this, I have followed a rather simple procedure, the second option referred to above. I took the individual units of the poem as a set and analyzed the occurrence of common features in the details of characterization. I discovered a pattern of seven components. This general pattern was then analyzed with respect to subtypes as specific variations of the general pattern, and I found that five subtypes emerged, each associated with an "office" (patriarch, priest, judge, prophet, king). It was with the peculiarities of these official subtypes of the heroes named and hymned that Ben Sira could work to turn a serialized poem into a specific and coherent review of Israel's history.

Before we continue, two important judgments have been made that need to be acknowledged. These judgments are about the set of heroes that belong to the poem, the set used to determine the heroes' profile. The first is that Simon the high priest belongs to the set, even though many scholars have argued that he should not be included in a "hymn to the fathers." The reasons for including him are given in appendix B. Three other passages, on the other hand, have not been included. These are the mention of Enoch in 44:16; the description of Elijah in 48:9–11; and the section on Enoch, Joseph, Shem, Seth, Enos, and Adam in 49:14–16. These sections appear to be later additions to the hymn, do not correspond to the pattern of characterization, and disturb the symmetry of the overall structure and plan. There are good reasons for deleting them, including manuscript evidence, and these reasons are given in appendix C.

THE GENERAL PATTERN OF CHARACTERIZATION

A casual reading of the poem will not stumble upon any profile of the heroic common to all of the figures hymned. This is because the poetry is vivid and the descriptions fascinating. The repeated evocation of scriptural accounts in the descriptions creates in the memory of the reader a full epic background against which the new poetic depictions appear to sharpen individual profiles rather than type them. Only when one begins to wonder wherein, precisely, the greatness of these figures lies for Ben Sira is one led to closer readings. The first close reading will probably continue to treat each figure independently and seek literary clues to elucidate his particular virtue, achievement, or mark of greatness. But this approach fails because the affirmations of glory never seem to be accounted for in relation to any particularity about the individual under consideration. Finally, however, and quite unexpectedly, one discerns aspects of characterization common to all of the figures and discovers that Ben Sira understood the glory of these figures to reside in a particular configuration of those common aspects. It is this configuration that I have called the pattern of characterization.[6] The seven components of the general pattern are (1) a designation of office, (2) mention of divine approbation or election, (3) a reference to covenant, (4) mention of the person's character or piety, (5) an account of the deeds, (6) reference to the historical situation, and (7) mention of rewards. The study of this list of components will show that it is the concept of office that determines the pattern as a whole. Since the several offices play significant roles in the development of the hymn, they may be regarded as subclassifications of the general notion of office itself.

It will be helpful to flesh this pattern out in some detail. There are specific nuances to each component that determine its function within the pattern. Only by working out these interrelationships will the profile gain that specificity of char-

acterization needed in order to determine Ben Sira's notion of
greatness. A detailed exegetical accounting for the derivation
of the profile would be tedious and distracting. Readers interested in a partial account of this work will find it in appendix D. A summary account will be given here in the form of an
integrative sketch—Ben Sira's profile of the hero.

Office

One is tempted to overlook at first the frequent mention of
a hero's office in the hymn. The most obvious and striking
thing about the hymn is that each of the great ones is introduced by name, and one looks immediately for particularities.
That a certain figure is a prophet, priest, judge, or king appears
to be touched upon almost in passing. These designations of
social roles are so traditional as to appear insignificant in the
context of a hymn in praise of select individuals.

But this assumption turns out to be wrong. The assignment
of a figure to an office is so consistently emphasized that one
must ask whether it is not the office that makes the man for
Ben Sira. An office is expressly mentioned for one half of the
figures hymned, and it is assumed for the rest. It is even the
case that the characterization of complex figures, such as Samuel, is achieved by attributing more than one office to them. So
a figure's office is an essential component in the pattern of
characterization. It is his office that sets a person apart from
others classed according to other offices, and it is his performance in a particular office that can distinguish him from others in the same class.

This means that Ben Sira reflected upon the various social
roles depicted in Israel's epic and historical literature. Office
has become a generic category within which these roles are
subsumed. These roles are constitutive for Ben Sira's characterization of Israel's great leaders. Taken as a set, they may also
be constitutive for his view of the structure of Jewish society.
As strange as it may seem, it is the office a given figure holds
for which he can be praised. The greatness of these heroes is
directly related to the great significance of these offices. All of
the offices are "glorious," including those of prophet and

priest, a notion most curious if greatness is being measured on a Greek model.

Election

Our curiousity is provoked further by the fact that these great figures are being praised as well for their election to these offices. This notion is emphasized repeatedly throughout the hymn, and it applies to all of the offices. It is as if their greatness had nothing to do with achievement. It is the divine choice of these figures for their offices that is the glorious moment they represent.

The terminology used to express the idea of election varies. In some cases, a particular form of election seems to be characteristic of those in a given class. Thus it is the prophets who are said to be "formed in the womb." Those in other classes are frequently said to be "found," "chosen," "separated out"—all variations on the theme of election. Without divine initiative, a figure would not be included in the roster of the great ones. There appears to be some grand design in Israel's history for which these leaders have been chosen to play certain roles.

Covenant

This impression of a grand design is strengthened with the observation that the notion of covenant belongs to the pattern of characterization as well. Ben Sira has expressly emphasized the establishment of covenants with the founding figures for all of the offices except that of the prophets (for whom the notion "formation from the womb" serves as substitute). It could appear, then, that participation in the covenants was a special case, reserved for founders, and of no special significance for later figures. This view would be wrong, however. Not only is there a necessary relation between the covenants and the establishment of offices, it is the idea of covenant upon which the continuity of office is founded. Each holder of an office is therefore directly related to the enactment and terms of the covenant upon which that office is based. Thus it can be said at the very end of the hymn that it is the "covenant of Phineas" that ensures the high priestly office for Simon and his descendents forever (50:22–24). The terms of a covenant set the standard by which the holder of an office can be judged. With this possibility of making judgments about how well a certain figure fulfills the covenantal terms of his office, one might expect that great achievements will be the mark of the hero's glory after all.

Virtues

One does expect in a hymn of praise that noble qualities will be mentioned. Ben Sira's hymn is no exception. The language of virtues characteristic for these great leaders is in evidence everywhere. One would think it possible to make a classification of virtues important to the author and to determine the way in which they have been used to characterize particular figures or offices. Such an endeavor founders, however, and one is required to take another reading. There are a number of observations that can be made.

For example, specifically ethical virtues are lacking, even though one might have looked for an emphasis upon such virtues as wisdom, obedience, and righteousness in a hymn written by a teacher-sage. Solomon is the only one said to be wise (47:12), and he turns out to be a figure of extremely ambiguous virtue. The only figure called "righteous" is Noah (44:17), and that characterization is given with the scriptural account (Gen. 6:9). Nothing more is made of it. As for the virtue of obedience, it is mentioned expressly only once. The instance refers to Abraham's obedience to circumcision as a sign of the covenant made with him (44:20).

There are, however, many attributions of what one might call religious virtues. Perhaps it is piety that would be emphasized in a hymn to the hasidim. But only of Joshua and Josiah is *hesed* mentioned expressly, and then it is not a mark of character, but the quality of an action to which reference is made (46:6; 49:3). This agrees with the ancient Hebrew meaning of the term: loyalty or solidarity in a social role. There is, in fact, no clear evidence anywhere that ascriptions of religious virtues to these heroes intend a delineation of what the Greeks would call character (*ēthos, aretē*). The attributions are simply made, affirmed without rationalization or illustration. It is rather the case that the affirmations of religious virtues tend to support another claim altogether, that is, the "virtue" of these leaders lay in a single fulfillment—the fulfillment of their offices.

Once this is seen, the several designations of religious virtue can be reduced to two main types, "strength" and "faithfulness." These terms occur with greatest frequency, and they are able to subsume other terms with similar intent, such as "zealous," "loyal," and so forth. It does appear that the ascription of religious virtues to these leaders serves primarily to characterize the quality of their leadership, their performance in office. They are understood to be "virtuous" only in this respect.

Deeds

We can turn now to the most forceful aspect of the poem. It is that great and glorious deeds are recounted in number. The achievements of these men have been recognized as worthy of praise. The poem is not simply a series of portraits of officials in their place and garb. They are all men of action, and the consequences of their actions are significant—significant as historical events.

When one seeks to trace these deeds to men of superior endowment, extraordinary skill, or resolute strength, however, one quickly loses one's way, for the glorious deeds recounted are also typed according to office. Prophets perform miracles and give prophecies; kings build temples and defend the city; priests minister and perform sacrifices; judges lead to war; and Moses (an office sui generis, as we shall see) teaches. The fathers perform no deeds at all. As with the virtues, characterization is still determined by the function of the office.

Because the poem draws upon the scriptural accounts for its data, there is great diversity in the description of deeds from figure to figure. This gives the reader the impression that individual characterization is intended. The impression is not unimportant, for the variety of specific deeds and special circum-

stances gives the poem color and texture and allows the reader
to consider each individual named on his own merits. Thus the
"sacrifice" of Phineas, for lack of other, more appropriate
data, is the slaying of the Israelite with the Midianite woman.
But all of the deeds are typed, and all of the deedtypes are
related to official functions. The great men are great perform-
ers only of deeds appropriate to their office. The poem is not
in praise of human figures who have won their right to fame by
personal achievements. These men are great because they have
faithfully performed the functions of those social offices ordained in divine covenant as constitutive for the
"congregation."

Historical Setting

It now becomes clear why a figure's setting or place in
history is so frequently mentioned. It too belongs to the pattern of characterization. One might think that a brief description of scene or context would be incidental to the depiction
of an illustrious one in a series of illustrious ones. But because
these men are praised for the reasons they are, the people for
whom the offices are ordained must be in view. It is in relation
to the well-being of the people that the performance of the
official functions can be judged. The social setting against
which these leaders and their deeds have significance is always
painted the same. It is the dark side of Israel's history— trial,
sin, violence, enemies, destruction. It is the plight of the people and the bleak background of threat that set the illustrious
leaders off. Their moments of greatness reconfirm the grand
design of the covenants and carry the reader through a study
of the official ministries.

Rewards

The reader is therefore astonished to find that the leaders
are repeatedly said to have been rewarded for their deeds and
virtues. But then it turns out that their "rewards" are (1) the
bestowment upon them of their glorious offices, and (2) the
honor they receive from the people because of that glory; so

TABLE 1. THE PATTERN OF CHARACTERIZATION

	Father (4)[1]	Moses (1)	Priest (3)	Judge (6)	Prophet (8)	King (4)
1. *Office:*	Father (4)[1]	Moses (1)	Priest (3)	Judge (6)	Prophet (8)	King (4)
2. *Election:*	found (2)[2]	found chosen	chosen (1) anointed (1)	formed (1) set apart (1)	anointed (1) formed (2)	chosen (1) (anointed)[3] (1)
3. *Covenant:*	blessing/ promise	law	priesthood			kingship
4. *Piety:*	righteous (1) faithful (1)	faithful strong meek merciful teaching	(strong) (1) (zealous) (1)	strong (2) pious (1)	faithful (1) strong (1) zealous (1) truthful (1)	strong (1) pious (2) obedient (1)
5. *Deeds:*		miracles	teaching (1) sacrifice (3)	miracles (1)	miracles (3)	

24

			(act of judgement/salvation) (1) (defense/restoration) (2)	act of judgment/salvation (2) defense/restoration (3)	act of judgment/salvation (5) visions/prophecies (3)	act of judgment/salvation (2) defense/restoration (3)
6. *Setting/Context:*	destruction (1) trial (1)	(oppression)	jealousy (1) sins (2)	sins (1) enemies (1)	sins (3) enemies (2)	sins (3) enemies (2)
7. *Reward:*	inheritance (1)	glory honor	inheritance (3) glory (3)	land (2) honor (3)		honor (3)

Notes

1. Parentheses under "office" give number in the class.
2. Numbers in parentheses elsewhere give incidence of occurrence.
3. Parenthetical characteristics indicate ascriptions that may be incidental.

the circle closes intact. There are no rewards that come from great personal achievements in pursuit of a noble, heroic ideal. But there is glory nonetheless, and glory in abundance. It is the glory invested in the offices of Israel by God's design, decree, and continuing manifestation on the one hand, and on the other, it is the glory attributed to the leaders in Israel by the people who recognize the fulfillment of the covenantal purposes in their leadership.

This pattern of characterization is summarized in table 1. The reduction of complex poetic material makes it necessary to use brief designations. Some of these are interpretive, giving a general term to cover a variety of descriptive details found to be functionally similar. But most are a shorthand reference to the actual content of the characterizations. Each office has been assigned a separate column in order to enable comparisons among the several offices as subtypes of the overall pattern. The significance of these variations will be discussed below.

THE CONFIGURATIONS OF THE PATTERN

The Special Characteristics of Each Office

The discovery of the general pattern of characterization satisfies certain questions with regard to Ben Sira's notion of greatness, but it is hardly sufficient if one wants to investigate the structure of the hymn as a whole. One is still left with a series of heroes depicted similarly. In order to discern the significance of the collection as a set, it will be necessary to have the particular profiles of each office clearly in mind. That is because the poem is given structure by the placement of certain offices in a carefully worked out set of relationships to the others. Since each office is a subtype of the general pattern of characterization, it will be a simple matter to sketch out its particular profile. This will be done, however, with an eye to peculiar or noteworthy attributions to individual figures. Peculiar attribution of an official characteristic is one of the devices frequently used to give a distinctive place to an individual in the sequence.[7]

The Fathers

The fathers include the figures of Noah, Abraham, Isaac, and Jacob. They are "fathers" in the sense that they are understood to be the progenitors of certain generic classifications of humanity within which all people may be counted as descendents. The divine covenants of promise were established with them, the effect of which is understood to be a continuing determination of the classes of humanity before God. Because of divine approval of his righteousness and the divine promise to spare humanity "for his sake," Noah represents all humankind as those who are privileged to be alive without threat of cataclysmic destruction. Abraham represents the division of humanity into "nations" for which there is a great potential to find divine approval, understood on the basis of Abraham's acts of obedience and of God's promise to "bless" the nations "in his seed." Isaac represents the line in which God's promise to Abraham is renewed, and in Jacob a nation emerges that is understood to be the locus for the divine manifestation of that blessing. Only in the case of Abraham are any deeds recounted, and that is in keeping with his double function as father of the covenant of promise and as example of one who accepts the law as the standard of righteousness. Only with Noah and Abraham is the divine election based upon human righteousness. Isaac receives the promise "for the sake of Abraham his father" (44:22), and Israel is blessed without mention of a reason at all. They are glorious as fathers of the covenants of promise, and their "reward," or "inheritance," is bound up with the destinies of their descendents and the continuing efficacy of the promises. It is not said of them, as it is said of others in the hymn, that they received glory and honor in their own times.[8]

The Priests

Those named as priests are Aaron, Phineas, Samuel, and Simon. Samuel is a composite figure who is designated as a priest because of his act of sacrifice, which occasioned a victory over the Philistines (46:16; cf. 1 Sam. 7:9). His inclusion

shows that Ben Sira saw the performance of sacrifice as definitive for the priestly office. It also shows that he wanted to keep
track of the priestly office through the period of Israel's transition from wilderness to kingdom. Phineas's act of "sacrifice" is
the slaying of the Israelite with the Midianite woman, that is, a
curious combination of priestly and warrior functions. This is
an interpretation of the statement in Num. 25:12–13 that because of his deed, which "made atonement for the people of
Israel," the "covenant of a perpetual priesthood" was given to
him.

Taking Aaron, Phineas, and Simon together as a class, it is
possible to see the particular pattern of office Ben Sira had in
mind. The priesthood is based upon a covenant made with
Aaron; the special office of high priest is established by covenant with Phineas. With Simon that covenant is understood to
continue in force (50:24). The primary priestly function is the
performance of sacrifice, and the sacrifice of major significance
is the making of atonement. Beyond this, there is special interest in the vestments as manifestations of the divine bestowal
of office and glory. It is important that this glory is recognized
by the people (45:20; 50:5, 11, 13, 20). Neither great deeds nor
special virtues appear to be constitutive.

The Prophets

The prophets as a class are distinguished primarily by their
great deeds, which manifest their peculiar function as agents of
the destinies of kings and kingdoms. They have a special form
of election ("formed from the womb") and are zealous and
faithful in character. There is no prophetic covenant although,
as will be shown, the line of prophets is understood to begin
with Moses. There is marked interest in the prophetic function
of "anointing" persons to be priests, kings, and prophets.[9] Of
particular significance is the extent to which prophetic agency
is understood to have been the means by which the judgments
of history took place. To Samuel's prophecy is attributed the
power "to blot out iniquity" (46:20); Elijah "reduces" Israel
(48:2); and Jerusalem is said to have been laid waste "by
(bĕyad) Jeremiah" (49:6).

The Kings

The kings and rulers have as their primary function the defense of the civil and religious institutions. They are praised for temple building, fortification of the city, and support of the cult. A peculiarity of the office of kingship, in distinction to all the other offices, is the fact that there are both "good" and "bad" kings. The bad kings are not mentioned by name, but they are mentioned; the good kings are praised in contrast to them. With kings, then, there is the problem of sin. Even two of the good kings are acknowledged to have sinned. David's sin is said to have been "put away" (47:11); but Solomon's sin "brought wrath upon his descendents" (47:20). That is why piety is so important as the appropriate virtue of a king. There is a covenant of kingship established with David, and Solomon is said to have succeeded him "for his sake" (47:12). But there are conflicting statements as to whether and how this covenant is understood to remain in effect for all time. In 47:22, it appears that the line of David will not be cut off. But in 45:25, there is a distinction made between the covenant and inheritance of Aaron, which belongs to all his descendents, and the covenant and inheritance of David, which passes only to a single son. What this may mean exactly is not clear, but the general intention seems to be the superiority of the covenant with Aaron and Phineas in respect to its mode of continuity and it assurance of perpetuity (45:24). Hezekiah is said to have "held fast to the ways of David" (48:22), but there is no mention of David or a covenant of kingship in the rest of the hymn.

Figures with Multiple Office

The conception of religious office is a determining factor in Ben Sira's patterns of characterization, and many of the individual figures may be classed quite easily as representatives of a particular office. Nevertheless, several of the most important figures are characterized by designations and functions taken from more than one office. The question is whether such composite characterization can be shown to have purpose in terms of Ben Sira's overall plan. Several of the more important composite figures will have to be analyzed with this question in mind.

Moses as Teacher, Prophet, and Ruler

Ben Sira has not named an office for Moses, and it appears that he may have singled him out as one who holds an office sui generis. It is important to ask about this. That Moses is given a prominent place in the series is indicated by the fact that he stands between the fathers "issuing from Israel" and the establishment of the specifically religious offices in Israel. His virtue, piety, honor, and glory are highly accentuated; he is "beloved of God and men" and "made glorious as God" himself (45:1–2). He is fully described in terms of the pattern of characterization, with the exception that a covenant is not mentioned. But in its place, there is an extremely detailed and explicit account of the revelation of God and the law Moses received. He is the only one to see God's glory himself and to have had placed in his hands by God the "law of life and understanding." This determines his uniqueness in the series. It also accounts for the various functions that are ascribed to him. These functions indicate that Moses was understood as teacher and prophet.

His function as teacher is based upon the reception of the law and is explicitly mentioned at the conclusion of the pericope in the statement of purpose: "that he might teach His statutes unto Jacob, and His testimonies and judgments unto Israel" (45:5). But if this is so, one wonders what has become of the office of teacher in the subsequent history of Israel's great leaders. We have already noted that the typology of the hasidim given in the proem is not easily correlated with the series of characterizations that follow in the hymn. In the proem, it is clear that the literati hold a place of honor. If one includes the description of the sage in 39:1–11 as an indication of Ben Sira's high regard for the teacher, it is all the more noticeable that one finds no emphasis in the hymn of praise of those who fulfill the office of the teacher-sage. Solomon's wisdom is mentioned, of course, but it had to do with "song and story and riddle," through which he became famous and

by which he astounded the nations (47:14–17). He is not cast
as a teacher.

There is, however, mention of a teaching function for Aaron
that agrees exactly with that described for Moses, and it is
probably here that one may see the beginning of a resolution to
our problem. In Sir. 45:17, it is stated that God "gave him His
commandments and invested him with authority over statute
and judgment; that he might teach His people statutes, and
judgments unto the children of Israel." Here the function of
teaching has been assigned to the office of the priesthood.
Because this is understood, there is no need or place for a
separate office of the teacher among those who define Israel's
religious-institutional history. Moses is the teacher par excellence, in the sense that he made known the knowledge of the
law to Israel at the beginning. But the office he founds in order
to institutionalize this function is not that of the teacher, but
that of the priest.

This is emphasized by Ben Sira in yet another way. At the
beginning of the section on Aaron, it is God who raises up
Aaron, Moses' brother, and bestows upon him the priesthood
as a perpetual office (45:6–7). This is followed by the description of Aaron's glorious investiture by God. But later on
(45:15), the account of Moses anointing his brother to the
priesthood in Leviticus 8 is taken as the occasion when the
"eternal covenant" with Aaron was established. Thus it is clear
that Ben Sira sees the priesthood itself as instituted by Moses.
That the priesthood assumes and continues Moses' function as
teacher is certainly in keeping with this view.

That Moses anoints Aaron may be taken as a sign of another
official function attributed to him, the function of the prophet.
For Ben Sira at least, anointing is something the prophets do.
Besides this act, there are three other indications that Moses
was understood to stand at the beginning of the line of prophets. His mighty deeds and his strength in the presence of the
king (45:2–3) are "prophetic" functions. In Sir. 46:1, Joshua is
said to be a "minister of Moses in the prophetic office." It is
probable that God's revelation to Moses has been aligned with
the prophetic motifs of vision and special knowledge.

Less clear is whether Moses is perceived to fulfill the role of king. In Sir. 45:3, after the mention of his being emboldened in the presence of the king, it is stated that "God put him in command (*Ṣiwwāh*) of the people." This certainly may refer to the function of a king-ruler. Ben Sira is conspicuously ambivalent about the office of kingship per se and has characterized the rulers of the restoration in terms used for the earlier kings. In the case of Simon, the duty of ruling is assumed by the high priest. It appears, then, that Ben Sira may have seen the kings as holding an office that obtained for a chapter of Israel's history, the function of which, however, had its origins before that time in Moses and continued after that time in the office of the high priest. If this is so, Moses may have been understood to incorporate in a single individual original aspects of all the major offices—prophet, priest-teacher, and ruler.

Moses' "office" then would be sui generis, for the revelation of the law needed no repetition, and the combination of functions he represented do not define a single pattern of continuing office. These functions, however, were not discontinued, but were assigned to other offices, which preserved them within the system of official ministries. Thus it is that Moses' characterization is fully in keeping with the pattern of characterization in general. It is composite on purpose; every element and function can be accounted for in relation to the office theme.

Phineas as Priest and Prophet

Phineas is problematic, since the story about him is hardly indicative of the priestly role and has been described in terms that are more appropriate to the characters and deeds of the prophets. But it is the story from scripture with which Ben Sira had to work. It was important to Ben Sira because of its mention of a covenant and its interpretation as "making atonement for the people of Israel" (Num. 25:10–13). It was here too, possibly, that a scriptural and covenantal claim for a line of high priests in Ben Sira's time was founded (cf. 50:24).[10] Ben Sira does praise Phineas for his zeal, strength, and piety

("his heart prompted him"), aspects of character not ascribed
to Aaron and Simon. But he emphasizes the covenant of atonement and high priesthood that begins here. In the first distich,
moreover, Phineas is called "third [in his line]" (45:23), which
can hardly be understood other than as a reference to his being
third in the series Moses-Aaron-Phineas.[11] If we take all factors into account, the composite nature of Phineas's characterization is understandable and does not seem to detract from
Ben Sira's consistent interest in the patterns of particular
offices.

The Judges

Joshua, Caleb, and the judges are very difficult to align with
particular patterns of office. This is probably because of their
roles as figures of transition who take the people into the land.
With the prophets, they share in the deeds of miracles; with
the kings, in the designations of piety; with the priests, the fact
that they "turn away wrath from the assembly, and cause the
evil report to cease" (46:7). The composite characterization
did not hinder Ben Sira from saying that Joshua was a "minister of Moses in the prophetic office" (46:1), and it is clear that
he has emphasized prophetic characterization throughout. But
the judges do not conform to the pattern of prophetic office in
their aspects as warriors, nor in their leadership of the people
into the land. These two functions set them apart, and it may
be significant that in relation to the description of each of
these functions, Ben Sira has added a purpose: "that all the
doomed nations might know that the Lord was watching over
his people's battles" (46:6) and "that all the people of Jacob
might know how good it is to be a devoted follower of the
Lord" (46:10). These are singular statements and make of
these figures the only "examples" to be found within the
hymn. That being the case, they do not contribute to the development of the particular patterns of the offices of institutional religion. Whether they describe an office in their own
right and what Ben Sira's interest in them may be—other than
in terms of his historical schema—are questions for which we
may not find an adequate answer. They characterize a figure

which appears to have been imitated in later hasidic and eschatological movements; but there is little in Ben Sira's book of wisdom that would suggest that he understood Israel to be in need of such leaders in his own time.

Samuel as Prophet, Judge, and Priest

Samuel is a fully composite figure, designated expressly as prophet, judge, and priest (46:13) and described in terms of functions taken from each office. As judge, he is said to have "commanded the congregation" (46:14); as priest, to have offered sacrifice (46:16); and as prophet, to have "established the kingdom," "anointed princes," and "declared unto the king his way" (46:13, 20). His primary office is clearly that of the prophet, and he serves in the series as the one from whose time the office of the king emerges. Saul, however, the specific king one expects in reference, is not mentioned by name, and it is therefore appropriate that in the figure of Samuel some form of each of the three classical offices be reflected, including that of the ruler. It is probably this interest in the continuity of official roles in the historical development of Israel that has determined the composite characterization. That Ben Sira has named the three offices and ascribed to Samuel functions appropriate to each indicates the combination is purposive.

David as King and Warrior

In addition to David's characterization as a king and praise for his proper stance toward the cult, a description of him as a brave warrior is also given (defending the flocks against lions and bears; defending the people against Goliath [47:3–5; cf. 1 Sam. 17:36]). This agrees with the scriptural account and is appropriate to the hymn. He is the only king who is described as a warrior, but he shares this function with his precursors, the judges, and thus represents the transition from conquest to defense, preparing for the time of peace when Solomon can build the temple (47:13).

Simon as Priest and King

The last figure in the series is also composite in characterization, and it is here that the purpose in ascribing several
official functions to a single figure may be tested most clearly.
Simon is, of course, the high priest, and the lengthy description of his vestments and liturgical performance on the Day of
Atonement shows that his glory is related to that office (50:5–
21). It is an exceptionally fine poetic narrative of the rite,
creating a brilliant picture of the splendor of Simon, surrounded by the other priests, his "brothers" and "sons," also
glorious, and in the presence of the "whole congregation of
Israel," who respond to the trumpets by falling down to worship the Lord and receive his blessing as Simon names the
Name. Because this blessing is the "pardon of God" (50:21),
the depiction of the high priest making atonement for the
people who are gathered around him in postures of praise and
worship provides a powerful climax to the hymn. This resolves
the question of threat that has provided the problem-context
for the entire series of figures from Israel's history. The next
question is whether Simon's office also is understood to climax
the series of religious offices and functions that the hymn has
developed.

The answer may be found in the introductory section
(50:1–4) and the concluding hymn of blessing (50:22–24),
which Ben Sira has used to frame the account of the high
liturgical moment. In the introduction, Simon is identified as
"the son of Johanan, the priest," in whose time several things
are said to have taken place. They include the renovation and
fortification of the temple, the building of the wall "with tun-
nels for protection like a king's palace," and digging a reser-
voir. It concludes by saying "He took thought for his people
against robbers, and fortified the city from the enemy." Ben
Sira was careful not to claim the office of the ruler-king for
Simon, but it is clear that he wished his readers to understand
that the primary functions of the king—building and defense
of the city and temple—were to be associated with him.

In the concluding hymn of blessing, it is also possible to see allusions to designations that were important in the description of earlier figures and offices. The blessing addresses God, "who exalts man from the womb," a combination of terms that the reader will associate with the idea of election in general and with the prophets in particular (whose special form of election is "from the womb"). Generalized and applied to the people, the motif appears now in a "democratized" form. The prayer continues for "wisdom" and "peace" within and among the people, qualities mentioned as present in Israel's history only during the time of Solomon. Then it concludes with the request that God's mercy be established with Simon and the covenant of Phineas be raised up for him forever. The evocation of the reign of Solomon, a time of peace during which the office of the prophet is not mentioned, and the attribution of the functions of the kings to Simon strongly suggest that the high priesthood is understood as the contemporary and sufficient locus of all of Israel's religious offices. It seems clear that Ben Sira saw it as a climax and fulfillment of Israel's glorious history as a whole.

The Structure
of History 2

In the course of the analysis, I
have made frequent reference to various relationships among
the offices and figures that suggest an overall structure to the
hymn. The series of great men presented in the hymn is more
than a listing of examples. It moves in strict chronological
order with many indications of sequences and successions that
appear to be of significance for its development both as a literary composition and as a reading of Israel's history.[1] In this
chapter, the structure of the hymn will be outlined, its narrative plot explored, and its view of history discussed.[2]

THE STRUCTURE OF THE HYMN

The overall pattern of the hymn has been outlined in table 2,
enabling us to make some general observations about its units,
themes, structure, and sense of development. The table consists simply of a list of the figures mentioned in the hymn
according to the sequence in which they occur. Headings indicate the development of certain themes in relation to the offices and can be organized in such a way as to reveal the
balanced structure of the hymn as a whole. The "history of
prophets and kings" is presented in a double column because

TABLE 2. THE STRUCTURE OF THE HYMN

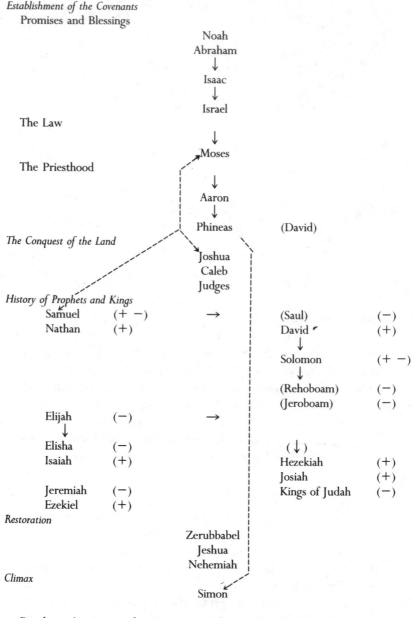

Establishment of the Covenants
  Promises and Blessings

                              Noah
                            Abraham
                               ↓
                             Isaac
                               ↓
                             Israel
The Law
                               ↓
                            Moses
The Priesthood
                               ↓
                            Aaron
                               ↓
                           Phineas   (David)
The Conquest of the Land
                            Joshua
                            Caleb
                            Judges
History of Prophets and Kings
      Samuel   (+ −)   →   (Saul)   (−)
      Nathan   (+)   David   (+)
                                            ↓
                                         Solomon   (+ −)
                                            ↓
                                       (Rehoboam)   (−)
                                       (Jeroboam)   (−)
      Elijah   (−)   →
        ↓
      Elisha   (−)   (↓)
      Isaiah   (+)   Hezekiah   (+)
                                         Josiah   (+)
      Jeremiah   (−)   Kings of Judah (−)
      Ezekiel   (+)
Restoration
                           Zerubbabel
                            Jeshua
                           Nehemiah
Climax
                            Simon

Prophets: + = saving function; − = judgmental or destroying function.
Kings: + = honorable; − = dishonorable.
→ = express mention of some form of succession.

of the marked tendency in the hymn to juxtapose a prophet and a king.

The Establishment of the Covenants

The first seven figures have in common the theme of covenant and thus may be seen to constitute a literary unit.[3] It is true that a covenant is not mentioned for Moses, but as the recipient of the revelation of the law he is clearly assigned an essential position among the founding figures. An indication that Ben Sira has intended this series as a unit is the mention of the covenant with David at the end of the unit (45:25). This passage is out of place chronologically and does not become the occasion for David's description and praise, which follow in place later (47:1–11). At that later point, there is allusion to his "rights of royalty" (47:11), but no discussion of the covenant. Covenant is mentioned at 45:25, immediately after the description of Phineas and the covenant of the high priesthood, both as an acknowledgement of yet another covenant that is to be included among "the covenants" (cf. "His covenant was with David *also*") and as a statement of contrast between the covenants of David and Phineas that ascribes some superiority to that of Phineas.[4] Another indication of the literary closure of the unit is the addition of a prayer of blessing upon Phineas that his "prosperity" and "power" may never cease (45:25b–26). This may be compared to the similar blessing of Simon with which the hymn is concluded (50:22–24). With the praise of Phineas, then, the first major section of the hymn comes to a close. It has to do with the covenantal basis of the divine promises and blessings and the emergence of the special offices within Israel by means of which those blessings will be actualized. In Moses, the functions of all the classical offices were begun, but it is clearly the priestly office itself that enjoys the privilege of being founded during this period of covenant establishment.

The Conquest of the Land

Joshua, Caleb, and the judges are figures of a period of transition and are to be considered together. The theme of

their sequence is of Israel coming into its inheritance in the
land. We have seen that the composite characterization of
Joshua and Caleb is in keeping with this historical function.
They are both warriors and carriers of the official functions
from the earlier period of foundation into the period of the
kingdom. The brief mention of the judges as a class (46:11–12)
may be taken as a conclusion to this interim series and compared with the mention of the twelve prophets as a class that
concludes the series of the prophets (49:10).

The History of Prophets and Kings

The second major block of figures has to do with the history
of the prophets and kings. This is an exceptionally fine review
of the history of Israel from the establishment of the kingdom
to the postexilic restoration, and it manifests several significant
narrative movements. Seen as a unit within the series of
praised leaders, it manifests an overall structure as well. There
is a marked tendency to correlate prophets and kings. In each
list, there are seven individuals and one collective designation
(the twelve prophets; the kings of Judah). Significantly, only
four of the kings are mentioned by name, those who are found
to be honorable and praiseworthy (David, Solomon, Hezekiah,
Josiah). The other four are not mentioned by name, presumably because they were found not to be worthy (Saul, Re-
hoboam, Jeroboam, kings of Judah). Of the prophets, five are
described as having performed functions that were basically
constructive (Samuel, Nathan, Isaiah, Ezekiel, the twelve),
three as having performed functions that were basically destructive (Elijah, Elisha, Jeremiah). One of the prophets (Samuel) and one of the kings (Solomon) combine both positive and
negative functions. The two lists may be correlated and balanced in terms of the values that Ben Sira has assigned to each
of the figures (see table 2).

The Restoration

The period of the restoration is prepared for by the positive
function assigned to the twelve prophets ("who recovered

Jacob to health, and delivered him by confident hope" 49:10)
mentioned at the end of the series of prophets and kings. It
consists of three figures (Zerubbabel, Jeshua, Nehemiah)
whose glories and deeds restore those of the honorable kings
and who are correlated to the three judges of the period of the
conquest.

The Climax

The climax of the hymn sets the description of Simon off as
a unit by itself, which singularly concludes the series. The
structure of the series of units as a whole may be visualized in
the following numerical sequence:

$$7 - 3 - \frac{7 + 1}{7 + 1} - 3 - 1$$

This pattern of literary units provides an extremely well-balanced structure both to the hymn as a composition and to the
history it recounts. It consists of three major units (Establishment of the Covenants, History of Prophets and Kings, Climactic Hymn in Praise of Simon) and two transitional units
(Conquest of the Land, Restoration) in chiastic or concentric
correlations. It may be viewed architectonically by regarding
the first unit as a foundation, the last unit as capstone. It may
also be viewed in terms of narrative or historical development
with beginning, middle, and end. If the beginning of the story
is understood as plan or mandate, the middle history may be
seen as the struggle to fulfill that mandate, and the ending as
the resolution or actualization of the quest. In either case,
aspects both of structure and of narrative development are
combined. This noteworthy combination of pattern and movement needs now to be explored. The place to begin is with
those literary devices by which Ben Sira expressly relates the
units sequentially.

THE CONCEPT OF SUCCESSION

Within the overall structure of the hymn, as well as within
the major literary units, there are repeated indications of sig-

nificant sequences and successions, which provide the hymn
with a sense of movement. In this section, several of these
indicators will be observed, and the principle of succession
determined.

Serialization

We can begin with the observation that, within the larger
literary units, there is frequently a serialization that links together several figures according to a theme. This serialization
can be demonstrated for each of the five major literary units,
but the discussion here will be limited to the first unit of seven
figures and the middle unit with its history of the prophets and
kings.

The first series of seven figures is replete with developmental schemata. The most obvious is the subseries from Abraham
to Jacob. It is held together by the theme of the promise of
blessing, which according to Ben Sira is renewed with Isaac
"for the sake of Abraham" and "comes to rest" on Jacob's
head. If one adds the figure of Noah to make a series of four
and notes the express mention of the classes of humankind in
regard to each, a second thematic development may be seen. It
is the movement of promise from all humankind to all nations
to Israel. At this point, Moses is introduced, there being no
room in the first series of seven for any other potentially significant figures between Jacob and Moses (e.g., Melchizedek or
the twelve patriarchs). Moses is said to "spring from" Israel
(45:1) and becomes the first of another subseries of three,
which runs from him through Aaron to Phineas (cf. 45:15,
where Moses anoints Aaron, and 45:23, where Phineas is said
to be the "third in the line"). Thus there is a series of seven,
composed of a single figure (Noah), plus two sets of three,
joined together by themes that make of them a unit. The obvious themes are those of covenant and office formation. The
not-so-obvious but equally important theme is the promise of
blessing. The negative promise ("not to destroy humankind")
and the positive promise ("to bless the nations") come to rest,
not only in Israel, but more specifically in the office of the high
priesthood. There it is realized in the act of making atonement

(cf. 45:15, where Aaron's covenant is "to minister to God, . . . and to bless His people in His name"; and 45:23, where Phineas's covenant is related to his making "atonement for the people"). There is thus a coherent theology determining the composition of this first unit. It has to do with some problem, some threat to human well-being to be resolved in the priestly office and lifted from the people in the priestly blessing (cf. 45:15; 50:20–21). This theology of promise and blessing will be discussed below.

Serializing does not play as significant a role in the second major unit on the prophets and kings, although the three honorable kings are mentioned as a unit in 49:4, and the three rulers of the restoration are handled as a unit in 49:11–13. But there are other principles at work that determine the sequences and trace out a patterned movement. The primary theme is the well-being of Israel, focused in the character of the king. The evil kings are not mentioned by name, but they and their effect upon the people are clearly acknowledged at three places in the history: at the beginning, where the "iniquity" that Samuel's posthumous prophecy "blots out" is a clear allusion to Saul (46:20); in the discussion of the series of evil kings of Israel that culminated in the destruction of the Northern Kingdom (47:23–24; 48:15); and in the passages on the evil kings of Judah who caused the destruction of Jerusalem (49:4–6). Against this background and within this history, the three good kings and Solomon are placed and praised. Correlating the prophets with this history, their functions as agents of judgment and salvation are given.

Samuel is an agent both for the establishment of the kingdom and for judgments upon its enemies and first king. Of the rest, the two prophets associated with good kings are recognized as agents of grace. Nathan served under David and, while his "service" is not described, his "putting away" of David's sin is (47:11; cf. 2 Sam. 12:13). Isaiah "added life unto the king," Hezekiah, and "comforted the mourners in Zion" (48:23–24). But Elijah, Elisha, and Jeremiah are all understood to have served under evil kings: Elijah and Elisha in Israel, Jeremiah in Judah (he is not associated with Josiah in the hymn). Their function is therefore one of judgment. Elijah "reduced" the number of Israel, "heard judgments of vengeance in Horeb," and "anointed kings for retribution" (48:2–8). Jeremiah was the agent through whom the city was burned after the corrupt kings had given their glory to a strong nation (49:5–6). It may therefore be quite significant that in the mention of Ezekiel and the twelve prophets that immediately follows (49:8–10), a note of hope is sounded. Of Ezekiel it is related that he saw a vision of the chariot, an image appropriate to the exilic context and the theme of hope. And of the twelve prophets it is said, "[They] recovered Jacob to health, and delivered him by confident hope" (49:10). That the twelve prophets are deliverers is striking both as a hermeneutical judgment and as a conclusion to the list of prophets in the hymn. This passage is followed immediately by a description of the deeds of restoration by Zerubbabel, Jeshua, and Nehemiah.

There is, then, a series of prophets composed of three who are clearly agents of judgment upon Israel (Elijah, Elisha, Jeremiah) and three who are agents of grace and hope (Nathan, Isaiah, Ezekiel). The series is headed by a prophet who combines both functions (Samuel), and it ends with the twelve who "restore" and "deliver" Jacob. The balance is even, the correlation with the series of the kings and rulers clear, and the sequential development significant. In contrast to the serialization of the first seven figures of the hymn, which charted a constructive development coming to climax in the covenant and office of the high priesthood, the serialization of the prophets follows a see-saw pattern that corresponds to the narrative theme of failure/restoration in the quest to actualize the covenant plan. That the sequence of positive and negative moments comes to rest at the end on a positive and hopeful note indicates that the oscillations of this interim series have not destroyed the potential for fulfillment.

Sequence and Succession

In addition to serialization, which gives both structure and movement to the composition, there are several other devices that Ben Sira has employed to create a sense of sequence and succession in the hymn and to unite its several literary units.

Sequence is frequently noted in terms of chronological placement in the series. Thus Nathan arose after Samuel (47:1), Solomon after David (47:12), and the kings of folly after Solomon (47:23). The evil kings led the people into sin until Elijah arose (48:1); after he was taken, then Elisha was filled with the spirit (48:12). The corrupt kings of Judah forsook the law until they came to their end (49:4), and so on. This type of sequencing indicates that Ben Sira's view of history is not devoid of chronology, but it is used primarily to place the principle figures of the history in relation to one another in a series of significant sequences. The history is read only in relation to these figures-in-sequence and does not become a subject to be recounted in and for itself.

Sequence becomes succession when certain notions of continuity are perceived. In the hymn, there are several such notions at work, all interrelated to achieve an overall sense of movement and purpose, for example, in the mention of a succession from father to son. This is expressed in the sequences Abraham-Isaac (44:22), David-Solomon (47:12), and Solomon and his sons (47:23). It is assumed in the sequence Isaac-Jacob (44:22–23), and Moses is said to "issue from" Israel (44:23). That this type of succession can be understood to transfer the power and promise of the predecessor's office onto the successor has been made explicit in two ways. In the sequence Abraham-Isaac-Jacob, the promise itself has been objectified and passed along (44:22–23). In the cases of Isaac and Solomon, there is explicit reference to their important position being "for the sake of" (ba 'ābûr) their fathers (44:22; 47:12). "For the sake of" could simply be a justification for inclusion in the series, of course. For Isaac neither deed nor virtuous character is mentioned, and Solomon is the one king included in the list of kings and rulers praised whose sin and its effect on Israel's history must be mentioned as well. But the phrase also occurs in a statement about Noah's effectiveness for his descendents ("For his sake there was a remnant" [44:17]).

Here it carries the connotation of cause or merit (cf. the parallel statement "And by reason of the covenant with him the flood ceased"). It is difficult, therefore, not to think that succession is being understood in terms of some conception of effective promise or influence that is determinative for the successors.

The term that has sometimes been translated as "successor" (taḥālîp) should also be mentioned here.[5] It is used as a designation of Noah (44:17), Elisha (48:8), and in parallel with "blessing" as the function of the name for judges that is involved in memory for their children (46:12). It does not appear as a noun in the Hebrew scriptures before Sirach. The verb form in the Hifil (yaḥălîp) means "to sprout again" (cf. Job 14:7). For Noah, "renewer" or perhaps "continuator" would be appropriate. But as used of Elisha, the meaning is clearly "continuator" or "successor." Elijah is told, "You anointed kings for retribution, and a prophet as successor *in your place*" (taḥteykā). The double connotation of successor (in relation to the predecessor) and effective agent (in relation to contemporaries and descendents) is noteworthy as an indication of the principle of power or influence that is understood to reside in the meaning of succession itself.

That Elisha was "anointed" to be a successor alerts us to another concept that Ben Sira may have recognized as an indication of succession. That the prophets anoint kings (Samuel, 46:13; Elijah, 48:8) probably means for Ben Sira that the office of the king is derived from and dependent upon the agency of the prophet. This would be in itself an important consideration for Ben Sira's understanding of kingship, but whether one should speak of succession here is not clear. Succession is certainly the intention in the case of Elijah-Elisha, of course; but since it is the only instance of such a relationship between two prophets, it is difficult to generalize here too. That Moses anointed Aaron, however, most probably signifies succession (45:15). It is the only mention of a relationship between them and is followed later by the statement that Phineas was the "third in line" (45:23).

It should be noted, though, that none of these conceptions

of succession has been used consistently in relation to any series of offices. It would be difficult to do so with the prophets. It is possible that there is a conception of a "line" of prophets.[6] But each is apparently elected individually, "formed in the womb," and so derives his office and place in the succession directly from God. With the kings after Solomon, both the ideas of succession and descent seem to evaporate. Only Hezekiah is placed in relation to David, but in terms of being strong "in the ways of David" (48:23), not in terms of succession or covenant.

Divine Intention and Promise

It is clear that Ben Sira has employed a variety of mechanisms in order to achieve the sense of movement with which he has invested his hymn. Thematic patterns that govern the construction of given series, temporal and genealogical sequences, and various indications of succession all attest to his express interest in sequential relationships that can guarantee the coherence and continuity of the structured history as a whole. But none of these several mechanisms for achieving movement has been used consistently or developed programmatically. This means the principle of continuity, if indeed there is one, must be discovered by an analysis of the structure and movement of the whole, giving due consideration to the pattern of characterization itself as that which provides continuity and the sequence of the offices as that which provides for the sense of development.

This means the conception of office itself can be adduced in support of the thesis that the idea of succession was important for Ben Sira. The evidence is found in the particular patterns of characterization for each of the offices. That an individual figure is described in terms functionally similar to those used of others, produces the sense of continuity of an office, whose holder acts as a tradent, that is, one in a series of successions. In tracing the derivation or origin of each of the offices themselves, however, it is clear that each is related to a founding moment of covenant or election. This founding moment, moreover, does more than merely inaugurate or establish a significant social role or function; it invests that function with divine purpose concomitant with the divine intention for the well-being of the people as an ordered community. Office becomes a given in one sense, a potentiality in another. Based upon divine covenant its status is quasiontological, that is, based "outside" empirical-social history. It can be "filled" only when the divine intention is actualized by means of it. This means that the principle of movement within the structure of the hymn and its view of history may actually be an assumed theologumenon. For Ben Sira, this divine intention appears to be manifest in the promise of blessing given at the beginning with the covenant with Abraham, and actualized at the end with the blessing of the Lord that Simon offers. If this is so, as will be argued below, the principle of continuity and movement that gives the hymn both its architectonic structure and its sense of dramatic purpose may be located ultimately in the conception of the divine promise as that which can actualize the potentiality of "office" and "covenant."

The notion of promise is certainly not obvious as a narrative theme in Ben Sira's hymn. But it is introduced at the beginning and appears to be foundational for the development of the notions of covenant, office, and their purposes. If one sees that the notion of promise mediates categories of intentionality and actuality, becoming a term for potentiality, it can also be seen that, as a historical and literary category, the idea may determine just such a developmental schema as we have in Ben Sira's hymn. The promise given with the structure of covenants and offices cannot be reduced either to history or to ideality. It expresses, rather, a guaranteed potentiality-to-be-actualized. The pattern of the covenantal offices does not, of itself, impell any historical or literary development of a dramatic or "quest" nature. But as a depiction of divine intention and promise, it does call for construction of the pattern (first unit), the *agon* of actualization (middle unit), and the celebration of fulfillment (final unit). It is now possible to ask more specifically about Ben Sira's understanding of sacred history.

THE CONCEPTION OF SACRED HISTORY

The Recasting of the Scriptures

The hymn reveals an impressive acquaintance with the scriptures and the major movements of Israel's history. It begins with Noah but assumes even then a prehistory. Then it follows the patriarchs, the events in the wilderness (with a brief allusion to the Exodus), the entrance into the land, the histories of Israel and Judah, the exiles and the destruction of Jerusalem, and the restoration. The order is strictly chronological. The use of the scriptural data is "correct" in terms of ascriptions, relationships, and settings being properly attributed.

Nevertheless, none of the major events, periods, and developments is taken as a subject in its own right. There are large blocks of material passed over without mention: the antediluvian period, the twelve patriarchs, the Exodus story itself, and the return from exile. Other major chapters of the history are acknowledged but not developed: the wilderness is acknowledged once as the setting for the threat of Korah's company to Aaron (45:18). But there is no mention of the wilderness-way, neither Moses nor Phineas is placed there, and the themes of testing and miracles in the wilderness are nowhere to be found. The period of the restoration is also only acknowledged in that Zerubbabel, Jeshua, and Nehemiah are praised. But there is no mention of the historical period as one of the restoration of anything lost or destoyed and no indication that their work should be understood in such a context.

The reason for this apparent lack of interest in many of the major chapters of Israel's history is, of course, that Ben Sira proposes a hymn in praise of the great leaders, not a history of the people. And yet, the series of great leaders is a reading of that history, and the people are always in view. This means the new reading that is achieved will recast the scriptural traditions, even in respect to the history of the people. If the well-being of the people is dependent upon the divine offices and the faithfulness of their holders, their history will now be given in the history of these leaders. If that history is intended as a history of salvation, that is, as a development of offices and the succession of officers in which and through whom well-being has come for the people, large portions of the history of the people themselves can no longer be relevant.

Thus the history must begin with the promise to Noah, and the antediluvian period can receive only an allusion as the context of trouble and threat (curse) for humanity. Of the patriarchs after Abraham, it is important only to know that the blessing is upon them. The Exodus and the wilderness-way— understood either as significant chapters in the history of the people or as paradigms for salvation events—signify the testing of the people by Yahweh, and they therefore must be reinterpreted. Only three threatening events from the wilderness period come into view. The first is the threat to Aaron's office by Korah's company, whom Ben Sira calls "strangers" (45:18). Here the test is put, not to the people, but to the office of the priesthood. The second is the need for Phineas's "atonement" for the children of Israel. The occasion for the action (the Israelite taking a Midianite woman) is not recounted, and of Phineas it is said that "he stood in the breach for his people." Here the people are the recipients of the benefits of a priest's sacrifice of atonement. The third instance is the response of the people to the report on the land (Num. 14:1–10). The hymn says that the congregation rebelled (46:7), which certainly puts them in a bad light momentarily. But Joshua and Caleb "stood firm," it says, "to turn away wrath from the assembly, and to cause the evil report to cease" (46:7). In the next set of two distichs it appears, moreover, that they were set apart from the people in order "to bring them into their inheritance" (46:8). The people of the wilderness-way have been portrayed as a congregation whose well-being is cared for in the faithful fulfillment of its offices by its leaders.

If we were to compare this finding with the history of the prophets and kings that follows, it would be possible to argue that the threat to the people has been transferred to the later period and has been focused upon the character of its kings. It is not that the kings are described as being tested. But they are the ones, of all the figures in the hymn, whose potential for failure is emphasized and whose achievements have been cast in terms of the virtue of piety. They and their office are by definition under judgment with regard to piety and obedience; they are symbols of testing. And the consequences of their unfaithfulness are shared fully by the people, both in terms of characterization (sin) and destiny (destruction and exile). After Solomon, "who brought wrath upon his progeny" so that "the people became two sceptors" (47:20–21), the history is essentially that of the foolish and corrupt kings "who sinned and made Israel to sin" (47:23). Two interludes of prosperity are associated with the good kings Hezekiah and Josiah. But even here, there is a marked reluctance to attribute salvation to the king. Hezekiah is praised because he fortified the city, but under seige it was the people who called unto God, who saved them by the hand of Isaiah (48:18–21). Josiah was "grieved at our backsliding, and put an end to the vain abominations" (49:2), but there is no mention of a time of peace and prosperity under his rule. Instead, the history of the kings of Judah who "forsook the law till the end" is summarized, culminating in the burning of the holy city (49:4–6).

The next indication of the well-being of the people is in the mention of the twelve prophets who "recovered Jacob to health, and delivered him" (49:10). Then follows the description of the restoration builders, but without any reference to the people. They are clearly in view once again, however, in the final picture of Simon's ministry. "He took thought for his people against robbers" (50:4), ascended to the altar of majesty "in the presence of the whole congregation of Israel" (50:13), and descending, "lifted up his hands upon the whole congregation of Israel," who receive from him the blessing and pardon of the Lord (50:20–21).

If the sacred history has been moving to this climax and the welfare of the people is understood to be assured only by means of the proper description and fulfillment of the high-priestly office, there can be no room for a restoration of the community on the basis of the acts of the rulers alone, nor on the condition of the people's own obedience and righteousness (cf. by way of contrast the Deuteronomic address, "If . . . then"). The history of the people has been subsumed completely in the history of Israel's offices and leaders, with priests "up" and kings "down."

The Glory of Israel's Leaders

The theme of glory is one of the most consistently encountered and striking characteristics of the hymn. Its source is surely to be found in the priestly traditions of scripture and Second Temple theology, where "glory" (*kābôd*) is used as a term for the majesty and manifestation of God. The glory of the Lord is manifest both in creation and in events of deliverance in history, but its special locus in the priestly theologies was understood to be in the cult, especially as a term for the divine presence in the tent or temple. That Ben Sira used this term to express the grandeur of the select leaders of Israel's history is most amazing. In the proem, Ben Sira may have anticipated the reader's reaction by the judicious statement that these men were "great in glory, the Most High's portion" (44:2). Their glory can be accounted for, that is, in terms of bestowal or election and thus not appear out of keeping with the divine aretalogical aspect of the hymn. Nevertheless, that Yahweh's glory is now bestowed upon and manifest in the majesty of these human figures indicates a momentous shift in the conceptuality of history and anthropology. The glory in the Lord, traditionally manifest in the history of the cult, is now to be seen in the succession of illustrious leaders—special men, set apart, through whom the salvation of Israel is to be actualized and to whom it is now possible to offer a hymn of praise. History now revolves around them and moves in the succession of their offices. It is a covenant history, marked by promise, actualization, continuity, and glory, manifest in the ministries of saviors. But what exactly is this glory and this ministry that moves and molds the people's history?

The Blessing and the Promise

We have seen that the theme of the blessing appears to have been developed creatively in the hymn. The priestly pardon can be identified with the priestly blessing in the conclusion, thus fulfilling the promise of the blessing to Abraham at the beginning of the hymn (50:20–21). What are the consequences of this for Ben Sira's view of convenant history?

The promise of blessing given to Abraham was found by Ben Sira in the content of the Lord's covenant with him (cf. the sequence from 44:20 to 44:21 and the "therefore"). It is this covenant and the covenant with Aaron that are the major foundations upon which Israel's history is to be constructed. The covenant with Noah is the negative statement of the promise and the context for understanding the significance of that given to Abraham. The covenant with David is criticized and compared unfavorably with that of Phineas, whose covenant is simply the special office within the priesthood of Aaron, and the revelation of the law to Moses is not understood expressly as a covenant. By emphasizing and joining together the covenants of Abraham and Aaron, Ben Sira announced a program.

The blessing promised to Abraham has two aspects. On the one hand, it has to do with the formation of Israel from his seed. This aspect of the promise is considered fulfilled when the blessing rested on Jacob. He was the "first born" and from him came the twelve tribes of Israel (44:22–23). On the other hand, the promise has to do with the resolution of some human dilemma, the negative statement of which had been signified in Noah. This aspect is not as clearly expressed, but it is implied in the sequence from Noah to Abraham. Nevertheless, the promise to Abraham is "to bless the nations in his seed" (44:21), and both the immediate context and the subsequent development of the theme of blessing as atonement indicate that this aspect is equally important for Ben Sira. Israel thus becomes the place where the blessing resides, but her function is to answer to the problem of sin and judgment. That function is fulfilled in the final scene.

The Theme of Location

Following the development of the history of Israel with the theme of location in mind, one can chart its progress by drawing a series of concentric circles, beginning with a large sphere

and moving toward a central focus. The story begins with all
humanity and the whole earth in view, and the promise to
Abraham's seed will be cast in terms of the eventual inheritance of the whole earth as well (44:18, 21). "Here" it is,
presumably, that Israel is formed (44:23), Moses receives the
law, Aaron and Phineas the covenants of the priesthood. If not
"here," in the vaguely visualized totality of the world, then
nowhere, for there is no other precise location or setting given
for these momentous events. A most amazing space or place—
simply the people and their founders in focus against the dark
background of the world in its vastness.

In the mention of the judges, "the land" comes into view,
and here it will be that the history is first localized. But in the
history of the prophets and kings, it is clear that the city is the
center of concern, and at the center of the city, it is the temple
and its cult upon which the major interest focuses. As the
hymn concludes, then, the city has been fortified, the temple
built, and the high priest has been placed in its precincts,
"coming forth from the sanctuary" (50:5), making "glorious
the court of the sanctuary" (50:11), to offer sacrifice and bless
(pardon) the people. All Israel is gathered around as the congregation, as are the priests, the "sons of Aaron in their glory"
(50:13). "How glorious he was when he looked forth from the
tent" (50:5), and in the blessing, "he glorified himself with the
name of the Lord" (50:20). Here one finds the people located
in the land (50:19), at the city, in the court of the temple. Here
one finds also the place where the office of glory is performed.
In the ministry of that office, the pardon of God in the blessing
is central. Thus both aspects of the promised blessing are fulfilled in this scene.

The people are "the whole congregation of Israel" (50:20),
that is, descendents of Abraham, the children of promise. The
priests are the "sons of Aaron," children of the priestly covenant who "bless the people" (45:15). The high priest is a de-
scendent of Phineas (50:24) making atonement for the sins of
the people. The themes of covenant, progeny, blessing, and
office climax here. It is the climax toward which the entire
history has been moving. Its glory is manifest in the figure of

Simon the high priest, whose "place" is at the center of it all in the sanctuary, whose office effects the formation of the congregation of Israel, and whose deed mediates the promised blessing of God to the people.

The Fulfillment

If this thesis is correct, there is a strong sense of historical fulfillment implied in the final scene. Not only is the history of Israel followed right into Ben Sira's own time, but the resolution of all of the major themes suggests that the history of promise and formation finally is being actualized. The sense of celebration and the motif of praise support this view. The scene reveals a very positive and optimistic assessment of Ben Sira's Israel as the people of God. The concluding hymn of blessing shows that Ben Sira was not unaware of the question of the future with its potential threat to the present arrangement: "May His mercy be established with Simon, May he raise up for him the covenant of Phineas, May no one be cut off from him, May it be to his seed as the days of heaven" (50:24). But from the future nothing more need be hoped for than that which is already fulfilled here.

The Israel that is actualized is, of course, the congregation of the temple cult. All of the major motifs and themes in the hymn, as well as some of the elements in the pattern of characterization, have been determined by cultic conceptions, concerns, and language. The themes of glory, piety, sacrifice, and atonement are obviously derived from this context. The relation of covenant to office and the functions and formations of the particular offices are also evidence for cultic concerns. The hymn and its interpretation of Israel's history can in fact be understood as a reading of the scriptures through the eyes of one whose picture of Israel-as-it-should-be is already given in the final scene. This picture has determined the constructions that have been put upon the past. The result is extremely creative and startling in its new conceptuality. It portrays the history of the deeds of God and the responses of his people as a dynamic development of cultic theocracy. The movement is highly structured and well balanced, showing that a single order has been superimposed on the otherwise manifold and disparate events of biblical history. The schema is organic in one sense, graphic in another. There is movement or growth from beginnings that reveal intentionality (promise) and potentiality ("*to* teach," "*to* bless"), through a process of formation and struggle to realize the ideal image, to a final achievement in which the model of the cult is actualized.

That human figures stand at the center of this model and are invested with the glory of its divine purpose, functions, and actualization is a new and daring conception. But this too can be seen as a projection upon all the hasidim figuring in the history of the special characterization of the high priest himself, through his role as high priest and especially with regard to his role on the Day of Atonement. He it is who enters into the presence of the Lord, shares in his glory, and mediates his mercy to the people. If this reading is right, the hymn may have functioned as a mythic charter for Second Temple Judaism.

THE HYMNIC HISTORY AS MYTH

Our thesis has been that Ben Sira understood the contemporary form of Second Temple Judaism as an appropriate climax to Israel's covenantal history. Only so has it been possible to account for the pattern of characterization, the overall structure, and the express intentionality of his hymn. We have also seen that the history has been cast in such a way that actualization of its reality and acknowledgment by the community can be claimed for Ben Sira's own time. It is a strange view of history indeed, without interest in sequential development at the level of contingent social-historical event. Each event is described as a moment of manifestation of glory. But each event also has been given a moment of promise or potentiality that points to a still more comprehensive and complete manifestation. It is when the several moments are seen in relation to one another that the full significance of any particular event is realized. The hymnic history, then, is to be taken as a whole, in the structure of which the completed manifestation is achieved.

Since the structure of the hymn is architectonic, each particular event of manifestation takes its place within the whole as an elemental component. Each event is related to each of the other events in two ways, however, depending upon the level at which the reading takes place. If one reads the sequences diachronically, disparate events can be related to one another as an accumulation of moments leading to the final manifestation. If one reads the sequences synchronically, the several moments can be related to one another as compatible and interchangeable signs in a single system of signs that manifests completeness. Since both of these readings are appropriate to the history, it can be seen that any given event may be read as a sign of some moment of actualization within the structure of the completed system or as a sign of a moment of potentiality for movement toward completion. If the complete system is the structure of the covenant community with its arrangement of institutions and offices organized around the temple cult and the role of the high priest, the purpose of the hymn appears to be given. It is a reading of Israel's history in just such a way as to disclose therein the evolutionary stages of the actualization in human-social formations of an essentially ahistorical theocratic-cultural ideal. This view of Israel's history can be designated "mythic."

The Synchronic View

In order to develop this suggestion, we should look more closely at the hymnic history as a coherent synchronic structure. The point has already been made that as a reading of Israel's scriptural history, the hymn reveals a high degree of intentional selectivity. It should be emphasized that this selection is marked by an extreme efficiency. Only the figures and the number of figures were chosen that were necessary to achieve the balanced structure intended.

The figures were chosen in keeping with their values as holders of the offices that structure the covenant community. In this ideal configuration, there is a clear notion of the community itself as a people and congregation determined by a divine election and blessing. This aspect of the structure of the covenant community is signified in the hymn primarily in the fathers. They are foundational figures both for the hymnic history that begins with them and for the image of the theocratic structure to be erected. Without them and the special character of the human community they represent, the superstructure of the theocratic ideal would have no place to appear. With four deft strokes, however, the covenant community does appear, carefully delimited and focused, emerging from the undifferentiated and chaotic mass of humanity, in the first four figures of the hymn.

To the structure of the theocratic ideal belongs, also, the notion of a mediator who stands high above the people, providing for them a central authority and access to the transcendent Divine. This structuring principle appears next in the hymn in the figure of Moses. As a composite figure, he represents the ideal archetype of all those as yet undifferentiated offices that must appear in the process of the structure's actualization. Through him, the community also receives the foundational "text" that will determine its special character. This appears in the revelation of the law.

With the mention of the law, an aspect of mediation comes into view that acknowledges the potential disparity between the ideal and the empirical, a disparity that must be resolved in the process of actualization. It is the priesthood as the highest office within the people, and the high priesthood as the highest office within the priesthood, that will mediate that disparity. The priests are derived from the Mosaic ideal. They depict the form of the office of mediation that will be appropriate to the structure of the community in its actuality, recognizable in its empirical manifestations.

With the presentation of the priests, the essential components of the structure of the covenant community are given. One is already able, therefore, to anticipate the final scene of the hymn and to recognize what is depicted there. That of course is exactly what the reader is expected to do. But the full significance of the correlation, its implicit verification of the legitimacy of the Second Temple institutions, is realized only when it is seen that both Aaron and Phineas belong still to the archetypal order of ideality. With them, it is true, the office emerges that will determine the shape of the empirical and actualized community in a way that the offices of the fathers and Moses do not. But its significance here is in its placement in the foundational epoch of covenants established with the first seven figures. The high priesthood has emerged, as we have seen, as the final image in a series that has moved through several shifts of focus as the structure of the covenant community comes into view. The unfolding of this structure constitutes a founding epoch, but it is important to see that the events of this epoch take place in no specific time or place. The picture comes into view against the dark and undifferentiated background of all time and all space, which is to say, "before" involvement with a particular history or location. Its function, then, is the manifestation of the formation of the theocratic community, and the structure that it reveals is an essentially transcendent and eternal order. It is, in the language of the phenomenology of religion, the sacred order imagined by the religious community and narrated in its myths.

That there are just seven figures chosen for this narrative function may now be given additional consideration. The number seven, as is well known, functioned for the Jews of Ben Sira's time as a code for completion, both in its connotation of quality (perfection) and in its connotation of time (full cycle). We noted in earlier discussions that the first seven figures form a unit by virtue of thematic development and formal periodizing. It can now be suggested that this unit of material is coded as well by the number seven, and in such a way as to enhance its capacity as an expression of ideality and completion. It is balanced, as we have seen, in the structure of the hymn by the concluding scene in which a re-enactment of this originary sacred order is depicted. That there is only one such scene focused on only one official figure does not destroy the balance at all. In the emergent image of the sacred order, the focus finally comes to rest on the figure of the high priest as the holder of the office that is to structure the covenant community in its empirical manifestation. Simon holds that office and is understood, therefore, to actualize the entirety of the sacred order manifest in the first seven figures. At the level of numerical code, the balanced correlation of the number seven with the number one achieves an additional significance. The number one also represents the idea of perfection, but in terms of unity or singularity. Thus to climax the hymnic history with this scene, which suggests a fulfillment of its covenantal intentions, does not violate the numerical code.

Still to be accounted for, however, are the middle sections of the hymn. These consist of three units, two units of three transitional figures each and a large middle section that relates the history of the prophets and kings. The balanced structure of the hymn as a whole is clear from these observations, especially when it is seen that the middle section itself is an internally balanced construction in which seven prophets and seven kings are placed against one another. What do these units contribute to the overall structure of the hymn and its function as myth?

The two units of transition (judges and restoration figures) bracket the middle section and thereby create a literary unit at the center of the hymn. This middle unit holds the first and last units apart and mediates between them. If, as we have seen, the first unit of the hymn creates the ideal image of the covenant community and the final scene depicts its actualization in time and place, it is already possible to anticipate the theme of the middle section. It will have to do with time and place and the process by which the ideal sacred order becomes actualized in human society. The theme of place is given immediately in the first unit of transition. It is "the land" into which the judges lead the people. This is given even greater specificity in the ensuing section: in the land, it is the city with its temple that becomes the locus for the struggle for actualization of the ideal. This struggle is, moreover, within the arena of human time or history, thus introducing the second theme. At the conclusion of this section, in the second transitional unit of the three restoration figures, the resolution of the process of actualization has been achieved in respect to specific human time and place, and the stage is set for the final ritual scene.

We have referred to the middle section as the history of the prophets and kings, and it is clear that in terms of narratve setting for each of the subunits, historical events are in view. But it has been noted also that certain events necessary for a full and continuous historical account are missing, and that a high degree of selectivity and systematization is in evidence. The significance of these findings for the hymn's synchronic structure can now be suggested.

The characterization of the two sets of transitional figures is composite in terms of office and ambiguous in terms of the architectonic structure of the covenant community. Their functions are therefore appropriate only to periods of transformation from one epoch (of history), order (of reality), or level (of structural systems) to another. Each set carries a single aspect of the process of actualization to completion (location in the land, security of the city and temple). There are three named in each period of transition, a numerical code appropriate to reiterative fulfillment and the distribution of effective function. They are necessary but provisional figures, signifying only those temporary moments at the beginning and the end of the conflict created by the coming-into-time-and-place of the ideal order.

In the section on the prophets and kings, then, this conflict is portrayed in terms of bifurcation within the structure of the covenant community itself. Oppositions both within it and in relation to its external environment are acknowledged and specified, and the dynamics by which these are to be resolved are studied. The bifurcation is what occurs in the emergence of the two offices of prophet and king. Each of these may be understood to be an aspect of the ideal mediator (Moses), derived from that figure by a process of differentiation. The division takes place immediately following the period of transition in which the ideal pattern is merged with the order of human time and place. It may be taken to signify the dysfunctionality that occurs between vision (prophets) and human achievement (kings), or between logos and praxis.

It may be recalled that there were no deeds performed by the figures of the foundational epoch, except the sacrifice of Phineas. In the first period of transition (judges), on the other hand, it is precisely the grand and glorious deeds of valor in war that are characteristic. With the kings, deeds of achievement continue to be normative, but they are now evaluated by a code that distinguishes constructive deeds from destructive ones. This code, however, is not available to the kings directly; it is rather the prophets who bring judgments to bear upon their deeds and call for actualization of the divine intentions. Thus the bifurcation of vision and achievement sets up a double system of oppositions appropriate to the theme of conflict between the ideal and the empirical. The first set of oppositions is that between prophets and kings and their significations; the second is that between constructive and destructive moments that occur in the course of repeated encounters.

There are seven prophets and seven kings in all, plus a collective designation for each at the end of the series. In the final collective designation of the kings, they are seen coming to their end (49:4); in the final collective designation of the prophets, the note of hope and deliverance is sounded (49:10). These statements do not resolve the dialectic between the prophets and the kings as such, for both are functional only within this unit of the covenant history, and within it, the covenant community has not been actualized. But the final statements do allow the opposition to come to rest with the prophets and their vision and hope. If now, by means of a second transformation (restoration), the hoped-for vision is realized, the opposition then will be resolved, and in such a way as to enhance the meaning of that realization as nothing less than the full integration of the human social order with the transcendental ideal. This can be appreciated and celebrated the more because the conflicts and potential divisions that accompany that merger have been disclosed completely and systematically, for the double series of seven indicates completion and is structured systematically. They have been disclosed as threats inherent within the community because the integration of leadership functions requires an integration of vision, institutional formation, and power difficult to achieve. Outside the community, there are other centers of human power that, if it does not achieve its own integration, can destroy it.

In the second transition and final scene, however, the integration is shown to have been accomplished. The office that is crucial for this move is the high priesthood. This office has been noticeably absent in the history of the prophets and kings, just as they are no longer in evidence in the final formation. We have seen the extent to which the depiction of Simon, though singularly that of the high priest, integrates nonetheless those aspects of the other offices that continue to be appropriate for the final configuration. The bifurcation of leadership functions in prophets and kings has been overcome, and the ideal that emerged in the foundational epoch has finally been actualized within the order of human history. Simon stands in the covenant of Phincas and performs the sacrifice of atonement in the intended place and at the intended time. He wears the robes of Aaron and thus displays the imagined glory of the originary investiture. He enters into the sanctuary and reappears before the people, an act of mediation that embodies the ideal seen only in Moses' glory. The promises to the patriarchs are manifestly realized in the "presence of the whole congregation of Israel" (50:13), which gathers to see the glory, hear the name, and receive the blessing and pardon of the Lord. All of this is included in the account, but only this. It is the precise function of this scene to realize the originary plan in the specified and central enactment of the Second Temple institutions of Ben Sira's own time.

The Diachronic Reading

The synchronic reading emphasizes both the balanced structure of the hymn and the various interrelationships of terms that this allows. But even as a system of signs, it has become clear that the hymn is not at all a structure *in stasis*. Even the ideal image of the structure of the covenant community created by the account of the first seven figures evolves by a series of moves that relate these figures to one another, not merely as a construction of disparate, accumulated parts, but generically. Each figure is seen to be derived from its precursors as a manifestation of an aspect of that which implicitly belongs to the covenant pattern coming into view. It is as if this series of moves was achieved by a set of lenses, each with a power that enables a yet deeper and more sharply focused penetration of the reality to be disclosed. If in the final figure a high priest (Phineas) and a specific act of sacrificial atonement are settled upon, it does not mean that the preceding perspectives are no longer in view. Thus the structure of the covenant community even as ideality contains within itself a dynamic moment. It is the structure of a promise-that-will-be-fulfilled, a seed-that-will-take-shape, a plan-that-will-be-constructed.

In the overall structure of the hymn, then, this dynamic works at another level. The evolutionary movement may be understood as the process by which the ideal (the dynamic) structure is actualized in time and place. This assumes, of course, a certain logic of sequences, which introduces a diachronic aspect to the structure. The structure continues to be balanced in spite of this; only so can the complete correlation of the levels of reality be maintained structurally (Second Temple institutions/originary pattern/the literary structure of the hymn itself). But it is a structure-in-movement. It is charged with an impulse that will generate, that wills the generation of these correlations. It has the capacity to sustain bifurcations and oppositions among its structural elements and to resolve them in the drive toward concretization. It is this forward thrust that gives the hymn its narrative quality and makes it possible to include Israel's history in the claim being made for the Second Temple institutions (the full incarnation of divine intentionality for Judaism).

One might even argue that it was the history itself, understood in terms of covenant and promise, that created the notion of a dynamic archetype. This, of course, would be true, but it would not account fully for the creative reflection that must be posited for this achievement. The history may have imbued Ben Sira's conception of pattern with the notion of dynamic evolution, but it is his predeliction for structuring that has selectively systematized the history. His rereading of the history has effectively erased the account and significance of all events that intervened and has connected those selected for inclusion in the hymn. For Ben Sira, time is therefore not a continuous series of contiguous events in the social history of a people. It is seen only in terms of moments in which the divine intentionality is manifest at some point in its evolution toward concretion. History has been structured and therefore spatialized. In this move, a systematic correlation of space and time has been achieved in a single grasp.

It is this understanding of order that marks Ben Sira's hymn as myth. It is intended as an account of those events that relate the evolution of the coming-into-being of the divine and eternal intentions for the structure of the covenant community as it is constituted in Ben Sira's own time. It becomes the myth by means of which that glory may be recognized as present in the ritual enactment of the covenant and community on the Day of Atonement. To participate in that ritual is to celebrate the actualization of the originary pattern. Given the conflicts necessarily suffered and overcome in the process of actualization, as recounted by the myth, the claims that are implicitly made for this ritual moment are enormous. The act is taken to be that toward which all time has moved; the high priest, the one around whom all space has aspired to be organized; the scene, as the final accomplishment of the divine intentions for human social structuring. Borrowing categories from Mircea Eliade, we may understand the hymn to have achieved a conceptual, systematic correlation of cosmos and history.[7]

The hymn began, as we have noted, with a section praising God's works in creation. This was followed by a recounting of the manifestations of his glory in Israel's history. In the final scene, it is therefore not insignificant that Simon is described, when he appears from the sanctuary in his glorious robes, as the very reflection of creation's splendor: "Like the sun shining on the temple of the Most High, and like the rainbow becoming visible in the clouds. Like a flower on the branches in the days of the first fruits, and as a lily by the water-brooks" (50:5–11). The glory to be seen is just that this correlation has been achieved—the glory of God's works in the order of creation reflected in the glory of his purposes actualized in the order of human history.

Part 2

Rhetorical Considerations: Reading and Writing

Reading: In the Place of Praise 3

Two patterns have emerged in the course of our analysis. The heroes have a profile; the history has a structure. Each pattern functions in relation to the other, taking its significance from the other by means of an interlocking system of signs. Unexpectedly, together they form a mythic foundation on which to imagine the edifice of Second Temple institutions.

If the study were left at this point, however, it could easily be misunderstood as an exercise in abstractions. If the patterns are really there, and if they do have social significance, it would be helpful to account for that significance in some other way. This can be done either by demonstrating their exemplary significance for some structuralist theory of culture or by a further exploration of the hymn's relationship to cultural (literary) and social history. To find the place of the text within its own cultural context, its relationship to other texts and systems of signs needs to be determined. If a sufficient number of intertextual relationships can be determined, this will serve both as a clarification and verification of the text's literary structures and as an index to its significance as a particular translation, transformation, and articulation of those systems of signs already available in its cultural context. It is this approach that will be pursued in part 3.

But to comprehend the significance of the text in its context, an additional exploration is required. We need to check our own reading of the text against plausible reconstructions of the way it may have been read by those whose text it was. A way must be found to imagine both the act of reading and the act of writing it as moments meaningful to those who were already well read in the systems of signs fundamental to their culture. By imagining the text's authorship and audience in a specific social setting, more precision can be given to questions about the way in which it gains significance in relation to other texts. In this manner, the accuracy of our literary analysis can be checked. The question is whether the text can be understood as a plausible rhetoric in its own context. If we find it possible to position it in this way, another perspective on the hymn's relationship to other "texts" will have been gained as well, because a precise social setting can itself be regarded as a system of signs within the cultural complex. Relationships established here will allow us to reconstruct yet another "translation" of signs and so determine their meanings.

DIDACTIC AND DEVOTIONAL MOMENTS

There are two features of the hymn that we need to account for and combine in any assessment of its social setting and function. The first may be called its didactic character, evidence for which is given in the scope of its historical review, the development of themes, the descriptive mode of much of its discourse, the patterning of characterization, and the implicit etiological purpose. There is great learning invested in this composition, and it is put forth clearly as a review and recitation of familiar material with specific interpretive theses. The reader is asked to listen, understand, and be instructed.

But there is a second feature of the hymn that certainly may be called liturgical, that is, an invitation to respond in postures appropriate to public religious occasions. This is manifest in the incipit (the announcement of intention for praise), the di-

vine aretalogical form, its association with the preceding hymn
to the Lord's creation, the language of cult and piety throughout, the movement to a final scene of ritual celebration, and
the inclusion of two blessings, one of which forms the conclusion to the hymn itself. There is deep religious fervor here, and
the reader is invited to share in it.

If we ask about the appropriateness of this hymn in corporate worship, however, or about its feasibility in a purely didactic setting, we can see immediately its limitations. A purely
liturgical function is made improbable by its descriptive style,
length, and especially by its theme—the glorification of pious
men. A purely didactic function is made improbable by its
heightened sense of assertion and authority, its manifestation
of religious certitude and commitment, and its invitation
throughout to honor, glorify, and praise. What, then, is its
function and where is it placed?

The combinations of liturgical and didactic modes of speech
in a poetic composition, a combination reminiscent of the didactic Psalms, suggests a mode of reflection that might be
called meditation. There is a sense of distance from active and
actual participation in corporate worship. Yet the mood of the
worshipper, the member of the congregation, continues to set
the tone for both the composition and the appropriate reading
of this piece. The reflection is studied, focused, and controlled
by this mood, and yet it is discursive. There is repeated invitation to pause, take note, and come again to see and assent to
the glory of this powerful history. It is a piece appropriate for
religious meditation, perhaps as preparation for worship; it is
literature of reflection that invites both understanding and
praise. We may thus be guided in our attempt to understand
the way in which the heroes of the hymn are intended to be
taken and its structured history affirmed.

THE READER'S DISTANCE FROM THE HEROES

The discovery of a general pattern of characterization in the
hymn raises the question of its function for the individual
reader. One is tempted to think of it as a model of piety for

personal emulation or aspiration. But our study of the pattern has shown that it is hardly appropriate as a model for individual achievement.[1] It is a study in ethos limited to leadership roles that are recognized as offices of authority in the structure of the religious community. This does not mean that such depiction is incapable of idealizing strengths and virtues to which the average individual might also aspire. In the case of Abraham, as we have seen, a rite and sign of obedience has been recorded that is also required of each Jewish male. By extension, many of the other religious virtues mentioned in the hymn would not be inappropriate for personal piety either. Thus the reader would see in the figures descriptions of piety that were recognizable and highly valued as descriptions of Jewish religious piety in general. By yet another extension, one might even say that election itself could be democratized in the reading and seen as a reflection in the heroes of a determination effective for all Jews. But just at this point, it begins to be clear that if read this way, the pattern of characterization functions as a statement of the religious identity of the Jewish people as already constituted by divine election and covenant. Neither within the pattern itself nor in the explicit mention of a relationship of the community to these figures is there any possiblity of seeing how one might come to achieve this ethos. It is simply and already given, expressed by their election.

In the case of the kings, there is a study of the risk of failure in terms of impiety, and one suspects that a standard other than that of election may be in play. That other standard may be indeed some form of Torah piety that the perceptive reader will no doubt detect. But we have noted the extent to which an ideal of righteousness in this sense is simply not in evidence in the hymn, and in the function of the office of the king, it is the fate of the people that is described as at stake, without any indication of their responsibility or choice in the matter. This leaves us with an idealization that functions paradigmatically, if at all, for judgments one might make about other holders of high social office.

These officers, then, are defined essentially in terms of social and institutional roles. In every case, they are figures through whom the purpose and agency of God for the constitution of the theocratic community is mediated to the people. Because the leaders are cast as mediators and benefactors for the well-being of the community, the people are depicted consistently in relation to them as recipients of their various ministries. This means that identity is understood in social, corporate, and institutional terms. The individual relates to these great leaders as one who already belongs to the congregation of the people, a corporate entity whose foundation and structure is celebrated in the hymn. The leaders function at first and primarily as holders of offices that determine the shape of the religious society. In reading the hymn, as Ben Sira suggests in the proem, the proper response to the memory of these great leaders is, therefore, to honor and to praise them (44:8, 15).

THE HEROES' EFFECT UPON THE READERS

But even if this much is so—that the heroization of the leaders is not intended to set up a model of piety for personal emulation and achievement—questions remain about the nature and purpose of the honor to be accorded to them. This is especially troubling in light of Ben Sira's explicit statement that the hasidim continue to exercise an effective influence upon and for the people in his own time.

The crucial text is in the proem at 44:7 and is cited here in the translation of Box and Oesterley:

7 All these were honored in their generation,
   And in their days had glory.
. . . .
10 Nevertheless these were men of piety,
   And their good fortune shall not come to an end;
11 With their seed their prosperity remains sure,
   And their inheritance to their children's children.
12 In their covenant their seed abides,
   And their children's children for their sakes;
13 Their memory abides forever,
   And their righteousness shall not be forgotten;
14 Their bodies were buried in peace,
   But their name lives unto all generations.

15 The assembly recounts their wisdom,
   And the congregation declares their praise.

Several themes developed in the hymn are announced here: honor, glory, progeny, inheritance, covenant, and piety. What is new is the programmatic statement of the continuing influence of these men within and for the contemporary community. The text consists essentially of five ideas: their honor and glory, their heritage, their covenants, their memory, and their praise.

Their Honor and Glory

The first statement is that the fathers received honor and glory in their generations (44:7). This is a comment on the past that may be compared with the concluding statement about their being praised in the present (44:15). This combination of the two moments of praise creates a sense of continuity. The theme of honor and glory announced in the proem is traceable throughout the hymn. It occurs mostly in keeping with the assertion that these glorious men were recognized and honored as such by their contemporaries. This is a very bold and striking interpretation of the past. It combines an idealization of the past with a remarkable notion of glory. Glory in this view is recognizable both by the leader and by his contemporaries. We might call it an objectification of presence. Glory, according to this view, is not the product of a subsequent generation's idealization of the past, as if Ben Sira were simply attributing glory and honor to these leaders. The glories of the past are at first recounted as moments of full recognition "in their generation." The reader is addressed as one looking on, called to recognize that it was so. As the hymnic account moves into Ben Sira's own present, glory is indeed manifest for him in the office of Simon (50:4, 11, 20). There is a sense, then, in which glory itself is understood as an effective principle of continuity within the history, for it has been manifest consistently throughout that history in the series of special men.

The response required of the reader is therefore quite complex. The notion of glory itself is dialectical with regard to the relationship it announces between hero and community (one has glory only in being glorified) and is therefore unstable as a concept. The reader is asked, however, not only to imagine such moments occurring in the past, but to understand as well that the recital of these imaginative moments in the present also constitutes a glorification of the heroes. For Ben Sira to make present the figures of the past for the reader in the act of glorifying them, and at the same time to describe that past in moments of objective glorification, destroys the perception of history according to developmental schemata and substitutes the notion of a continuous (though dynamic) presence throughout all time. It will be important to keep this in mind as other statements about the effective influence of the pious are explored, statements that appear more beholden to an empirical reading of the history.

Their Heritage

The second idea expressed in the proem is that the good fortune, prosperity, and inheritance of the pious continue to exist as possessions of their descendents (44:10–11).[2] If taken literally, there is nothing in the hymn to which this can refer.[3] It expresses a view of material reward for virtue that reminds one of an earlier statement in the proem about "stalwart men, solidly established and at peace in their own estates" (44:6). Taken together, these two statements reflect a social and economic concern for the security of property, a concern that Ben Sira certainly may have shared. To address this concern, most probably aristocratic and conservative but possibly political as well, by appeal to legacy from the hasidim is a striking claim and may indicate the degree to which Ben Sira understood the history and model of Second Temple Judaism to include given social structures and economic institutions. How it might be that the economic form of Ben Sira's society could be imagined as legacy from those praised in the hymn is difficult to see. In the tradition of the Hellenistic encomium, it is true, a person's achievement of goods and property was recognized as appropriate for eulogy.[4] But in the school traditions of philosophical ethics, the relationship between goods (*ta agatha*) and virtue (*aretē*) had become exceedingly problematic.[5] If Ben Sira was influenced here by a Hellenistic convention, it has been combined with the Jewish idea of inheritance. If this combination of ideas derived from a Deuteronomistic conception of the relationship of piety to the inheritance of the land, a bridge might be posited that could make some sense of Ben Sira's assertions. But this sense is not expressed, and it would be in any case difficult to correlate with the kind of piety attributed to the leaders hymned. We are left, then, with a simple claim of legacy curiously unhelpful for our question about the manner in which these special men continue to exercise influence in the community. But it is clear that the effectiveness of the sacred history (notice the plural "their" at 44:10–11) is understood in relation to the social and economic structures of the time.

Their Covenants

The third idea expressed is that the descendents of these men continue in their covenants (44:12). The theme of covenant is fully developed in the hymn, as we have seen. As a theological idea, it contains within itself the notions of originary moment and continuous promise. If the effective influence of these men has to do with the continuing validity of the divine covenants with them, the principle of continuity and agency is ultimately that of divine initiative and faithfulness. This is an extremely complex notion in its own right, providing as it does, not only a certain view of God, but a theological claim about a people's continuity in history. That both of these notions are contained within the singular concept of covenant as that which continues makes it possible to see how this concept can be correlated with that of glory. The idea of covenant is certainly at work, and it is very important as an indication of the essentially priestly theological frame within which Ben Sira stands.[6] But if this is so, the effectiveness of the men-so-praised in the hymn is qualified as functional to this theologumenon. This is fully in keeping with our discussion of the pattern of characterization.

The claim made at 44:12 is that the progeny of these men do continue to be counted among those included in the original intention of the covenant. In chapter 2, it was argued that the themes of covenant promise and genealogical descent announced in the first section of the hymn were conjoined creatively again in the concluding scene. This agrees with the assertion here and lends further support to our contention that Ben Sira's purpose in the hymn was to create a theological charter for a specific form of Judaism in which the temple institutions stood at the center of a complete social system. But the phrase "for their sakes" (44:12) alerts us to the fact that this charter is not to be expressed except in terms of the efficacy of those men of glory with whom the covenants were established and in and through whom they continued to be manifest and actualized. Our question about the mode of this effectiveness has been answered theologically by the reference to covenant, but it has not been answered in such a way as to account for the form of the hymn.

Their Memory

The fourth idea is that the hasidim continue and will continue to be remembered (44:13–14). Here, finally, we encounter a statement that may have direct relevance for our question about the function of the hymn itself. The mention of burial, name, and memory is to be understood at first as a common form of expressing a general Jewish aspiration. The aspiration has, of course, deeply religious significance and grows out of the theological conception of the covenant people. It has been understood traditionally as the Jewish analogue to Hellenic conceptions of apotheosis or immortality. To be remembered implies the continuance of the community. Remembering itself is, in this specific sense, a mode of perception characteristic of human existence. As a category of historical continuity and influence, then, memory can be understood to function in analogy to the concepts of glory, inheritance, and covenant. It is objectified here in Ben Sira's statement insofar as it is "their memory" that is said "to abide forever."

In the hymn, there is also repeated mention of this motif.

To have a name and a memory is one way in which a glorious leader may be said to have received his reward. Ben Sira was also careful not to mention the names of those found unworthy of depiction as ideal leaders. This carefulness alerts us to the function of the hymn itself in the propagation of the memory of these glorious men and shows that Ben Sira was aware of that contemporary function. As with their glory and covenants, so with the names of these great men. The hymn's mode is that of historical description, but its function is to facilitate the leaders' memory in the present time. How exactly this may be intended is not indicated here (44:13–14), but in the immediately succeeding statements additional significant clues are given.

Their Praise

The fifth and final statement that Ben Sira makes about the effective influence of the men of piety is that "the assembly recounts their wisdom, and the congregation declares their praise" (44:15). Here it is that a concrete setting (assembly, congregation) and specific actions (recounting, praise) are mentioned as particular occasion and means for the contemporizing of the memory of the glorious men. This is very helpful because it indicates a corporate and religious context within which the acknowledgment of the greatness of these men takes place. If we were able to be more precise about this occasion, and especially about the role that Ben Sira's hymn might play in relation to it, our questions about the way the influence of the great men was effected for the individual and the congregation could finally be addressed.

The problem with Ben Sira's statement is that, even if we take it literally, we do not know to what occasion it may have referred. Middendorp has analyzed the two terms for assembly in Sirach (gāhāl, ʿēdāh) and concluded that both are used to refer to public gatherings of the people in Jerusalem for essentially political functions after the manner of the Hellenistic ekklēsia.[7] He notes that Ben Sira's grandson may have distinguished between the two, in that ekklēsia is used to translate gāhāl, whereas synagōgē is used to translate ʿēdāh.[8] This would prove helpful, however, only if we had other evidence for the existence of a synagogue-like institution in second-century Palestine, and if we knew also that the term *synagōgē* (instead of *proseuchē*) was current in the second century in Egypt as a technical designation for some extra-temple Jewish institution of a religious nature, either in the Diaspora or in Palestine. Neither bit of information is available to us, however, which means that Ben Sira's usage is probably in keeping with older scriptural usage in which no distinction is made between the two terms.[9] But is Middendorp's conclusion about the essentially political nature of these gatherings acceptable in the light of 44:15 and 39:10?

Reviewing the references to these terms in Sirach as a whole, one is struck by the degree to which it is one's wisdom that is said to be of paramount importance in this context.[10] Middendorp understands the references to wisdom to refer to the rhetorical demands for wise and considered speech appropriate to a deliberative body. He argues, not only for the practice of rhetoric appropriate to the deliberation and jurisprudence of these assemblies, but also for the practice of encomiastic speeches in analogy to Hellenistic declamation. For this period, Hellenistic influence on the structure and political function of such an *ekklēsia* is, of course, probable. But it is not at all clear, nor probable, that Jewish practice would have therefore conformed in every way with Hellenistic analogues. The evidence from Ben Sira is that even a very open appreciation of Hellenistic models of social governance, education, cultural forms, and thought has not destroyed essentially Jewish concerns for theocracy, Torah, tradition, and wisdom.

We may assume, surely, that the Jewish practice of rhetoric in jurisprudence, for instance, would have been determined by the particular nature and requirements of Jewish law. Since the only evidence we have for anything that can approximate the Hellenistic encomium for this period is Ben Sira's hymn itself, extreme caution must be exercized in the question about the practice of declamation strictly on the Greek model. The hymn as we have analyzed it does not correspond fully to the form of the Hellenistic encomiastic speech, nor does it share in those cultural and anthropological assumptions that set the stage for declamation. But the telling consideration here is that ultimately the congregation itself is said to recount the wisdom of the pious and declare their praise. It is also the congregation that declares the praise of the sage himself (39:10). It is this corporate dimension to the act that is not illuminated sufficiently by Middendorp's thesis and that therefore calls for another consideration.

THE ASSEMBLY AS THE PLACE OF PRAISE

There are three aspects of this occasion that must be accounted for and combined in any compelling thesis. The first has to do with the nature of the assembly itself; the second with the linguistic-literary form in which the pious are recalled; the third with the nature of the praise attributed to them. Each of these aspects is difficult to determine, especially if taken up separately. But taken together, a plausible group of settings can actually be imagined. Our task is to relate the discussion about the assembly to a consideration of the nature of the memory and praise made possible by the hymn.

We may begin with the observation that Ben Sira's hymn is composed entirely of biblical material. The assumption might be, therefore, that the primary occasion for remembering these historical figures would have occurred in the reading of the scriptures at certain times of assemblage. It is unfortunate that we know even less about the place and extent of scriptural readings among the Jews of Palestine during this period than we do about the forms of religious assemblage themselves. The evidence from Nehemiah 8 and 9 has been taken to indicate that Torah was read publicly during this period, at least on the days of high festival and pilgrimage.[11] Ben Sira does not mention such an occasion. But it is clear from the evidence in Sirach itself that Torah was known, studied, and interpreted at this time as a basis for Jewish ethic, jurisprudence, and if Middendorp is correct, for constitutional law respecting Second Temple institutions.[12] Certainly the biblical stories were known as well, recalled and retold in some way by the people. It is probable also, that Torah was read as epic credo in some form on certain religious occasions (cf. the homiletic summary in Nehemiah 9) or even within the course of instruction in some school setting. If so, the mention of these figures would have occurred in the normal course of the reading, and it would be to that occasion that Ben Sira refers. He would not be saying, necessarily, that it was the practice of the community on such occasions to eulogize the heroes formally. Neither would his statement have to mean that the scriptural accounts in which these men figured were understood by the community as eulogistic in intention. He would be saying that it was on these occasions that the memory of these men was kept alive in the "congregation" and that one might view the congregation's activity on these occasions as "recounting their wisdom and declaring their praise." This would mean, of course, that Ben Sira's statement would be taken, not as literally descriptive, but as an interpretive assertion. Is this plausible?

It has been argued that the didactic intention of the hymn determines its appropriateness as a meditation and preparation for worship. By focusing now upon its midrashic character, we can see that one aspect of its didactic capacity has to do with an interpretive rereading of the scriptures from a certain point of view. Insofar as members of the people-as-congregation shared this interpretive reading with Ben Sira, a possibility given with the reading of the hymn itself, Ben Sira's statement about "recounting their wisdom and declaring their praise" would be apt. It would be an assertion of the influence of the hymn on those other occasions in which Torah was recited or recalled. It would not have to refer to the use of the hymn itself as a component of religious service, nor of any specific practice of Torah reading as intentional eulogy. It would indicate rather the effect created by the correlation of the Torah and the hymn in the mind of the reader on any occasion of recitation or recall.

But if this is so, the act of praise to which Ben Sira refers also must be understood essentially as a response to such a recitation, a response that therefore combines both reflective and liturgical moments. It must also combine appropriate con siderations of both the human and the divine aspects of the hymnic history. In both its Hebrew and Greek connotations, "praise" is capable of expressing just such a combination of moments. In the Greek (*epainon, epainein*), the notion is essentially a designation of eulogistic speech with reference to worthy figures. In the Hebrew (*tᵉhillāh, hillēl*), the appropriate object is God and the divine manifestations. It is the Hebrew connotation, of course, that alerts one to the need for thoughtful consideration, lest one be tempted to take the term in strictly Hellenistic connotation. As liturgical response to hymns and the reading of the scripture, however, praise may merge in the Hebrew with the notion of blessing (*bārak*). Blessing does occur in this sense in Sirach both at the end of the creation hymn in chapter 39 (39:35) and at the end of the hymn in praise of the fathers (50:22). This blessing (50:22–24), which begins with reference to God but continues as prayer for the continuity of Phineas's covenant with Simon, follows immediately upon those verses in which the priestly blessing and pardon are described. Here the themes of the promise of God's blessing to Abraham and the priestly functions of blessing and atonement were found to be conjoined in the climactic scene as Simon "glorified himself with the name of the Lord" (50:20).

It may now be suggested that the daring shift in perspective in Ben Sira's composition, whereby the human figures of Israel's history can be glorified and praised, probably took place in the context of priestly reflection about the contemporary cult. In this context, a correlation of the notions of glory, blessing, and praise was possible that, understood as a cultic moment of divine manifestation, priestly office, and congregational response, could mediate between ascription to the divine and description of the human exactly as we have found it to occur in the hymn. The hymnic descriptions of Israel's leaders as glorious would have been possible, according to the view, as projections upon them of the glories of the high priest himself in his performance of high liturgical functions.

It should be noted, though, that in the final scene, the people do not actually praise Simon. It is Ben Sira who praises him

in his description of the scene. This description does suggest
that the people are in the presence of Simon's glory, and the
reader may conclude that the people recognize it. But it is
important to see that this conclusion occurs at the level of the
reading of the hymn. Thus Ben Sira's praise, both of Simon and
of all the leaders, is accomplished precisely in the composition
of the hymn (45:5). When he asserts in the proem, then, that
the congregation declares their praise (44:15), it must be praise
in keeping with the function of the hymn itself.[13] There is, in
fact, a statement made within the context of the hymn itself, at
the end of the proem, that is intended to attest the leaders'
glory by asserting that it is recognized by the congregation. But
the actual occasion of the reading of the hymn takes place, not
during congregational worship itself, but in a displaced setting
of instruction and meditation.

If the praise of which Ben Sira speaks is just that praise
enabled by his hymn, it must contain the moment of reflection
and assent that the hymn's interpretive and didactic functions
entail. It is this moment that allows the term to be used at all
in reference to Israel's leaders and that gives the term its capacity to evoke Hellenistic thought and practice. But it does
not cease for this reason to be a fundamentally religious act
that is determined by its pre-displacement setting in "the congregation," a religious community constituted liturgically. The
reflective moment is what happens to the heroes when their
memories are recalled by the composer and readers of this
hymn as members of that congregation. If the moment of composition and meditation takes place in some setting other than
that of a temple liturgy—in, say, some scholarly and instructional setting—it does not mean that the idea of the congregation is no longer applicable. The meditation itself is upon the
structure of the religious community and its history. The act of
praise is attributed to the community precisely because the
meditation cannot take place outside it. This means, finally,
that the community effectively mediates the significance and
glory of the leaders to the individual. This is fully in keeping
with our analysis of the pattern of characterization and structure of the hymn. The heroes are depicted only in relation to

the community and its history. The individual is not placed in direct relation to these great men but stands at a distance from them as a member of the congregation. The act of praise is possible only on the basis of incorporation within the community, and the effectiveness of the glorious ones is realized in the act of praise, which acknowledges thereby the community's own theocratic foundation and existence.

PRAISE AND POLITICAL HISTORY

We have encountered a rather complex rhetoric in our attempt to understand the function of Ben Sira's hymn. To praise Israel's leaders as the hymn suggests, one must read the hymn, of course. But for that reading to work its way, at least two other occasions must be in the picture. One is a public occasion for the reading of the scriptures themselves. The other is the public occasion of high-priestly performance. To distinguish these three moments in the act of praise called for by the hymn is to notice its essentially reflective nature. It is also to notice the text's dependency upon other systems of signification, as well as its manipulation of them. The purpose of this recasting of these prior "texts" is to combine them in another, more comprehensive system of signs, that is, the hymn's own system of signs. Thus Temple and Torah have been integrated in a single version of Israel's history by the text's careful selection of details from each system. The act of praise called for by the new vision requires some perception on the part of the reader of this accomplishment.

But is it possible that yet more must be in view? If our reading of the hymn is right, more than Israel's epic historiography has been appropriated and more than the high holy Day of Atonement has been reflected upon. If the hymn is a mythic charter for Second Temple Judaism, the function of its invitation to praise may be more complex than we have imagined. We must therefore assess its significance in relation to the larger context of social and political history in the Palestine of Ben Sira's time.

Middendorp has explored Ben Sira's relationship to the political structures and events in Jerusalem during his time and concluded that he stood with those who favored the position of Simon II over those who sought other configurations of power.[14] Simon's position, briefly, was to accommodate the foreign powers ruling Jerusalem as long as Jewish institutions such as the gerousia, courts, and temple could continue to function on the basis of Mosaic law. He was therefore able to support Antiochus III as power shifted from the Ptolemies to the Seleucids. Others, however, represented by the Tobiads, at first took the side of the Ptolemies, with whose government they had strong relations, then sought to take advantage of the Seleucids' desire to Hellenize the political structures of Jerusalem in order to enhance their own positions of power within the international political and economic order. Their political power in Jerusalem is indicated by the fact that Onias III, successor to Simon II, took their position, thus setting the stage for the massive religious and political conflicts that centered on the temple and the office of the high priesthood.

Middendorp has argued convincingly that Ben Sira favored Simon's position. He was partial neither to the Ptolemies nor to the Seleucids. Of course, he was not threatened by their rule as it had been experienced up until the time of Simon II. Threat would occur only in some move to integrate the religious and political powers of the city on the basis of a Hellenistic *nomos*. As for openness to Hellenistic thought and culture in general, Ben Sira's book reveals the marks of an erudite cosmopolitan, confident in his ability to accept and understand his world in a way that supported his deep religious piety.[15]

This position, dependent as it was upon the relative autonomy of the temple institution as it was privileged to exist at the turn of the second century, could not have been maintained in the immediately subsequent decades. This being the case, the hymn must now appear as a preposterous claim made in the face of all odds of impinging historical vicissitude. If he composed the hymn after Simon's death, as the descriptions in Sir. 50:2–3 would lead one to believe, he cannot have been unaware that the institution of the high priesthood was in danger. What then are we to make of such a composition?

The thought that there may have been an element of apology, if not political program, in the writing is difficult to suppress. Middendorp has not found any evidence of a political program as such in Sirach. But he has noted the curious lack of expressly theocratic formulations in the book and has concluded that Ben Sira was being extremely cautious in this regard.[16] Kings are mentioned throughout, of course, as befits a wisdom book, and it does appear that for Ben Sira, a king is a king whether in Israel's history or among the nations or as foreign sovereign in contemporary Palestine. The concept is accepted, and the fact of royal power acknowledged. But it is not justified or glorified in any way, except in the context of the specific function assigned the king in the hymnic history. The wisdom sayings about kings in general, as well as about taking positions in the service of the king, express a deep reservation about the influence royal power has both upon the society as a whole and upon its individual members.[17] The rule is accepted—"as is the king, so are the people"[18]—but this is hardly a basis for hope, though it may allow for the inclusion of traditional wisdom, which takes the form of advice to the king.

It must therefore appear all the more significant that Ben Sira assigned the only royal function worthy of glory, the establishment and defense of the city-temple, to the high priest Simon. If this analysis of the intention of the hymn is correct, the theocratic ideal for the covenant community is fully constituted in this office and there is no longer any need for another kind of king as well. This appears to be cheating a bit on Ben Sira's part, in that the function of the kings who were actually ruling Palestine is missing from his picture. One would expect that under the circumstances, this problem of the bifurcation of power would have to be addressed and reflected in the hymnic depictions. But there is no indication in the hymn either that the high priest's power was, say, destined to expand until one day kings in Palestine would be no more or that the high priest's sphere of authority was recognized to be limited to a religious order separate from the king's. It is this, then, that creates the hymn's anomaly.

Insofar as it glorifies the Second Temple institutions represented by Simon, it could be taken as a political program, of course, but only within the context of an internal Jewish debate about the nature of the high priesthood, and then only by making its point negatively, that is, by glorifying Simon's specifically religious significance without addressing the question of how far his authority might be imagined to extend out into the economic and political structures of the community. This hardly would have been sufficient as political manifesto, even though as a document written from an implicitly political point of view, its mythic claims would have registered an amazing degree of seriousness and commitment in its support.

So the hymn appears to be something more, something else. It is in the office of the high priest that all is at stake. The lack of polemical overtones in the hymn and the celebration and glorification that climax in the final scene speak, then, for a piety that, even though the troublesome problem of kingship and kingdom was recognized as real, preferred to see in the religious order a sufficient arena for covenant-community actualization. This means from our point of view that the mythic claim was itself an idealization of the Second Temple institutions. They were being glorified, not on the basis of the actual state of affairs in Palestine, but in spite of them.

This achievement bespeaks deep piety and profound learning at the same time. It is to be understood as the work of one who had his place within the institutional structures of the religious community as scholar and sage. The power of its implicit claim is based upon its audacious affirmation and its intellectual achievement. A priest and scholar, schooled in the traditions of Torah and wisdom, would be the appropriate office, a priestly school the appropriate context. It is perhaps, after all, a wisdom composition, born of the strange capacity that Jewish wisdom teachers seemed to possess, to affirm God's wisdom and the reality of his created order-for-good in spite of all evidences to the contrary.

Writing: The Glory of the Scholar-Sage 4

If one were to imagine Ben Sira's view of his world iconographically, the final scene from the hymn would probably dominate the foreground. Not highlighted in the picture, but acknowledged in one way or another by disclosures and assumptions, most of the obvious features of Jewish social life would be there in the background. Estates and libraries, assemblies and courts, priests and scholars, commerce and conflicts—all of it is there, assumed, and some of it is partially seen, bustling around the temple in the center of one's vision. What Ben Sira does not have in the picture, however, is any clear depiction of the larger Hellenistic world within which Second Temple Judaism had to fight for its existence. In the first sections of the hymn, there was a dark background against which the glorious figures and moments were painted. But in the final scene, and in Ben Sira's book of wisdom as a whole, one has trouble catching sight of the kings and commanders, interests and ideologies, conflicts and intrigues that were threatening to destroy his social world.

This shifts our attention to the other side of the rhetorical equation, away from the reader of Ben Sira's poem and onto the author himself. If he invested the interest in the composition of this hymn that may be suspected from its rhetorical potential, whence the literary and mythological resources to do so? Whence the commitments and energies to sustain its view in spite of the realities of its context? Can it be that there is more to the hymn than has been discovered, something about it that could support its obvious invitation to celebrate the glory it sings, even though one knew, surely, that the vestments and foundations of the high priesthood represented by Simon were the subjects around which ruthless political forces raged? In short, where is the mythic vision anchored?

The suggestion has been made that Ben Sira's place was in a temple school. This accords with a consensus of scholarship, even though there is little evidence for such an institution at the time except for Ben Sira's own book of wisdom.[1] It would be helpful to know more about this school, and about Ben Sira's activity as a scholar-sage at work within this context— his haunts, his library, his desk and students, his place within the social structures, and his authority as one who could dare such a composition and hope for its hearing. If our thesis about the hymn's intentionality is correct, interest in its author is not idle curiosity. If it is possible to see more clearly the author at his work, one might be able to see more deeply into the hymn's promises and purposes. But it is not possible to begin with the hymn for this investigation because, as we have already noted, the role of the teacher, though modeled at the beginning of the hymn by Moses, drops from sight in its subsequent study of the social roles in Israel's illustrious history. This means that Ben Sira's role as teacher is not in view in the scene that sets the foreground for our picture of his world. But though the teacher is not in view, he is within hearing as the author who lets the reader stand beside him, looking on at that grand scene. So author, hymn, and religious occasion are intimately conjoined. Somewhere outside the picture, the author takes his stand. We need to find that place and to locate it in relation both to the final scene of the hymn and to the larger-world within which that scene takes place.

There are three sets of literary clues at our disposal for this exploration. One set has to do with general observations from

Ben Sira's book about his learning. Another is given with a fine poem about the scholar-sage in Sir. 39:1–11. The third is the relationship of Ben Sira's picture of the scholar-sage in Sir. 39:1–11 to his depiction of the hasidim in the proem to the hymn.

THE MARKS OF BEN SIRA'S LEARNING

Ben Sira's book of wisdom has long been recognized as a compendium of rich learning. This study cannot be the place to enter into any detailed discussion of its themes or content, although aspects of its teaching will be taken up in the final chapter. But one point can be made that will advance our quest. An amazingly broad scope of literatures must have been read and mastered by the author of this book. These literatures include both Hebrew and Hellenistic texts. Ben Sira's acquaintance with Theognis, as well as with Stoic and Cynic commonplaces has been shown.[2] His knowledge of Hellenistic literary genres, including maxim collection, hymn, encomium, biography, and history is in evidence.[3] He reproduced and reinterpreted a Hellenistic hymn to Isis, combined Greek maxims creatively with Hebrew proverbs, and found a way to relate wisdom mythology with the Hebrew scriptures.[4] There is less clarity among scholars about the book's arrangement of materials. Middendorp, especially, has argued for its loose arrangement and its appearance in stages. But close reading detects blocks of material in theme units, and the book as a whole may be structured by a sound organizational principle.[5] It is quite possible that it is arranged on the model of a handbook for teachers in the Hellenistic schools.[6]

Ben Sira's thorough knowledge and critical reading of the Hebrew scriptures also cannot be doubted. This reading extends far beyond the literature of Hebrew wisdom and the Torah of Moses, as the analysis of the hymn in chapter 5 will show. Not only are the later historical writings in his library, but he uses language in the depiction of the heroes that reflects the Psalms and Prophets as well. And in every case of allusion, reminiscence, and appropriation of themes, the author's creative hand is to be discerned.

The impression one receives from reading the book without consideration for the author's library, however, is that the compositions are his own. He does not cite precursors; nor does he express his indebtedness to other literatures in the normal course of writing. His work is set forth as his own wisdom, and it is marked by a mastery of literary skills in the creation of a fine poetry. But when one takes note of the evidence for his extensive scholarship, his accomplishments as an author begin to take on another, rather exciting, dimension. He now can be seen as a man of letters upon whose desk a full range of the literatures of the Hellenistic age were welcome. This openness to Hellenistic culture expands the borders of Ben Sira's world beyond the picture he paints of it. It shows him to have been a much more complex person than we may have thought, and it suggests that the texts that meet in his hymn of praise may belong to a cultural fabric much more intricately woven than we have yet discerned. We must now trace out some of those textual appropriations in the composition of the hymn. But first, we need to see if our suspicions are correct. We need to know if Ben Sira would agree, if he has acknowledged anywhere the scope of his undertaking. He may have done that in a fine poem about the scribe, to which we now turn.

IN PRAISE OF THE SCHOLAR-SAGE

In Sir. 39:1–11, Ben Sira has given a description of the scribe at work that contrasts him with those who ply the trades. The text is as follows, given here in translation based upon that of Box and Oesterley:

1 Not so he that applies himself to the fear of God
  And to set his mind upon the Law of the Most High;
 Who searches out the wisdom of all the ancients,
  And is occupied with the prophets of old;
2 Who heeds the discourses of men of renown,
  And enters into the deep things of parables;
3 Searches out the hidden meaning of proverbs,
  And is conversant with the dark sayings of parables;

4 Who serves among great men,
  And appears before princes;
  Who travels through the lands of the peoples,
  Tests good and evil among men;

5 Who is careful to seek unto his Maker,
  And before the Most High entreats mercy;
  Who opens his mouth in prayer,
  And makes supplication for his sins.

6 If it seem good to God Most High,
  he shall be filled with the spirit of understanding.
  He himself pours forth wise saying in double measure,
  And gives thanks unto the Lord in prayer.

7 He himself directs counsel and knowledge,
  And sets his mind on their secrets.

8 He himself declares wise instruction,
  And glories in the Law of the Lord.

9 His understanding many do praise,
  And never shall his name be blotted out:
  His memory shall not cease,
  And his name shall live from generation to generation.

10 His wisdom does the congregation tell forth,
   And his praise the assembly publishes.

11 If he live long, he shall be accounted happy more than a
   thousand;
   And when he comes to an end, his name suffices.

As the description unfolds, the scholar and his activity are
introduced as taking place within the sphere of piety. The
theme of the scholar's piety frames the whole by the mention
of his "fear of God" at the beginning (39:1) and the honor he
receives in the congregation at the end (39:9–10). Imbedded
within the poem are additional notices about his prayer for
mercy (39:5), the divine source of his inspiration (39:6), and
his preoccupation with the law (39:1, 8). Thus his piety is
shown to be the source of his wisdom and the controlling
motivation that guides his activity as a scholar. This activity is
outlined in a sequence of three general movements. The first is
his quest for understanding (39:1–5); the second is his reception of the spirit of understanding from God (39:6); the third is
his transformation into one who is able to provide for others
the wisdom he has found (39:7–8).

This three-part schema is easily recognized as the quest for wisdom that ultimately comes from God. In Jewish wisdom literature, the schema is found dramatized in several ways. Wisdom may be objectified, described as hidden and as the object of human quest, or it may be depicted as seeking out those who will recognize and receive it.[7] If the focus falls upon the human figure, the quest itself may be dramatized or the schema may simply take the form of exhortations embedded among other wisdom sayings and instructions "to seek" after wisdom.[8] But the wisdom writings before Sirach are remarkably cautious about depicting a scene of resolution to the quest. In those cases in which wisdom is said to be achievable, the mere assertion that it is so seems to be the point. How one actually comes to find it, however, is conspicuously absent from the earlier literature. That in Ben Sira's hymn a resolution to the question is claimed by the scholar must be regarded as most remarkable. How was it understood to have been achieved?

Research as the Quest for Wisdom

In the scholar's quest for wisdom, the objects and means of scholarly research are given. This immediately shifts attention from the schema of the wisdom myth and focuses it upon modes of learning that are quite familiar. The scholar is preoccupied with the study of literature on the one hand and the accumulation of observations about the political and social arena on the other. Taken together, these activities define a Hellenistic commonplace on the learned man and thus appear too mundane as vehicles for the quest for divine wisdom. That the scholar's research is not understood to be misguided, however, is evident. Not only is the first text cited the law of the Most High, the eventual result of the research will be none other than the scholar's own coming-to-speech as the author of just such texts as he has been reading.

There are several observations that can be made about those texts. First, there is a trace of canonicity in the listing of them, noticeable initially in the priority given to the law and by the mention of the wisdom of the ancients and the prophets. This has been taken to refer to an early classification of Jewish scriptures along the lines of the later canonical view.[9] However, the list does not conclude with these three corpora. It continues with the discourses of famous men, specific forms of wisdom composition, and then moves easily into the category of experience won in the international scene. This scene is also presented as a "text," that is, as an articulation of "good and evil among men" that the scholar also must learn to "read" ("test," 39:4d). Thus the scholar's canon is not conceived as closed. The most that one might say is that it is weighted at the top and devolves through layers of other texts of lesser significance. But this view too, though it might be appropriate in some respect, fails to see the significance of the range of texts as a whole. If it ends with the human situation itself, the range of texts is ultimately being determined by a notion of the articulations that disclose that situation. This means that the "text" of the human situation has a fundamental place in the scholar's canon. This should come as no surprise to scholars of the literatures of wisdom. The noteworthy phenomenon is the combination of observation, wisdom texts, and Torah that Ben Sira's resources present.

One needs to notice also that the manner of designation of these texts is very general, not specific, with the exception of the "Law of the Most High," to which we shall return. The wisdom texts, which scholars have taken to refer to Jewish wisdom literature, are called "the wisdom of all the ancients"; the discourses are simply those "of famous men"; and the prophets are those "of old." It would not be unthinkable that if indeed Ben Sira has intended these designations to refer primarily to the Jewish corpora, he has purposefully phrased them in such a way as to allow association with Hellenistic classifications of literary activity and genre as well (legislation, philosophy, poetry, histories, collections of aphoristic wisdom). Nevertheless, he has nowhere acknowledged any indebtedness to Hellenic authors.

That these objects of the scholar's investigation are understood as authored texts is also to be noted. There is specific mention of "the ancients," the prophets, and "men of renown." If the subsequent mention of parables, proverbs, and riddles is made without indication of authorship, it does not mean that they are not perceived also as composed speech, that is, as authored texts available for investigation. The anonymity of Hellenistic gnomological collections was not taken to mean that they were not authored. They were, in fact, understood to have been authored by (the ancient) sages. This view of texts as compositions, and its corollary that the scholar reads them both as exegete of others' work and as one who aspires to take his place among other authors, introduces the conditions for a new and specific problem in the transmission of Jewish wisdom, indeed of Jewish thought and literature as a whole. With the consciousness of authorship, the stage is set for the notion that culture is tradition, that questions of authority must be resolved in terms of literary accomplishments. Only here, with the emergence of the idea of authorship, can one speak properly of a "wisdom tradition." Before Ben Sira, as far as we can tell, there was no wisdom tradition in the sense of scholars' awareness of precursors as authors and of the work of interpretation as the price for taking one's place in the line as tradent and author in one's own right. Now, with authority recognized as authorship, tradition begins and struggle begins. Texts become the field of exploration and conflict. They contain the wisdom that has been found, but they belong to others whose texts they are until one has appropriated them. What one seeks is their wisdom. But it must be wrested from them as from those who have captured a treasure and will not let it go. Another's wisdom is at first hidden from those who read his texts, seeking to understand them.

Thus these authored texts are enigmatic, as is the human scene as text. The scholar's task is to search them out, enter into them, converse with them, and become occupied by them. What he seeks to find in them is meaning, wisdom. This meaning is hidden in their depths. As a critical reader, the scholar will attempt to analyze these texts and discover the wisdom that is beneath and beyond them all. Here, then, is the hermeneutical program as well as the principle of the scholar's canon. All of these texts are "wisdom texts." They form a canon of disparate genres held together by the scholar's common investment in them. He will study them to win a single vision. That single vision, moreover, will encompass the deep structure of things that orders all reality from God and his world of creation to human good and evil. If he succeeds, he will have overcome. No longer is he exegete and scholar merely, interpreting the texts of others. He will make those words, those texts, his own and find a voice for himself as an author.

The result of this research, then, overlooking for the moment the hiatus of inspiration, will be that the scholar himself comes to speech. The forms in which this speech will be composed are, moreover, familiar to us as forms of wisdom speech: wise sayings, advice, knowledge, and instruction. In verse 7, the scholar is described "setting his mind on their secrets," which shows the degree to which his own wisdom is still understood to be related to his reading of the texts of others. The question is whether he will become a critic of others' texts or an author in his own right. It appears that he will become an author. The secrets of his precursors are now his own. He will "pour" them "forth" in speech. This speech becomes, as we shall see, another text, his own composition.

The Spirit of Understanding

We may return now to the middle section of the poem, in which the scholar receives the "spirit of understanding" from God. At first reading, this section appears to emphasize the piety of the scholar as it manifests itself in the midst of the scholarly endeavor itself. That of course is so. But the nature of this piety is most unusual. If we compare the marks of the scholar's piety here with that depicted in the hymn in praise of the fathers, we can begin to see its peculiar configuration. In the hymn, aspects of piety were attributed to the great leaders in keeping with the functions of their offices. In the poem about the scholar, it also appears that those aspects of piety attributed to him are cast in ways that will enhance his own special role and status. That he "applies himself to the fear of God" could be taken as a commonplace, of course, until it is noted that this motif does not occur in the hymn. It is probably to be understood as a formulation in keeping with his special status as wisdom's child. For the reader of wisdom texts, the fear of the Lord is the "beginning of wisdom."[10] The scholar's prayer for mercy also contrasts with the prayers recorded in the hymn. There the call upon God was for aid in the fulfillment of high covenantal office for the people. It was motivated especially by the need to perform grand and glorious deeds of defence. Here the prayer is highly personalized, not mediated by covenantal office. It takes place immediately "before the Most High" and is understood as a move that must be made in order to come to speech.

There are three speech acts recorded in verse 6, and they occur in a specific and significant sequence. The first is the prayer for mercy; the second is the speaking of wisdom itself ("in double measure"); the third is the thanksgiving. This means that the prayer for mercy and the prayer of thanksgiving frame the moment of inspiration. Wisdom speech is therefore viewed as divinely inspired, as speech that is possible only in the context of prayer. Because this is so, the scholar's prayer is not merely the mark of a general piety, but a personal claim to inspiration. The same is true of his preoccupation with Torah. As a mark of piety, orientation to Torah is nowhere to be found in the hymn. Naturally, to "set one's mind upon" Torah or "to glory in the Law of the Lord" may be taken as customary ways of designating piety in general. But spoken of this scholar, they mean something else. They mean that the Torah belongs to the scholar as his special domain. The scholar has invested Torah with canonicity, and thus his piety is peculiarly that of the sage.

In that he is filled with the spirit of understanding as a benefaction from God, the scholar's piety is ultimately a special form peculiarly suited to his vocation. By means of it, he can lay claim to immediacy of vision, divine presence, and finally, to wisdom. This resolves the quest in and among the many enigmatic texts. Piety means that the scholar has prevailed and now will take his place among the sages. Clearly there are associations here with older views of inspiration by the spirit of Yahweh. One thinks immediately about the prophets and prophetic inspiration.[11] In the hymn, also, it was the prophet whose vision was possible by the presence of divine spirit. The text that the prophet read, however, was the human situation; the logos that resulted had power to create and to destroy kings and peoples.[12] In the description of the sage, vision is a winning through to the presence of wisdom in and beyond the texts, and the spirit is designated as the "spirit of understanding."

The concept of prophetic inspiration has been recast in two ways. First, it has been evoked as a moment that occurs in the context of prayer for mercy, thus verifying the scholar's piety and making the claim for superior understanding. Second, this moment itself has been cast as the bridge between research and authorship. It has become a claim to having seen the divine wisdom encoded in the scholar's texts that he himself may now "pour forth." It would therefore not be inappropriate to think here of the Hellenic poet's muse or of the romantic sublime as phenomenological analogues.[13] But because the moment is so clearly that of the scholar engaged with texts, the appeal to divine inspiration at this point implicitly transforms his relationship to those texts. He is, using the description of Harold Bloom, the "later poet . . . who opens himself to what he believes to be a power in the parent poem that does not belong to the parent proper, but to a range of being just beyond that precursor."[14] This power is manifest in two ways: he now understands, and now he can speak.

The Scholar as Author

That the scholar is said to come to speech should not be taken as evidence against his primary orientation to texts. To come to speech is a recurrent theme in the book as a whole. It marks the highest achievement of the scholar-sage and indicates the proper medium for his own effective function within the community. Certainly it is true that as this function is described, it is understood as a moment of living speech in which wisdom is disclosed. Yet there is a curious failure in Sirach as a whole to distinguish between written and oral modes of speaking. One need only refer to Ben Sira's introduction to the hymn of creation, which follows this account of the scholar's coming to speech. He promises himself to make his instruction "shine forth" (39:12) and asks the pious (his readers) to "hearken" and lift up their voices with him (39:13–14). Then follows the "living speech" poured forth as a carefully composed text. At the end, he acknowledges that this is so: "When I considered it, I set it down in writing" (39:32).

One way to understand this would be against the background of the Hellenistic view of texts as scripts for reading and hearing. But there appears to be more involved than this. In chapter 24, wisdom is portrayed as coming to speech and is identified with the "Book of the Covenant of the Most High God: the Law which Moses commanded" (24:23). As the poem continues, the book itself is described as "filling men with wisdom" (24:25–27), and continuing the metaphor, the author says, "I will water my garden, . . . again pour forth teaching as prophecy, and leave it for eternal generations" (24:31–33). That the "I" here is no longer referring to the personified figure of wisdom is made clear in the final lines: "Look and you will see that I have not labored for myself only, but for all those that diligently seek her" (24:34). Thus the scholar's texts, both those over which he has labored and those he has wrought, are wisdom texts and thus inspired. As such, they are described in terms of living speech.

This notion is startling precisely because one of the scholar's books, the Torah, is actually attributed to the "Most High." What this means for Ben Sira is not at all clear. He nowhere says expressly that he understands the Torah to have been written by God. But neither does he say, as Philo will later, that the five books were written by Moses. In the hymn, Ben Sira says that God "placed in [Moses'] hand the commandment (*miṣwāh*), even the law (*tōrāh*) of life and discernment; that he might teach His statutes unto Jacob" (45:5). This is midrash upon the story of the tablets, to be sure, and thus should not be used naively to elucidate Ben Sira's view on the larger corpus. But the designation "law of life" (*tôrat ḥayyîm*) does appear to broaden the reference to allow for the inclusion of more than the Ten Commandments. In Sir. 24:23, the "Law

which Moses commanded" is called "the Book of the Covenant of the Most High God." In Sirach, neither the term Torah
nor "the Book of the Covenant," can be taken definitely as a
specific reference to the five books of Moses as canon.[15] But
one cannot avoid the suspicion that some close association is
being made here between the Torah of God given to Moses
and the books of Moses that record the epic Ben Sira has in his
hands and that the wisdom song interprets. If the scholar
claims, therefore, to read these books with understanding, and
then comes to speech himself, the status of that speech, his
own texts, is given. He is more than a scribal interpreter. He is
one whose wisdom, as Ben Sira says, "increases wisdom"
(38:24). We shall want to ask later on what this might mean
for the status of his hymnic history as myth in relation to the
Torah itself.

BEN SIRA AS THE SCHOLAR-SAGE

The picture Ben Sira has given of the scholar may be viewed
as the portrayal of an ideal type. The larger literary context
(38:24–39:35) shows that the scholar's work is a profession
that may be contrasted with the trades. The description itself
focuses upon just those matters essential to distinguish the
profession and achieves a well-balanced profile of the activity
by which the community can recognize the superiority of a
given scholar within its midst. That activity is defined as mastery of literary traditions and the composition of wisdom writings. We may call this scholar a sage.

If we bracket now those aspects of the sage's piety that
reflect distinctly Jewish concerns, we can see that the depiction of the scholar-sage includes many features that invite
comparison with Hellenistic analogues. The picture itself is
Ben Sira's own construction, of course, combining characteristics of a number of Hellenistic types engaged in the transmission of philosophical, literary, and educational traditions.
The resulting configuration may therefore be an idealization of
a scholarly function with Jewish provenance in mind. It might
assume quite particular views of canonicity, authorship, and
ethics and wisdom instruction. But indebtedness to Hellenistic

modes of learning is nevertheless the most probable explanation both for the idea of such an ideal type and for the
emergence of such a self-consciousness about social role within
the educational institutions of Judaism.

The indebtedness to Hellenism is indicated primarily in the
express combination of scholarship, authorship, and the offering of instruction—all aspects highly prized in the Hellenistic
culture of literature and *paideia*. The listing of the scholar's
canon is an additional nuance of Hellenistic consciousness
about literary corpora.[16] The notice about "testing the good
and evil among men" recalls a motif particularly associated
with Cynic practice.[17]

It is, however, in the mention of rewards for the scholar's
labors that the telling evidence for Hellenistic influence is
given. This is the honor the community is said to give to the
scholar-sage. Glory, fame, and memorial are deeply rooted in
the Hellenic tradition as the goals of heroic endeavor and the
reward for the achievement of excellence. As the arena appropriate to the achievement of excellence shifted from battlefield
to the games, and on to the polis and the gymnasium, the
literary forms appropriate to the depiction and praise of the
respective protagonists were transformed as well. The moves
can be traced from epic poetry through the odes of the lyric
poets to the prose encomia of historians and rhetoricians and
on to the biographers of the empire.[18] The triad of warrior,
king, and athlete as appropriate subjects for praise determined
the early formation of the encomiastic tradition and continued
on through to the lives of kings and commanders of the Roman era. But as the cultural ideals shifted first to include, and
then to prefer, those who figured as embodiments of *paideia*,
philosophers, orators, and poets were honored with encomia
as well.[19] Praise and honor were involved always and, especially in the self-consciousness of the lyric poets and the
composers of prose encomia, under a double aspect. The first
aspect was the express purpose of the composition to achieve
honor for the person praised or sung. The second, rooted in
the Hellenic penchant for competition and the panegyric con-
test as the occasion for such display, was the praise and honor

sought by the author himself. It is this development that suggests a Hellenistic influence for Ben Sira's hymn of praise for the scholar-sage.

Once it is seen that this poem about the scholar-sage is motivated by the encomiastic motif in verses 9–11, the goal toward which the whole has moved to find its appropriate climax, Ben Sira's book itself may be read again in a new light. Especially noticeable now are, not only the sense of authorial performance in the exceptionally fine poetic compositions throughout, a performance marked consistently by great care and the pride of perfected accomplishment, but also the frequency with which the motifs of praise, glory, and fame are used to mark for his students that standard by which the seeker after wisdom will be known to have arrived.

In the poem in praise of the scholar, Ben Sira cannot, of course, make reference to himself. But as we have seen, he moves immediately to self-reference in the hymn in praise of creation and concludes with a notice that it is his own written composition that he has shared. Throughout the book, his consciousness of authority as scholar-sage is evident as well, especially in those cases where he employs the first person for heightened claims to wisdom or for the introduction of hymnic material.[20] The apparent effacement of self-reference in the scholar poem should not be taken, therefore, as an indication that Ben Sira did not understand himself to have aspired to, or even achieved, the ideal. The fact that he created this ideal type as an encomium of the scholar-sage may mark a significant move in the conscious conceptualization of the scholar's role in his time. This role probably should be seen as just coming into prominence as a recognizable office within the structure of Jewish society. Its idealization is achieved, not by archaizing, nor by appeal to ideational or ontological investments, but by reduction to and concentrated focus upon those aspects of the scholar's moment that are seen to be definitive. That moment is, of course, significant in its claim to divine inspiration, and it is here, no doubt, that Ben Sira's comfortableness with the psychology of oriental wisdom comes through. But the simple ease with which even this is depicted, indeed the manner in which the whole is blithely recounted, reveals the status of this ideal as fully achievable. We may take it, then, as Ben Sira's self-portrait. He was conscious of being an author.[21]

Ben Sira and the Heroes

A striking feature of the poem in praise of the scholar may now be noted. It is the degree to which it corresponds to the proem of the hymn in praise of the fathers. Both fall easily into two major parts connected by a transitional section, and both end with an announcement of memorial in the assembly. In part 1 of the proem, the types of those to be praised are listed according to their definitive virtues (44:3–6); in part 1 of the poem, the scholar is depicted according to his definitive virtue or occupation (39:1–4). A transition is given in the proem with the notice that there were others who received no memorial (44:7–9); in the poem, a transition is given with the notice that the scholar prays and receives the spirit of understanding (39:5–6). It is this that constitutes the major difference between the sage and those who labor with their hands (cf. 39:24, 31–34). In part 2 of the proem, the lasting achievement of the pious leaders is given (44:11–14). In the poem, the achievement of the scholar-sage is announced as the instruction he can give (39:7–8). Both passages end, then, on the theme of eternal renown, and the concluding distich for both is the same: "The assembly recounts his [their] wisdom; the congregation declares his [their] praise" (39:10; 44:15).

This literary correspondence is all the more suggestive when it is noted that among those worthy of praise listed in the proem, three of the six are distinguished by their wisdom. We have had occasion earlier to remark about this listing and the fact that the promise to write only in praise of these leaders did not seem to be fulfilled in the hymn itself. Such a discrepancy should not be taken as an indication of literary failure, of course. It is possible to make some correlations between the hasidim of the proem and the figures praised in the hymn. In any case, the proem is intended to validate the notion that there are men worthy of praise, not to offer a programmatic

outline of the typology to be followed in the hymn. Yet the
listing is strangely disproportionate in its emphasis upon those
engaged in scholarly and literary activities. Of the three remaining types of those worthy of praise, only two might fall
under the category "kings and commanders" (44:3a, 4a). The
third, "men of resource" (44:6), appears to have taken an encomiastic motif and transformed it into a social role, a curious
construction. But it also could refer to the scholar. The encomiastic motif itself must have been very closely associated
with the office of the scribe-sage for Ben Sira. Therefore it was
in reflection about the scholar's work and social significance
that literary forms influenced by the Hellenistic encomium
could be employed.

But if this is plausible, the social function of the sage in
Jerusalem, indeed the status of Ben Sira and his book of
wisdom themselves, may be far more significant for our understanding of the religious institutions of the time than his hymn
has disclosed thus far. We may return now to our thesis about
the hymn and its function as mythology of the Second Temple
institutions structured around the office of the high priest. In
our analysis of office and its significance for the narrative development of the hymn, we noted that among those mentioned in the first series of seven, Moses' office appeared to be
the archetype that combined and unified aspects of all those
offices later to be derived from it by processes of differentiation and bifurcation. It may now be recalled that in the subsequent development of those official functions—fragmented in
the history of the prophets and kings but resolved in the re-
emergence of the high priestly office of Simon—one aspect of
Moses' office did not reappear. This was his role as teacher.

Given our thesis about the etiological and mythical function
of the hymn, not only for the high priesthood, but for the
structure and constitution of the theocratic community itself,
the failure to include a major official function in the scene at
the end is troublesome. This might be accounted for in two
ways. One is that Moses and his office were understood to be
only originary and foundational, not re-enactable in the actualized community. The other is that the transference of the

responsibility to teach the statutes and judgments to Aaron (45:17) was assumed to continue in force as a priestly function in the Second Temple institutions and thus needed no reiteration as long as the high priest was recognized as legitimate. But it appears that elsewhere in Ben Sira's book and earlier, the reader will have already had ample opportunity to ponder the glories of the scribe-sage, undoubtedly a priest, in regard to his place within the community.

This displacement may be of some significance. In genre, force, and implication for the social structure of the religious community, the poem in praise of the scholar-sage belongs "in the picture" that it is the intent of the hymn to depict. But the poem does not occur within the hymn itself. Its place is outside of it in spite of the fact that the Mosaic office is the absolutely pivotal configuration for the originary pattern of the community, and that its own formation is based on the moment of revelation and reception of the law as constitution for the community. When, therefore, in Ben Sira's description it is his preoccupation with the law, reception of the spirit of understanding, and subsequent role as teacher within the community that mark the scholar-sage for praise, one can hardly avoid concluding that it is in the office of Moses where the priestly scholar-sage is to stand.

This conclusion can be supported by a further consideration. We saw that in the office of the prophet a counterpoint to the king was posited and that the marks of the prophet were essentially a capacity for vision and powerful speech. If now, in a form more appropriate to the cultic ideal, the scholar-priest also is marked by vision and speech, the "prophetic" aspect of the office of Moses continues in force. The counterpoint has been transformed, as it were, by a double effacement by the sage himself: (1) no longer does he stand in opposition to the ruling office, for he himself is a priest, and the high priest is worthy of praise; and (2) he need not name himself in any case because if he achieves his end, his name will be remembered by the congregation.

Such effacement does not bespeak uncertainty about one's role. There are clearly two offices of constitutive significance to be recognized by the community. Both are worthy of praise and memorial. The praise of the one is dependent upon the praise of the other. For those who are ranked among Ben Sira's students and readers, the glory of the high priest cannot be seen save through the sage's eyes and words. The didactic and meditative aspects of the hymn, which create that sense of distance from actual participation in the rite and allow it to be seen through its poetic depiction, now gain their full import. The reader sees the scene, not as it is in its literality, but as the poet-sage says that it is. He too is not in the picture but stands with the reader looking on, seeing there what he has seen by virtue of his studies in texts and his wisdom and words. Simon is glorious only insofar as the wisdom and the words of the sage make him so, just as the scholar's texts are enigmatic until the spirit of understanding lets him produce another. Ben Sira has discovered the power of a poetic text and the glory of authorship. His rather objective manner of describing the scholar's vocation should not mislead us. Acknowledgment of the significance of the sage's profound authority and its social implications are fully revealed in the displaced encomium on the ideal scholar and the resulting double effacement of Ben Sira's own authority as author within the community. The office of the priestly scribe cannot be considered to have emerged only in Ben Sira's time, of course. But its transformation via Hellenism into the office of the teacher-sage, whose authority rests ultimately on his scholarship, wisdom, and his way with words, may be a *novum* indeed.

Part 3

Hermeneutic: Text and Cultural Contexts

The Hymn as Jewish and Hellenistic Text 5

W e return now to the hymn as a literary composition. Its obvious dependence upon the Jewish scriptures has been noted, as well as its selectivity with regard to those figures and events helpful for its own purposes and its interpretive distance from the scriptures upon which it draws. It has been suggested that a study of the text's relationship to other texts might tell us how this was achieved and why. Something of the why has been discovered by pursuing the text's relation to its social context. But the how is still to be explored. Perhaps a study of the text's relation to its precursor texts will help with this question.

In the description of the scholar, features that could account for a recasting of a precursor literature were noted. The scholar's literary canon, though centered in the Torah, was quite extensive, perhaps even including Hellenistic literatures helpful for the task of instruction in wisdom ethics, religious values, and what might be called their philosophical foundations. Ben Sira's knowledge of certain Hellenistic literary traditions has also been mentioned, and in the case of the encomium, a genre and its particular function has been identified as a probable influence on his conception of the scholar and his understanding of his own work. We must now focus upon the composition of the hymn itself.

Specifically, those literatures read and studied by Ben Sira need to be identified, literatures that may have had direct bearing upon the creation of the hymn. We shall begin with a consideration of the Hebrew texts, then move to a discussion of possible Hellenistic prototypes, and finally address the question of the role of wisdom texts as well. The effort is directed by the desire to see more clearly the particular lineaments of the hymn as a purposeful poetic composition, to mark its indebtedness to precursor texts, as well as to determine its new conceptualizations and creativity. That creativity can be defined as a moment of its intertextuality.

PRECURSORS IN THE JEWISH TRADITION

The evidence from Ben Sira's book as a whole is that, in addition to his preoccupation with the book of Proverbs, he had read most of the Hebrew corpus known to us to have been extant. For the hymn, however, direct dependency is limited almost entirely to the Pentateuch and the historiographic literature. It is possible, therefore, to limit the study at this point to a consideration of just these texts.

The Pentateuch

The place to begin is with Ben Sira's reading of the Pentateuch. We have noted the problem of reference with respect to his use of the terms "Torah" and "Book of the Covenant" and the literature he intended to designate by them. But this uncertainty need not keep us from pursuing our investigation. It is clear that Ben Sira did have what we understand as the Pentateuch before him as text or texts among other texts. This is documented in his use of all five books in the composition of the hymn (as well as elsewhere in his book). Whether he understood these five book as a unit and whether it was that unit that was intended by the designation "Torah," are matters that may or may not be clarified to our satisfaction. We shall posit such a unit in order to investigate it as a possibility. In asking about it, some clarifications may emerge.

There are references to Torah as ethical code in Ben Sira's book. This naturally raises the question of a Torah piety in Sirach, a piety that may have been based upon a certain view of the books of Moses. The Deuteronomic redaction immediately comes to mind. Marböck, however, has found that those references to Torah that could be taken in the sense of a Deuteronomic code are few and that most of Ben Sira's ethical instruction is put forth without appealing to Torah at all.[1] This suggests that Ben Sira found some way to correlate Torah, piety, and wisdom ethic other than on the basis of the Pentateuch as a book of ethical instruction. There is no evidence that he sensed any tension between what he understood by Torah as wisdom ethic and what he understood by proverbial and philosophical wisdom as ethical instruction. Because there is no evidence for a Deuteronomistic rationale for the Pentateuch as wisdom ethic, if Ben Sira understood it as a foundational document at all, he must have done so in some other way.

This might have been as constitution and code for the Second Temple institution, which also would have meant a reading from a particular point of view, in this case with cultic and constitutional interests in mind. For this, the book of Leviticus could have provided the major focus, supported of course by indications of cultic concerns throughout the Pentateuch as a whole. The references to temple, priesthood, the commandments given to Aaron (45:12), and the importance of cultic piety throughout the book indicate that the Pentateuch was indeed understood essentially as cultic constitution. But even if this is so, it is important to see that Ben Sira has not appealed to it expressly as such an authority nor interpreted it primarily with cultic legal codes in mind. From Leviticus is taken only (1) certain aspects of the description of Aaron and his office for use in the hymn and (2) the commandment concerning love of one's neighbor as an instance of wisdom ethic in the earlier parts of the book.[2] As many have noticed, Ben Sira has also taken several specifically cultic operations, including sacrifice and atonement, and declared their efficacy to be functional within the practice of a wisdom ethic alone (cf. 3:28b; 34:1–4;

40:24b). The Pentateuch, then, was for Ben Sira more than a cultic code.

A third possibility presents itself. It is a reading of the Pentateuch, but especially of Genesis and Exodus, as epic literature. This is suggested in the early accounts of Adam (17:1–14; 15:14–20; cf. 40:1–17), as well as in allusions to the account of creation and other narratives of Genesis and Exodus throughout the book.[3] One has the impression that Ben Sira was intensely interested in this material as an account of primordial events that determined and disclosed the basic condition of human existence. This should not surprise us. That is what the Pentateuch essentially is. Given Ben Sira's knowledge of Hellenistic literature and learning, the probability is therefore quite strong that he recognized it as epic and regarded it as significant mainly as an epic. But as is the case with the study of Homeric epic in the Hellenistic schools, and especially among the Stoics,[4] Ben Sira's reading of the Pentateuch is marked less by an interest in the narrative and historical-etiological features of the epic than by a quest to discover therein traces and reflections of certain contemporary philosophical and ethical concepts. Thus he merely assumed the epic nature of the Torah. He nowhere indicates that it was or should be read just as narrative. Instead, it was to be studied, and the concerns that were to guide the study are manifest. They have to do with ethical anthropology and the degree to which a wisdom view of the world and of the human situation may be detected in the epic account of the beginnings of things. Thus the foci of interest, were one to mark the places in the Pentateuch taken up in Sirach for comment, are those human figures, beginning with Adam, in whose events the human drama of wisdom and ethics may be discerned.

This at least is clearly the concern in Ben Sira's reflections upon Adam. In Sir. 17:1–14, the divine bestowals upon the human creature are listed and come to climax in the gift of a "heart to understand" (17:6b). This gift corresponds to the bestowal of wisdom upon all flesh "in measure" in the opening hymn of the book (1:10a). It is this wisdom that allows the recognition of God's glory in creation (17:8–9). Then, however, the gift of the covenant, "the law of life," is mentioned (17:11). It is grounded in another moment of revelation (17:12–13), which corresponds in turn to the gift of wisdom "without measure . . . to them that love Him" in the opening hymn (1:10b). The ease with which the reflection upon Adam is expanded to include the covenant, a combination of motifs from Genesis and Exodus facilitated by a notion of wisdom that comprises both knowledge and ethical capacities, shows us that Adam is understood to be a symbol of all humankind. His typological significance is even more pronounced in the reflection in Sir. 15:14–20. It may be suspected to have played a role in anthropological-ethical formulations throughout the book. In the hymn in praise of the hasidim, however, it is not Adam but Noah who stands at the beginning. Given our thesis of the epic nature of the Pentateuch for Ben Sira and the fact that he had devoted considerable study to the significance of Adam, how can we explain the change?

Both the depictions of Adam and the characterizations in the hymn show that the epic figures have been cast as types. This is normal for the study of epic literature in the Hellenistic period. But Adam is typed as the representative of humankind, while the hasidim are typed in terms of special roles, which we have called offices. This distinction appears to be important. If it were pressed a bit further, in keeping with our thesis about the function of the offices for the structure of the covenant community, the relation of Adam to the hasidim would be that of all humankind to the elect community. Noting that Noah is a bridge figure, and that the covenant with him occurred in the "season of destruction" as a sign that God would "not destroy again all flesh" (44:17–18), we can add the element "human problematic/divine solution" to the general distinction between the two groups. It is true that Ben Sira has not developed the narrative of Adam's sin expressly, preferring to emphasize his human capacity for wisdom as a universal endowment instead. But neither has he depicted Adam as a primal figure of ideal type (e.g., as a royal figure) in whom the conditional aspects of human existence are overcome. Adam does stand for the positive capacity of human beings for wisdom and obedience (God's yēṣer; 15:14). But this does not guarantee that wickedness will not emerge, as indeed Ben Sira repeatedly acknowledges. Adam, in addition to the gift of capacity for wisdom, is in need of the benefits the covenant (the community) can provide (17:11–14). The hymn in praise of the hasidim is a reading of the epic with this second benefit in mind and thus cannot begin with Adam.

In the hymn, only the first seven figures praised are taken from the Pentateuch, but they constitute a unit with a particular function within the development of the hymn as a whole. That function has to do with the establishment of the covenants in a founding epoch before history in the land begins. Can anything more be inferred from this about the status of the Pentateuch for Ben Sira? If one correlates Ben Sira's designation of Torah as the Book of the Covenant (24:33) with the observation that the Pentateuch provided only those first seven convenantal figures for the hymn, the special status of the Pentateuch for him is given. He has read it as epic, the first chapter of a genealogical history. The mythic aspect of the first section of the hymn, together with its internal development of the covenants and their studied interrelationships, brings to mind the theogonies and anthropogonies at the beginning of Hellenistic histories and encomia.[5] That Ben Sira treated the Pentateuch in just this way indicates that, for him, its wisdom was a function of the way in which it could be read as originary narrative of the archetypal patterns of human existence and the divine intentions for human community. It thus becomes the Jewish analogue and counterpoint to Hellenistic views on the origins of the human race.

The Priestly Redaction

It has been suggested that a reading of the Pentateuch as epic literature should occasion for us no surprise. This observation may now be expanded to suggest a place for Ben Sira in a Jewish tradition of epic historiography.[6] The point of departure is the degree to which his hymn highlights those concerns known to have determined the priestly redaction of the Pentateuch itself. In that redaction, Israel's epic was read or reshaped as the history of the covenants that founded Israel's cult. The covenant with Noah was understood as the promise and possibility for all humankind to be included in the economy of divine favor. The promise to Abraham was understood primarily in terms of the land that his seed would inherit. Both the priestly writer and Ben Sira mention as well the sign of circumcision, which began with Abraham. Moses was recognized as having received the law by audition and vision, a mode of revelation that Koch sees as coming from an old theology of the tabernacle.[7] But in the priestly redaction, the focus is rather on Aaron, who was ordained to the priesthood, invested, and given authority for cultic orders. On Sinai, Yahweh's glory was manifest in the sanctuary, and the first sacrifice was performed. The people were viewed as obedient recipients of the benefits of these institutions, primarily the sacrificial means for forgiveness and cleansing. With the establishment of the cult at Sinai, institutional history began.

That Ben Sira's hymn reflects a view of the Pentateuch very much like that of the priestly redactor indicates that the reading must have continued in priestly circles as a tradition. In some form, it became available to Ben Sira. In his reading, Moses' importance has been expanded and emphasized, the covenants have been interrelated systematically, the archaic epoch has been dehistoricized, and the subsequent history has been systematically interpreted as a time of struggle coming to resolution and climax only in Ben Sira's own time. These of course are the very features that distinguish his hymn as a new reading and indicate its provenance in a new time and place.

The Histories and Chronicles

From the figure of Joshua on, the hymn shows dependence primarily upon the books of Joshua, Samuel, and Kings. There is, however, occasional indication of acquaintance with Chronicles, especially in the descriptions of David, Solomon, and

Simon.[8] It is probable, too, that Ben Sira knew the books of
Ezra and Nehemiah, as the mention of Zerubbabel, Jeshua, and
Nehemiah shows, even though the information about Zerubbabel and Jeshua was available in Haggai as well. The question
is whether anything more can be said about the way in which
he read them.

There are four aspects of Ben Sira's treatment of Israel's
history that compare with Chronicles. The first is the way in
which he clearly distinguishes between the acceptable and the
unacceptable kings. The second is that David's significance is
seen to lie primarily in his care for and ordering of the liturgy
of the cult. The third is that his conception of history includes
a recounting of events right up and into his own time. The
fourth is that a rewriting of the history of Israel and Judah is
undertaken in support of a cultic-institutional view of postexilic Judaism. It is plausible, then, that Ben Sira shared in a
traditional rereading of the Deuteronomic history of Israel
along the lines of that achieved by the chronicler.

But the differences between Ben Sira and the chronicler are
also significant. Ben Sira's selection of acceptable kings is
smaller, numbering only three. Solomon is important for Ben
Sira because he built the temple and was associated with
wisdom. But he is not included in the list of faithful kings
because of his sin, which is also recounted. The chronicler
avoids any mention of Solomon's sins. The covenant with
David, though mentioned by Ben Sira, is devalued in favor of
the covenant with Phineas, which alone continues in force. For
the chronicler, all theocratic institutional validation is traced to
the covenant with David. Chronicles is also marked by a nar-
row Levitical interest for which Ben Sira gives no evidence, so
that a totally different conception of Israel's cult is revealed.
But the scope of history in Chronicles, from Adam to Nehemiah, as well as its cultic-ethiological intention, shows it to be
a precedent of sorts for Ben Sira's hymn. Momigliano has discussed the genre of historiography known as chronicle and
placed it in the Hellenistic period.[9] It cannot account for the
grand design of Ben Sira's hymn, but its availability as a recognizable mode for recounting the history of a local institution

(e.g., a city or temple) may have provided a framework within which Ben Sira began to work.

Ezra-Nehemiah

Ben Sira's knowledge and view of Ezra-Nehemiah is much more difficult to ascertain. If he took the information about Nehemiah restoring the walls from this literature, which appears to be the most probable assumption, his failure to include Ezra in the list of great men and his apparent lack of interest in the history of the restoration as such must indicate some aversion to this literature and these traditions. His failure to include Ezra is particularly interesting in light of Ezra's role as scribe and priest, exactly the role that Ben Sira praises and knows himself to hold. But as we have seen, there may have been reasons not to include the scholar-sage among those praised in the hymn, and this may have been enough not to have mentioned Ezra.

Nevertheless, there are several considerations that indicate more may have been at stake. First, Ben Sira did not share in the exclusivist notion of Jewish identity and ethic reflected in Ezra-Nehemiah. Second, the harsh judgment upon the sins of the fathers and the people and the call to repentance and to Torah piety that pervades this literature run counter to Ben Sira's view of Israel's history.[10] Odil Steck has shown that the covenant-renewal ceremony in Nehemiah 9 was shaped by a homiletical program based upon what he calls a Deuteronomistic view of history.[11] He has traced its influence as living tradition through the period of the Second Temple and shown it to have been pervasive in much of the literature in the form of prayers, homilies, redactions of the prophets, and other literary forms. In this tradition, the exile was understood as a judgment of Yahweh, deserved on account of the sins of Israel during the pre-exilic period of the kingdom. This judgment continued in force upon the postexilic community and called for a collective confession of sin, repentance, prayer for mercy, covenant-renewal, and obedience to the law as preconditions for restoration. Within this schema, the pre-exilic prophets as a class were considered to be sent by Yahweh to preach repentance, but they were rejected completely by the people. Steck theorized that this theology was at home first in Levitical circles, then among the later hasidim.

Marböck has suggested that Ben Sira also stood within the Deuteronomistic tradition.[12] He argues this because Ben Sira shares with the Deuteronomist the understanding of Torah as instruction and wisdom (Deut. 33:1; 41:6–8), as well as certain other themes, for example, election, inheritance of the land, rest, the commandment to love God, and so forth. It would indeed be surprising if Ben Sira did not share some views with Deuteronomic traditions. He correlated Torah with wisdom and righteousness, knew about judgment upon sins, and could call for repentance and the keeping of the law. But his wisdom ethic does not reflect a specifically Deuteronomistic Torah piety, and the telling point is that the contemporary form of the tradition demonstrated in Steck's work is not in evidence anywhere in Ben Sira's book.[13] Steck's finding agrees with ours that another view of history is at work in the hymn, where the sins that destroyed the kingdoms are attributed to the kings. The prophets are not rejected by the people (though Jeremiah is said to have been persecuted by the king [cf. 49:4–6]). There is no place in Ben Sira's conception for a collective confession of sins or a Torah piety as preconditions for a restoration of Israel. The conclusion must be, therefore, that he constructed his hymn without recourse to a Deuteronomistic view of Israel's history.

In summary, the hymn demonstrates a certain reading of the Hebrew epic and histories. It stands in the tradition of the priestly redaction of the Pentateuch and shows some formal similarities to the work of the chronicler. But its most distinctive features have not been clarified by comparison with these precursors. We turn, therefore, to a consideration of possible Hellenistic influence.

PRECURSORS IN HELLENISTIC LITERATURE

There are three forms of Hellenistic literature with which Ben Sira's hymn has been compared: historiography, biography, and the encomium.[14] All three may be traced back well before the time of Ben Sira, and all three flourished during his time and throughout the Hellenistic period. On the evidence of school handbooks, unfortunately extant mostly from later centuries, all three genres were mined for educational purposes. It is plausible, therefore, that acquaintance with Greek *paideia* in early second-century Palestine would have involved instruction in the reading of these literatures. All share in the Hellenistic preoccupation with social roles of leadership, characterization of ideal types, and portraits of personages. Each, as we shall see, may have contributed something to the composition of the hymn.

Historiography

The question of Ben Sira's indebtedness to modes of Hellenistic historiography is made difficult by the fact that as a reading of Israel's history, the hymn obviously continues a Jewish tradition. But we have noted its uniqueness within this tradition, and it is not improbable that some features of its composition were crafted on the model of the literary conventions of Hellenistic historiography.

The evidence for a reading of the Pentateuch as primordial epoch is very suggestive as a case in point. In both the tradition of encomia and in the development of Hellenistic historiography, it was not unusual to begin with an account of archaic origins.[15] This section of the history included mythological, legendary, and genealogical materials that were intended to trace primordial origins. To begin with originary accounts was understood not merely as a claim to tradition, although it was occasionally articulated as such. It was also intended as definitional, a sort of historical diaeretic that anchored the person, the race, or the culture. This at least is evident in the later Hellenistic historians (e.g., Diodorus Siculus and Nicolaus of Damascus, both first century B.C.E.). For these later historians, philosophical considerations with a generally Stoic concern for universalistic anthropology, as well as reflection on the significance of the Roman *ecumene* and the question of cultural plurality, may have been the most immediate conceptualities.[16] But the phenomenon of archaizing is already in evidence programmatically in the early third-century work of Berossus; and it is present as well in the history of Ephorus in the preceding century, even though he himself may have understood his point of origin, the return of the Heracleidae, to be not "mythic" but "historical." Ben Sira's hymn may be placed on a trajectory somewhere between the archaizing histories of the fourth and third centuries on the one hand and the universal histories of the first century on the other. He did not share the programmatic purposes of a Diodorus Siculus, for they presuppose the emerging Roman order. But similar predilections are already in evidence, especially in that Ben Sira has found Stoic anthropological and ethical commonplaces helpful to elucidate his Jewish wisdom ethic. This, together with his reflections upon Adam as definitional type for humankind, indicates a reading of the Pentateuch very much like that of the somewhat later Hellenistic histories.

Historiography itself, in its Hellenic and Hellenistic forms, was impelled from the beginning by cross-cultural experience, which evoked curiosity about other peoples as well as reflection about cultural values and traditions.[17] Within this general frame, even the so-called minor histories of local institutions, based upon chronicles and archives, came to be cast as commemorative accounts of their own illustrious traditions. The consciousness of cultural pluralism was the prevailing horizon for all histories of the period, and even where not explicit, competition of claims to represent superior cultural values was present. There is little in the nature of an overt cultural competitiveness in Ben Sira's book. But there are aspects of his hymn that appear as minor historiography, and in this, a second point of comparison with Hellenistic historiographic literature may be noted. His consciousness of cultural pluralism is reflected elsewhere in the book, especially in the sayings about kings and rulers; and his implicit claims for the archaic and divine origins, as well as for the illustrious history of the high priesthood and its temple, bespeak a purpose not at all out of keeping with this function of the historiography of the Hellenistic period.

That he reviewed this history primarily in terms of leaders

and their contributions to institutional history also is indicative of Hellenistic influence, as is the degree to which conflict, war, defeat, and victory provide the subthemes and arena for much of the history from Joshua on. Kings, commanders, wars, and cultural conflict provided the basic and enduring ingredients for Hellenic and Hellenistic historiography from the beginning, even after topics and concerns of much broader scope came to be included. Ben Sira has not cast his history in a narrative and descriptive mode, with discussions of cultural conventions and depictions of personages at war in strange lands. But it seems to reflect a specifically Hellenistic assumption about rulers and men of power as the major vehicles of history and thus as the major figures of historiography.

We may summarize, then, by saying that certain aspects of Ben Sira's hymn do reflect acquaintance with Hellenistic historiographic literature and gain their significance by participating in the assumptions that gave this literature its purposes. These purposes include studied assessment and commemoration of the values of a culture or of a subcultural institution in implicit comparison to other cultures. History was helpful to this end by providing descriptive data of those leaders and functions illustrative of an institution's existence and tradition. Insofar as values could be manifest in strong leaders and seen to be repeated throughout a history, both a sense of definition and a quality of endurance could be achieved. Tracing such a pattern back to mythic origins achieved even more, namely, the grounding of those values in the order of things understood to be originary, ideal, universal, or divine. Historiography also presented a means for describing cultural conflicts, accounting for cultural change, and investigating cultural threats and options, as was evidenced already in the great histories of the fifth century. From this point on, both epic and chronicles as prior modes of recalling and recounting the past could be taken up into a new reflection, which might be called a cultural anthropology. The definitional moment that was the object of the quest is the Hellenistic notion of *aretē*.

Ben Sira's hymn shares in these assumptions about historiography and in this quest for cultural and humanistic definition. But its particular pattern of characterization, its architectonic structure, notion of continuity, style of description, and other features are not crafted on the Hellenistic model. These must be accounted for some other way. That other way, it has been suggested, calls for comparison with Hellenistic biographic literature.

Biography

It is the most obvious feature of the hymn, namely, its manifest preoccupation with characterizations of the human agents of Israel's history, that has called for comparison with the biographic literature of the Hellenistic period. In order to gain some clarity here, it will be necessary to distinguish between the generally pervasive biographic interests in the historiographic and encomiastic literatures on the one hand and the beginnings of biographic literature in the narrower sense within the Aristotelian tradition on the other. Biographic literature in this sense appears to have emerged within the arena of competition among the philosophic schools of the fourth century and their chief spokesmen.[18] It consisted initially of anecdotal material that highlighted the personal characteristics of individual philosophers and teachers. It does not appear to have been encomiastic. Indeed, much of it was gossipy or even derogatory, designed perhaps at first as personal or philosophical polemic. At some point, however, this type of material was recognized as being of value for elucidating the relationship of a particular philosophy to a particular manner of life (*bios*). The assumption was that a teacher's manner of life should correspond to his philosophy. Stories about what he had said or done, together with brief accounts of his habits, personal characteristics, sayings, and relationships with others, could be collected in a kind of portrait of the man known to have espoused this or that philosophical teaching. This emphasis upon personalia and espousal of a teaching sets this literature apart from both historiography and encomia. In both of the latter, but especially in historiography, personal touches, anecdotes, and sayings might be used on occasion. But the emphasis here was rather upon the description of strong actions and the delineation of qualities of character, rather than upon personal philosophy and the integrity of one's manner of life. The difference is due, no doubt, to the fact that historiography and encomia were focused primarily on kings and commanders, for whom deeds and achievements were definitive; the biographies had as their subjects philosophers, principally, for whom teachings were definitive. As we shall see, the items included in an encomium present a rather complete outline of a person's life and achievements without recourse to the anecdotal material characteristic of the Peripatetic "lives." These lives were not biographies in the sense of a full accounting of the course of a person's life. They were at first merely collections of disparate "biographic" materials. There were numerous examples of this genre written throughout the Hellenistic period, apparently as a tradition quite distinct from that of the encomium. Its survival well into the Roman period is documented in the work of Diogenes Laertius.

This tradition is not reflected in Ben Sira's treatment of the great men he praises. There are no anecdotes, personal touches, or interest expressed in an individual's personal characteristics. Only those items useful for a characterization in keeping with official functions are included. There is, indeed, no place within the conceptuality of office in the hymn for consideration of the correspondence of one's espoused philosophy and one's mode of life. In the case of the scholar-sage, the "office" most analogous to the Hellenistic philosopher-teacher, Ben Sira chose not to depict a specific scribe at all, but to cast up an ideal type.

Nevertheless, there is one aspect of Ben Sira's hymn that compares with the biographic literature. It is the theme of succession, which is introduced repeatedly in a variety of ways. Succession does not appear to have been an important notion in Hellenistic historiography in general,[19] but it did become a significant organizing principle for the biographic material when it came to be treated historically. It surfaces as program in the title of the work of Sotion of Alexandria (*Diadochē tōn philosophōn*), written roughly at the same time as Ben Sira's hymn, and determines the genre from that point through to the work of Diogenes Laertius. In this tradition, "succession" refers to the sequence of philosophers as heads of schools and comes to be used for charting the assumed derivative sequences of the philosophical schools themselves, from a point of origin with Thales as the first sage on through the entire history of their leadership. It is therefore based upon the notion of philosophy as tradition and works primarily with the relationship between teacher and student, the student viewed as successor and tradent of the philosophy, the school viewed as vehicle of the tradition.

Ben Sira did not achieve such a coherent conception of sequence as succession. Nor would this have been achieved easily, given the variety of offices, events, and history he needed to integrate. It is therefore all the more noteworthy that he found a variety of ways to introduce the notion of succession at telling points throughout the hymn. Especially interesting in this regard is the sequence from Moses through Aaron to Phineas, "the third in line" (45:23), as well as the notice that Joshua was a "minister of Moses in the prophetical office" (46:1) and the repeated emphasis upon the prophets as those involved in activities that determined the sequences of leadership throughout the history.[20]

We have had occasion to wonder about Moses' office as teacher, and whether Ben Sira's hymn indicates any reflection about its continuation in the process of the actualization of the covenant community. The conception of Moses as the first of a line of prophet-teachers is not worked out expressly nor carried through in the hymn, and there are several considerations that may account for its improbability as a major theme or organizing principle. One is the contingency that Ben Sira attributes to the period of the prophets in keeping with his mythic schema. This militates against the theme of continuity, say, of Torah teaching from Moses through the prophets and on into Ben Sira's own time. Another is the difficulty of superimposing the tradition upon prophets understood to be, not scholar-teachers, but visionaries. In that Ben Sira himself became conscious about what it means to be an author and understood the process of creative composition to be the result of divine inspiration, his role falls somewhere between that of the prophet and that of the scribe. His seriousness and creativity as a thinker lies in the fact of his noticing the task of the wisdom scholar and scribe as he took up such precursors as Moses (and his vision and books) and the prophets (and their visions and utterances). But the hymnic history did not provide Ben Sira with an opportunity to study and trace this new conception of office back to Moses adequately. If it had, a rather painful reflection would have been required in the attempt to distinguish the uniqueness of Moses as author in relation to Ben Sira himself.[21] Such a reflection on the relationship of scribal and Mosaic authorities did eventually occur, and it produced a most creative solution among the Tannaim. But this resolution could not take place, could not be used to rewrite the history, as long as the Second Temple model for Judaism was dominant.

Nevertheless, the ideas of authorship, teaching as tradition, faithfulness to a vision, and succession are all there in nuce in Ben Sira's book and are carried quite far even in the hymn as a motif that underlines the importance of sequence and continuity in the series. This may be seen, therefore, as an early appropriation of a concept from Hellenistic biographic literature that was later to be developed by other Jewish historiographers.[22] As is well known, the principle of a chain of tradition became canonical with the Tannaim. In the tractate Aboth, the prophets are the link in the chain that carried Torah from Moses, Joshua, and the elders through to the men of the great synagogue and on to the Tannaim at the end. Bickermann has argued convincingly that this schema is indebted to the idea of succession worked out in the schools of philosophy and used to organize the biographic literature in the Peripatetic tradition.[23]

It now appears that Ben Sira also was influenced by this idea of a succession of philosophers, albeit at a very early point in its conceptualization, and that he used it, though quite haltingly, as an organizing principle in the hymn. That it occurs at all in the hymn indicates that he was aware of the importance of Moses in ways analogous to Hellenistic views of the importance of the founders of philosophical schools. The implications of this for determining the point at which cross-cultural correlations began for the Hellenistic Jewish intellectual are clear. The first correlations between the cultures would have been discovered at the level of *paideia* and wisdom as literary and educational enterprises.

The Encomium

The indications are, then, that Ben Sira was acquainted with Hellenistic historiography and biographic literature in some degree and that certain general features of the hymn were influenced by his knowledge of this material. But more than this cannot be claimed. As historiography, the hymn is most peculiar, and there is very little in it analogous to the Hellenistic biographic genre. With the encomium, however, to which we now turn, the results of a comparison are quite different. Here one finds numerous and substantive parallels in style, form, content, and intention—parallels sufficient to warrant the thesis that major aspects of Ben Sira's hymn have been crafted on the model of this Hellenistic prototype.

The encomium can be traced from its origins in Hellenic epic, through significant developments in the lyric poetry of the classical period and the prose of the first sophistic period, and on through its flourishing as commemorative speech during the Hellenistic period.[24] It was a form recognized as both literary and rhetorical, it was invested with formal and critical theory in the schools, and it was found useful both for commemorative public occasions and for educational exercises. Its purpose was to praise the virtues of persons and institutions worthy of commemoration as those who incorporated the cultural ideals. Its subjects were originally epic heroes and victors in the pan-Hellenic games; then kings and commanders, as those upon whom an entire cultural tradition rested and in whom its values were once again tested and reaffirmed; and eventually, rhetors also and poets, philosophers, and others with roles of social significance were taken up for eulogy, as were cities, cultural institutions, and cultural and ethical values themselves. The encomium articulated the Hellenic aspiration for excellence, achievement, recognition, and reward. It was a basic vehicle for the transmission and translation of the Hellenic spirit during the Hellenistic period. Its formal characteristics and rhetorical expectations were familiar to a wide spectrum of experienced listeners in the populace, both Hellenes and Hellenists, wherever the institutions of Hellenistic culture spread. It was a form for entertainment, but with serious implications as well, inculcating in those who listened the very virtues rehearsed in the commemoration of the important personage or institution.

It is not surprising, therefore, to learn that Ben Sira was quite familiar with the encomium as a specific genre of rhetorical composition. We have already noted the extent to which he compounded the community's act of praise by including the scholar-sage alongside all of the great leaders of the past and recent present as worthy of honor and glory. This, as we have seen, was reminiscent of encomiastic tradition and practice. Though its ostensible purpose was obviously to enhance the image of the commemorated person, the encomium was also understood to be an occasion for the display of the rhetorical skills of the speaker. That Ben Sira's scholar-sage receives glory is fully in keeping with this convention. That one of his compositions is an encomium itself follows quite naturally.

The purpose of the hymn and the purpose of the encomium are, at least formally, the same. This is indicated clearly in the express intention of the author to sing praise (44:1), as well as in the repeated mentions of glory, fame, memorial, public recognition, acclaim, and festival occasions throughout the hymn. On the surface, then, the hymn is clearly encomiastic in its intention, and it is just this feature of the hymn that distinguishes it from its Jewish precursors. Probing a bit further, one can see that certain stylistic and compositional devices have been employed that were common in, and definitive for, encomiastic rhetoric. The use of comparison, contrast, the claim to being unsurpassed, and an illustrious genealogy in the depiction of a person all accord with common rhetorical practice. Rhetorical questions, hyperboles, and exclamations of awe may also be mentioned as tropes especially appropriate to the encomium.

But the telling consideration is the degree to which the biblical figures have been cast according to a common pattern. This indicates that the same conception of the typical has been superimposed upon all of the biblical accounts and has governed the way in which characterization has been achieved. Noting that the type reflected here is official, manifests its virtues in great deeds, and is responsible for the well-being of the social order, we can now suggest the source of that pattern of characterization. It was conceived along the lines of the Hellenistic encomium with its primary orientation to social leaders, kings and commanders especially, in whose deeds of achievement the social order was understood to have been defended and preserved.

In order to visualize the formal correspondence between the Hellenistic encomium and the pattern of characterization in Ben Sira's hymn, we may summarize the main divisions of the encomium as they are set up in table 3. This summary is based upon discussions of the encomium in rhetorical handbooks (*technai*) and the *progymnasmata*. It reproduces the major sec-

TABLE 3. THE PATTERN OF CHARACTERIZATION
AS ENCOMIUM

ENCOMIUM	*PATTERN OF CHARACTERIZATION*
1. PROEM	
2. BIRTH/GENEALOGY	2. ELECTION
3. ACHIEVEMENTS:	
A. PURSUITS	1. OFFICE
B. VIRTUES	4. PIETY
C. DEEDS	5. DEEDS
D. BLESSINGS	3. COVENANT
	6. SETTING CONTEXT
4. CONCLUSION	
A. DEATH	7. REWARDS
B. MEMORIALS	

tions of the speech form that may be shown to have shaped the encomium from the beginning, were expanded upon during the Hellenistic period, and continued to provide its outline for the Roman and Byzantine periods.[25]

A correlation with the pattern of characterization in the hymn can be achieved by assigning each item of the pattern to a corresponding topic in the encomium outline. Only item 6 in the pattern of characterization ("setting/context") is difficult to match. As discussed earlier, the setting is probably a function of the historicism of the hymn rather than of its encomiastic intention, and thus it does not have an analogue in the encomium. But it is not out of place, for the encomium regularly included mention of social context and tradition at appropriate junctures throughout the speech. The kind of setting depicted in the hymn, consistently a threat of moral and political destruction, is a thematic matter related to the hymn's specifically Jewish and religious provenance.

The proem of the encomium included mention of the person's name, the occasion for the speech, and the author's acceptance of the task of eulogy. A proem for each figure has not been included in the pattern of characterization, but it is important to see that it could have been. Each hymnic unit begins by introducing the person by name with some indication of his praiseworthiness. This makes it possible to speak of a formal correspondence with the encomium proem. One should note also that the other items included in an encomium proem, the statement of authorial intention and reference to occasional assemblage, are present in the proem of the hymn as a whole.

The second section of the encomium had to do with a person's birth and genealogy. Topics appropriate for this section were the illustriousness of one's nation, city, parents, as well as one's genealogy, which could include legendary and divine ancestors. This was expanded in the later Hellenistic and Roman periods to include one's upbringing and education. In the hymn, there is little interest in these kinds of material because there is little interest in the persons praised as individuals. But just because the figures praised in the hymn are important, not

as individuals, but as office holders, that is, as those who manifested the ideal type of specific social functions, the theme of
election (to office) may be seen as the appropriate correlate to
the Hellenistic categories of birth and genealogy. It represents
the specifically Jewish-religious counterpoint in keeping with
the hymn's larger mythic and theological concerns. In addition
to the theme of election, other hymnic material having to do
with one's birth, parentage, and genealogy belongs here also.
There is a noticeable emphasis upon this theme throughout the
hymn, which does suggest a formal correspondence with the
encomium.

The third and major section of the encomium was the re-
hearsal of qualities and achievements. The lists of topics and
their classifications vary somewhat from handbook to handbook, as do the orders suggested for their development. At an
early time in the tradition, a distinction may be noted between
a chronological arrangement of one's achievements and a top-
ical arrangement of one's qualities or virtues. Later classifications according to various typologies—for example, the
distinction between physical qualities and external resources
("goods")—also came to be used, sometimes to simplify,
sometimes to compound the problem of arrangement. But the
four items mentioned in table 3 (pursuits, virtues, deeds, blessings) appear to cover the major concerns and content of the
encomium throughout the Hellenistic period. Under the topic
"pursuits" (epitēdeumata), attention came to be focused upon
what we would call one's vocation. This was thought of in
terms of roles such as "statesman," "philosopher," and so on,
and thus corresponds to our category "office." Naturally, the
offices of significance for Jewish social history were particu-
larized for Ben Sira. But one suspects even so that where it was
possible to make a correlation between one of these and some
Hellenistic role, the similarities were explored. This is especially noticeable in the case of the judges as commanders and
the kings.

The item designated "piety" corresponds readily with the
delineation of moral virtues in the encomium. The repeated
mention of "strength" as a noteworthy quality in the hymn is

especially reminiscent of Hellenistic encomia, where physical prowess, spiritual courage, and vocational authority and power were regularly mentioned as worthy of praise. That the form of piety praised in the hymn is essentially a capacity to be faithful to one's calling-in-office, not a paradigm of Jewish religiosity in general, supports the thesis that an encomium prototype is at work.

That characterization is achieved in the hymn mainly by means of the recounting of deeds is also an encomiastic trait. In the tradition of the encomium, in distinction from the biographic tradition, characterization was achieved primarily by means of the narration of deeds as achievements. Some of the deeds mentioned in the hymn, for example, the fortification of the city, are Hellenistic commonplaces in the encomiastic tradition.[26]

Under "blessings," natural and fortunate endowments could be given as well as a listing of resources, property, and of all worldly signs of success. It is not clear whether these were understood primarily as gifts or achievements, and thus whether they should be discussed at the beginning or at the end of the main section; but that they were signs of a person's virtue, and thus praiseworthy, was not questioned. We have seen that in the hymn also, those items listed under the category "reward" are actually endowments. Indeed, the tension here between reward (or achievement) and endowment (or gift) is so dialectical that even the basic endowment of blessing and covenant can be described as what one receives as reward for virtue or virtuous deed. The dialectic is heightened by reading the hymn against its Jewish precursors, with their theologies of divine initiative and their anthropologies of faithful obedience. But a clearly sequential relationship between human efforts and just rewards was not characteristic of the Hellenistic encomium either. In this respect, the hymn shares what might be called the mentality of the encomium, even though the specific items mentioned as rewards (covenant, inheritance, land) are particularly Jewish values.

At the end of an encomium one's manner of death and memorials may be mentioned, as well as prayers offered. In the pattern of characterization of the hymn, "rewards" include memorials, glory, and honor. This is a striking feature and the most explicit similarity with the Hellenistic encomium and its ultimate purpose. Death as a theological and philosophical issue was troublesome for Ben Sira, as evidenced elsewhere in the book, and some aspects of that problem are no doubt related to the availability of Hellenistic views and reflections on the question.[27] But he could be comfortable with the concept of memorial and, in the hymn, has emphasized this aspect of the death of the pious—an idea in keeping both with encomium practice and with Jewish anthropology. One also might mention in this regard that the two blessings that conclude the praise of Phineas (45:25c–26) and Simon (50:22–24) correspond nicely to the prayers that conclude many Hellenistic encomia.

In a recent dissertation, Thomas Lee reviewed the question of Ben Sira's knowledge of Hellenistic literary genres and concluded that it was the encomium to which he was principally indebted. Lee's thesis is that the hymn was Ben Sira's encomium on Simon II, written to persuade Onias III to continue in Simon's tradition. Lee presents an outline of the major sections of the encomium with which to compare the structure of the hymn. In his analysis, the encomium can be divided into four parts: the proem, the genealogy (*genos*), the deeds (*praxeis*), and the epilogue. He was able to correlate the hymn's proem and final blessing (50:22–24) with the proem and epilogue of the encomium outline. The main body of the encomium, that having to do with achievements, he compared with the hymn section on Simon (50:1–21). This left the bulk of the poem to be accounted for as the "genealogical" section. Lee could show that aspects of the depictions, especially of Moses, Aaron, Phineas, and the kings, are indeed similar to the description of Simon and that some connection was intended. He showed also that a review of one's ancient and historical ancestors did pertain to one's glory and was thus relevant as an element in the Hellenistic encomium. But in order to understand the extremely long series of historical figures that the hymn gives,

Lee had to point to another genre, to what has been called a *Beispielreihe,* a series or collection of examples. He was able to show that the example series was compatible with the function of the genealogical section of the encomium, but the problem of the disproportionate space given to the "genealogy" in the hymn in relation to the "achievement" of Simon, he could not answer. This leaves one uneasy with his thesis as a sufficient explanation of the structure of the hymn.

Nevertheless, Lee's work is very important, and his thesis can be accommodated. The encomium pattern is in evidence in each of the smaller units of the hymn and provides an explanation for the proem at the beginning and the blessing at the end of the poem as a whole. Lee's study also supports several other conclusions we have reached. He offers an additional explanation for the panegyric occasion that plays so large a role in the final scene of the hymn, a setting and description in agreement with encomiastic tradition. He argues for the necessity of including the section on Simon in the hymn and sees the hymn as a whole to have its intended climax there. He observes that many of the figures in the hymn are described in ways that appear to be similar to the description of Simon.

But just here the problem with Lee's thesis begins to tell. The reason the "genealogy" section of the encomium is compatible with an example series is that both of these literary forms entail a review of history for making their points. The genealogy does this in order to enhance the illustriousness of the personage eulogized. The example series seeks to establish the credibility of a certain kind of human achievement. Ben Sira may have modeled his hymn with an eye to both genres, but neither literary form really is sufficient to account for the peculiar way in which his figures are characterized, linked, and used to trace a complete, schematic history. The structure of the poem we have proposed indicates a larger purpose than an encomium on Simon.

Simon is praised, to be sure. But the "genealogy" is not his alone, nor is all of it relateable to him as a personage, certainly not, as Lee suggests, as a personage whose "character" is reflected in all of the preceding examples of "fidelity to the commandments."[28] It is rather his office that is in focus, not simply as a given social role within a culture with a consistently paradigmatic history, but as a product of that history that recounts the costs of its conception and actualization within a complexly structured community. Thus the proem of the hymn does not mention its telos in Simon's appearance on the great day. The poem begins with figures of extremely broad significance, develops its themes dynamically, studies the interrelationships among the offices throughout Israel's history, and moves toward a conclusion about what it is to which all of the history has been purposefully moving. This is more than encomium, even though features of the encomium are clearly in evidence throughout.

Placed at the intersection of Hebrew and Hellenistic literatures, Ben Sira's hymn manifests an amazingly complex intertextuality. We have seen that Ben Sira was conversant with Hellenistic historiography, biography, and the encomium, but that each provided models only for certain aspects of the poem. From the emerging genre of universal history, Ben Sira took the notion of the primeval epoch and read the early history in Genesis and Exodus in its light. He read the subsequent history of Israel as a chronicle of events and leaders marking Jerusalem's destiny. He made his selections on the basis of specific social roles and conflicts found to be significant for the institution of the temple cult. His characters were portrayed on the pattern of the encomium and linked by themes taken from the biographic histories of the Aristotelian tradition. The result is a poem with decidedly encomiastic traits. But it should not be called simply an encomium, any more than a chronicle or epic historiography. It is an epic poem that cannot be reduced to any of the genres thus far noted as precursor literatures.

Since that is the case, another look at the hymn's architectonic structure is called for. The key to its coherence and mythic function has not yet been discovered, that is, what it was that called for the correlation of history and encomium to begin with. Though each precursor text has been found to contribute something to the composition, none has provided a rationale sufficient to explain the hymn's evocative power. Perhaps there is yet another "text" with which the hymn can be compared, a text that can clarify the particular configuration Ben Sira has given to his epic poem.

Wisdom as Text and Texture 6

Of the partial alignments of hymn and precursor texts that we have explored, none has been able to elucidate the particular schema of ordered history that the hymn presents, a schema that enabled the integration of the many texts in a single vision. The question is whether the rationale for Ben Sira's creative intertextual and cross-cultural reading can be determined. Was he a reader of yet another kind of text, a text available to us as well for our own exploration of that rationale?

That other "text," I would argue, is a "wisdom" way of viewing things—a reading of the world from a certain perspective, determined and enabled by a certain way with words. Concretely, that other text is Ben Sira's book of wisdom itself, and especially those poems and hymns within it that achieve a marvelous and mythic self-reflection. In them, certain basic moments in the mythic pattern of this particular reading of the world are disclosed. In them, the act of perception of the world has been transposed into myth and recited as a series of events in the encounter of a personified wisdom with the world. We shall see that this pattern and this personification provide us with the text we seek and that the myth of wisdom can account for the hymn's mythic structure and its theme of glory.

To read the hymn as a wisdom myth is, of course, a bit unusual. There is no internal evidence, linguistic or referential, that demands comparison with the wisdom hymns. On the basis of all the conventional scholarly views on wisdom, the likelihood of correspondence is not great.[1] In fact, it has always been a puzzle that a hymnic history was included in a book of wisdom at all. Wisdom thought and language, insofar as it has been understood to delimit a given horizon of interests and concerns within Jewish tradition, has not been associated with theologies of history, preoccupations with midrash, theories of prophecy, defense of the culture, and so on— all obvious features of the hymn. Nevertheless, our literary analysis of the hymn and our attempt to account for its composition on the basis of its rhetoric, assumed setting, and intertextuality have not disclosed the impulse or vision that guides its formation. Nor have they revealed that passion out of which the hymn attributes glory to the pious. We will attempt now to discover that passion and vision. I maintain that read as a wisdom text, all features of the hymn cohere and are clearly marked by a deep commitment to find a rational basis for human social organization.

WISDOM AS A MODE OF THOUGHT

We have no designation, other than the term "wisdom" itself, for that place and function within Jewish society taken and played by a book like Ben Sira's. It has been customary to speak about a "wisdom tradition" as if there were a social institution or literary tradition that traded mainly in wisdom as a body of knowledge and transmitted it as such. But recent scholarship has found it necessary to question the assumption of a wisdom tradition understood along these lines.[2] It has not been possible to identify a specific class of sages who functioned primarily as tradents of wisdom in any specific, continuous social setting within Israelite history. This means that the analogy of the prophetic, priestly, and Levitical traditions, for instance, can no longer be used to conceptualize the placement and transmission of wisdom as a separate stream of philosophical, theological, or ideological thought as scholars have been wont to do. There does not appear to have been any such distinct and self-conscious program characteristic of any particular social institution invested with the concerns of sages alone. As for the literature usually identified as wisdom texts (Proverbs, Job, Qohelet, some psalms, etc.), they singularly lack placement and even concern for placement in any specific nexus of cultural or subcultural activity of preserving and transmitting wisdom itself. Until Ben Sira took them up as precursor texts, moreover, nothing like a literary canon seems to have existed. No author seems to have regarded previously composed wisdom writings as literary precursors in a tradition of wisdom discourse at all.[3] This does not mean that the phenomenon of wisdom discourse and thought in ancient and early Judaism is insignificant as a characteristic of its culture. But it does mean that we must reconceptualize its function as a mode of perception available to (and perhaps determinative for) the culture as a whole, not a special class of scholars. Gifted individuals in a variety of settings and subcultural traditions were capable of using such discourse creatively and reflectively. But as a mode of discourse, wisdom was probably more pervasive in the culture than we have imagined it to be.

To speak of a mode of wisdom discourse is, however, already to delimit the range of reference to the term itself. Wisdom (ḥokmāh), it should be noted, can be used to refer to a very broad range of human skills, capacities, perceptions, and behavior. It is a generic term for "knowledge" or "knowing" and requires modification by attribution or context in order to gain any specificity at all. Thus one might speak of mantic wisdom, craft wisdom, crafty wisdom, proverbial or life wisdom, ethical wisdom, and so on.[4] In each case, recognizable experience and observable behavior might be understood as evidence, and certain linguistic formulations or genres might become customary for communication and transmission of the knowledge claimed. When, then, in the literature under discussion, reference is made to wisdom, an extremely indeterminate linguistic sign is employed. That reference is made at all to wisdom as an object of observation and thought is, of course, the problem. The question for us is whether we can understand more precisely what knowledge or knowing in this mode may have been.

We may begin with the observation that at the basic level of proverbial speech forms, wisdom refers to some skill in the assessment of and response to human and social circumstances. This skill has to do with the correlation of circumstance with convention in the interest both of preserving social conventions and of achieving personal status and well-being within the social order. Thus we speak of wisdom from experience, articulated in proverb and available for utterance or enactment upon an appropriate occasion.[5] The proverb itself is a product of generalization from many experiences and tends to characterize human beings in terms of typical behavior. But the status of the typical is quite problematic, at least for contemporary Western mentality to grasp, because it is merely descriptive and related to "cases" instead of to "causes." The cases themselves, though forms of broadly universal human experiences, are nevertheless culturally conditioned and assume a particular cultural stability and ordering of social life. Insofar as a proverb distills what is at stake in the typical circumstance and refracts from it options and consequences, it itself is the wisdom intended in linguistic form. The wisdom available in a proverb can be taught and learned, provided that the social order remains stable and the proverb's own linguistic occasions (for being said, recalled, re-enacted, reaffirmed) remain conventional and functional.

A collection of proverbs, then, does represent an accumulation of wisdom that has been won by means of certain methods of observation, testing, and classification. The definition of certain constants in a given social structure with its own patterns of human behavior is involved. Its linguistic formations are appropriate to the preservation and communication of these insights. As a mode of thought, speech, and action widely available to a culture, proverbial wisdom can provide a way of making sense of things. It can provide a perspective and method for reflection, capable, ultimately, of encompassing all or-

ders of perceived reality if organized around the anthropological focus and its concern for well-being. Understood in this
way, wisdom thinking can provide an entire culture with an
"intellectual" capacity capable of being shared and understood
by all.

But this mode of thinking is prescientific, existential, and
humanistic. There is no capacity or interest here for a radical
analysis or critique of the mechanisms that might guarantee or
account for the occurrence of the typical, nor a need to develop a conception even of that order or structure of things that
is assumed implicitly in the program. Wisdom is therefore dependent upon the givenness of a social order with its conventions. It may function in the formation, defense, and continuation of a culture's social values, but it is incapable of radical or
scientific investigation for adjudicating competitive values or
for grounding a system of values in another arena of discourse.

Should a shift occur in a cultural tradition, or should there
be a major social change or breakdown, the viability of the
accumulated wisdom will be sorely tested.[6] Insofar as the
wisdom accumulated is knowledge about human experience,
wisdom is transferrable from one social order and its particular
conventions to another. Insofar as the typical is a circumstance
in which behavior determines the outcome (e.g., deed-conse-
quence), there is an understanding available to the wisdom
mode of perception itself that can facilitate assessment of contingent situations. But this is true only up to a certain point.
The contingent can be managed by wisdom only if it is relative
to a set of closely related, typical possibilities. The contingent
then becomes at most a sort of mild surprise as to which one
of the numerous typical occasions arises. If the possibility of
the typical were to be erased by drastic cultural changes, the
possibility of wisdom itself would be threatened.

WISDOM CRISIS AND THE EMERGENCE OF MYTH

Conventional wisdom was threatened by social crises at one
time or another in all of the cultures of the ancient Near East.
In each case, the agony registered in the literature marks the
importance of a people's wisdom as the intellectual fabric of its

social discourse and cultural etiquettes. A series of questions and reflections set in about the status of wisdom in the situation of social confusion. These reflections took many forms, governed as they were by the full range of human attitudes toward cultural chaos, from despair and cynicism, through a range of rationalizations, to imaginative endeavors to make sense of things again in spite of it all. One of these endeavors resulted in the creation of a mythic figure.

The personification of wisdom as a mythic figure emerged in Hebrew thought and literature much before the time of Ben Sira. It is customary to regard Proverbs 1–9 as the earliest evidence for this phenomenon, and it is there that we can discern the result of what must have been a daring self-reflection. Not only did the crisis of conventional wisdom force an honest assessment about its inability to function as before, its own critical capacities were called upon to give an account of its failure and to broach some solution. This social-intellectual crisis for wisdom, most probably to be set in the exilic or early postexilic despair over the end of Israel's monarchies, has not been thoroughly explored in the scholarship. Von Rad examined the way in which later scholars (e.g., Ben Sira) discovered the logical limits beyond which a wisdom mode of inference and deduction could not go. He concluded that this effort was made possible by turning the logic implicit within wisdom thinking in upon itself. He was quite right about the courageous dialectic of this self-reflection, but he did not explore sufficiently the social conditions that impelled it or the full range of intellectual activity that accompanied it. This is because he viewed wisdom thinking on the model of the history of ideas and could find no way to relate its discourse to social history once the bond of conventional wisdom with everyday life was broken by cultural crisis. Nor could he account for the emergence of the mythic figure of wisdom itself.

A careful study of the emergence of this figure shows, however, that it was one of the primary results of the crisis that tore the social fabric away from the knowledge about the world that wisdom discourse once represented. In this case, more clearly than in the case of later analyses on the limits of wisdom logic, the full extent of the crisis can be reconstructed. The mythic figure stood as an attempt to give an answer to the many questions forced by the crisis. But it was not a simple, intellectual product of the investigation of these questions. Critical thought had to be given to every aspect of the crisis in order even to imagine such an answer. There must have been a serious attempt to conceptualize the system of etiquette conventional wisdom represented as system. This would have been forced upon thinkers by the rupture between conventional wisdom as a way of recognizing the familiar patterns of human behavior in a stable society and the breakdown of its social orders. The distinction between wisdom as a system of knowledge and society as a vulnerable structure, then, would have been the first agonizing acknowledgment. But the desire to make sense of things would have required other distinctions as well, explorations of the tenuous relations between what we have learned to call the orders of things: the divine, the natural, the social, and the ethical. This forced analysis would have been very difficult, because conceptual categories would have to be created in order to imagine these "orders" as distinguishable components of what was once viewed as a totality. Conventional wisdom, dysfunctional in the wake of the destruction of its assumed social stabilities, would need to be rethought as well.

One way of rethinking was to acknowledge the dislocation of wisdom from the social fabric, but to affirm that its insights and concerns were valid nevertheless. Such a process of reflection could result in the mythic personification of wisdom that we have in Proverbs 1–9. It should be regarded as a first-level abstraction of the enduring value of the system of conventional wisdom. This system was now concentrated in a single symbol that stood over the social arena. However, the social arena had lost its capacity for conventional wisdom discourse, and so the figure of wisdom was imagined no longer to be related to contemporary social discourse. It was cast, rather, as coming to speech for itself, and its speech was the call for social sanity of a figure imagined not to belong to society any longer, having its location in the divine ordering of the natural world.

Wisdom now was imagined as belonging to God, related in some way to the act and order of creation, appearing only epiphanically in the streets and public places of the city, and calling out to the foolish to accept her teaching (Prov. 1:20–33). The desire to affirm the presence of a wisdom no longer at home in society is obvious here, as is the attempt to affirm its reality by means of a mythic projection upon the larger screen of the world of creation. This was apparently the only "order" of things actually imaginable any longer (Prov. 8:25–31). Because the other "orders" were not yet imaginable as orders, the myth reduced them also to agents who could represent them: God, the resistant market place, the fool. Wisdom was imagined as an agent in order to relocate the stability it represented in the next larger order of things imaginable, the natural order.

That wisdom became a mythic figure, an abstraction in a prophetic call for realignments of the orders, was not poetic fantasy. It was the result of a deliberate reflection about a real state of affairs. Wisdom had to be imagined this way because that was all that was left of it—an absent agent, hoping to claim authority for some system of order and sanity in the world in order to survive at all. But the "reappearance" and "acceptance" of wisdom within the sphere of human life was required as an additional moment of perception. Thus the projection of wisdom upon the larger world as an "order" of creation was an assertion about wisdom and order previously unexplored.[7]

Wisdom became a name for that passionate desire to retain some notion of the social sense of things. But that could be done only by anchoring it, not in the social order itself, but in the structure of the world. The social order was gone and, though the concern was to see it (or another social order) reinstated, its absence determined that the projection of orderliness, only now imagined as a category at all, be upon the universal screen. The assumption of a societal order was canceled out in the very process of thinking of "order" itself. Human well-being had to be imagined first in relation to a cosmic order of things.

It may be, of course, that some mythic correlation of cosmic and social orders (e.g., Maat) was the proximate source of the idea that wisdom was still present, if only in the realm of creation. The mythic conception of wisdom was partly a discovery and disclosure of structures implicit to and originally merely assumed by wisdom thought, partly a new linguistic creation. The desire to retain the sense of things in spite of the breakdown of a society's structures is, of course, understandable. That it was achieved by abstracting, projecting, and personifying wisdom, however, marks a profound and tragic experience of despair and indicates just how important a culture's wisdom actually was. The picture that first resulted did not include wisdom in the social order. It depicted the figure of wisdom at creation (i.e., "located" outside both the social and natural orders), claiming involvement in creation and seeking re-cognition in society.

It was undoubtedly due to a social crisis and its threat to a body of conventional wisdom that such a self-reflective moment occurred within Jewish cultural history. With the possible exception of Proverbs 10–31, all of the literature normally designated as wisdom writings bear the marks of this process. The separation between the wisdom of the social order (now threatened with destruction) and the wisdom projected upon the created order (now affirming its presence) was radically experienced. But the myth that resulted from this reflection was strong, as strong as the desire to find wisdom in the world again, and as strong as the God with whom wisdom was joined at the beginning of the world.

According to this myth, wisdom is that which orders or even creates the world, articulates or even guarantees its typicalities (and those values that derive from orderliness, such as rightness, equality, and peace), and is available or even desires to be known or manifest (in the social order). In the process of mythologization, new linguistic formations were produced (e.g., the naming and mythic characterizations of the personified figure of wisdom itself), conceptual categories were created (e.g., the idea of "creation by wisdom"), narrative schemata were imagined (e.g., the "appearance" of wisdom in the world), and additional literary genres were requisitioned (e.g., dialogue, prophetic address, hymn).

If we look closely at this myth, we can see that it represents the process by which wisdom can be reappropriated. But insofar as it was concerned to answer the question of wisdom's absence, it inverts the sequences of the process by which wisdom was won in the first place. To acquire conventional wisdom there was (1) the drama of the human quest for learning about wisdom and the typical in the social arena, (2) its articulation in proverbs so that transmission and repetition could occur, and (3) the assumption about the goodness of the order in things. The myth, in contrast, narrates first the creation of order by wisdom, then its entrance into the human arena and its speech of presence, and finally its invitation to the listener to accept it.

The conception of wisdom and its order in the world, related though it was to older naivetes in the structure of wisdom thought, was not an abstraction of older wisdom views about the world; nor was it a conception about the world that had been won by some investigation of it that ascertained its principles of regularity and order. It was a new view of wisdom, a linguistic and imaginative achievement born of the desire for, the will to affirm, what ultimately had to be a divine (i.e., extrahuman) knowing and ordering of the world. This happened in such a way as to make it possible to call for an ordering of human society that corresponded to the divine will. The passionate projection is a profound and beautiful affirmation of what had to be so in the face of social experience that told otherwise. But it is extremely important to see that it is a mere abstraction, a naming of that which is not known, without reference to any empirical, logical, or philosophical data to serve as its grounding.

In the Hellenic tradition of philosophy, the attempt was made to discover the physical basis for natural and social ordering. The Hebraic conception of a wisdom ordering of creation was not based upon such a move. It was not argued but affirmed. Thus it stood for the tenacity of the desire for social order in the moment of its lack. It called, not for an investigation of the verifiability of a certain kind of order in creation, that is, a "wisdom kind," but for a renewal of social ordering and stability itself. Nevertheless, once this thought had been achieved, namely, that the world was ordered by wisdom and that this was the reason and model for human social ordering, a kind of logic was given to the quest for social ordering and a powerful rhetoric could emerge to call for it. But the rhetoric needed additional rationalization in order to persuade.

One further observation needs to be made about the wisdom myth before asking about Ben Sira's reflection upon it. It is that the narrative sequence we have given, which begins with God at creation, moves into and through the natural order, and ends in the city with wisdom's call, is our own reconstruction, a combination of motifs presented separately in Proverbs 1–9. This reconstruction is justified on the basis of comparative mythology closely associated with the wisdom literature of Israel's neighbor Egypt, a mythology that has been shown to provide the imaginative stimulus for many details of Israel's mythic wisdom. But it has not been set forth in just this way in any early Jewish wisdom writing. The narrative depictions remain episodic, exploring aspects of the myth at certain critical moments. These moments are invariably at the rifts and seams between the several orders of reality that wisdom must reunite: God-world, God-city, world-city, wise-fool, and so on. At each junction, wisdom personified stands in the gap between two orders, representing the desire to link them together again, to see them related. But that is all. There is no narrative logic other than desire to any of the episodes of mediation, though they are hauntingly attractive as images. They invite, in fact, further reflection on the problem of how one might see things integrally related again. All subsequent wisdom mythology can be understood in just this way, as junctures explored in the interest of working out the problem of fragmentation (Prov. 8:22; Job 28, 38; Sirach 1, 24; Wisdom 9, 10; etc.). But the mythic episodes themselves do not relate how the gaps actually are to be bridged. They cannot do this until three conditions are met: (1) A full narrative logic must be discovered that can relate together again all of the orders now apart; (2) the orders must be conceptualized structurally, systematically, and in such a way that they can be combined in a single complex system; and (3) a new social order must be actualized and rationalized in accordance with the wisdom myth. We are now ready for Ben Sira.

WISDOM MYTH AND THE QUEST FOR A LOGIC

Ben Sira's book of wisdom is a major witness to intellectual endeavor accomplished in a wisdom mode. It is replete with a broad spectrum of wisdom genres, engages a wide range of basic issues in Jewish ethical and religious thought, makes a proposal with regard to the purpose of creation and human existence, and argues for a certain view of Jewish cult and piety by claiming that they are supported by the most profound manifestations of wisdom itself. His book is clearly not a product of some "precrisis naivete" about the validity of conventional wisdom and the stability of a given social order. The great catastrophes that brought an end to the pre-exilic monarchial orders were still vividly in memory, and the consequences of these events for the culture's accumulated wisdom were known. Ben Sira does not acknowledge expressly the possibility of skepticism and cynicism that could and did emerge in postexilic reflections about the reliability of a wisdom view of things, but it cannot be that he was unaware of them.[8] His own position, which was positive in its affirmations about wisdom, appears on a first reading to be put forth in a quite straightforward manner. In actuality, it is highly rhetorical and apologetic in purpose, dealing in hyperbole, generalizations, and attempts to ground the case for wisdom by observations that move beyond the customary limits of wisdom discourse. This indicates that Ben Sira worked within and against the context of conscious and articulate critique of conventional wisdom and the adequacy of its logic.

In order to counter this critique, the wisdom myth was at hand. But merely to continue to recite the myth in the face of its critics would have been inadequate. A further rationalization was required, as we have indicated, to explicate its narrative logic, reimagine its symbols, and work out its correlations with some social order within which another wisdom discourse could make sense, instruction could be given, and human well-being achieved. It was just such an effort that Ben Sira invested in the wisdom myth. He did this in the interest of what might be called a wisdom theology for Second Temple Judaism. The narrative logic was worked out by correlating the myth with Israel's history on the one hand. On the other, the narrative episodes were taken as occasions to reflect on several categories of mediation capable of bridging the gaps between the orders of things. The symbols representing the several orders were expanded and diversified in order to find aspects of them that could be correlated, the notion of system was introduced and refined, and Second Temple Judaism was idealized and grasped as a centered structure in order to see within it the reflections and manifestations of the glorious arrangement of God's intentions for the world.

This intellectual achievement needs to be examined more closely. Our analysis and discussion will lead eventually back to the hymn, which it will be argued, may be one of the finer achievements of Ben Sira's intellectual efforts in a wisdom mode, even though the figure of wisdom no longer appears there. But other hymns and poems in his book show him always at the larger task as well. We need to explore these, for there it is that Ben Sira's struggle for a firm foundation on which to build his rationalized order of things can be discerned. In this exploration, as we shall see, his interest in Hellenistic modes of thought will finally be explained. It was not a flirtation with a culture somehow more attractive than his own. It was a quest for logos, for another, supplemental abstraction with which to undergird his myth of wisdom, and it was absolutely crucial to his enterprise. The new assertion of wisdom's presence in society and the world had to be grounded by arguments and considerations from other, expanded fields of observation and reflection on the nature of things. The claim to find wisdom in a given social order in the postcrisis situation and under cynic critique required more than the identification of a social concretion with a mythic abstraction. The abstraction still would be only an empty cipher for the desire that there be an ordering of things in the world. So unless additional considerations were forthcoming about the rationality of the myth, one would be left with mere assertion, capable only of the rhetoric of desire.

The first need, noted above, was to work out the narrative logic of the mythic episodes. It can be seen that Ben Sira has explicated the narrative capacities of the wisdom myth in certain significant ways. One is that wisdom has been depicted as a creation of the Creator himself, who "poured her out upon all His works," as well as "upon all flesh" (1:9–10). This mythic datum theologized the wisdom order in terms familiar to Jewish conceptuality and in such a way as to indicate that there was a basic correlation between the world and the human capacity for understanding it, anchored in divine intention and activity. If left here, of course, this would add merely another assertion to the assertion about wisdom itself, and thus will require some further substantiation. But to bridge the gaps between Creator and creation, as well as between creation and humankind by means of the single narrative image "pouring" is already helpful. Another expansion of an older mythic episode occurs in the narrative of wisdom's quest to find a home in the world among a particular people. The narrative ends when the Creator tells wisdom to settle down in Jerusalem (24:8–12) and she obeys. This localizes wisdom and claims her presence within the social institutions of Judaism. The relationship between these two expansions of the myth (manifestations of wisdom in creation as well as in the human order of things) is that between capacity or potentiality to recognize wisdom and its actualization in a social construct. Taken together, they give a simple narrative logic, and both expansions are capable of further elaboration, as will become clear.

Another requirement noted above, identification of wisdom with a social order, is also already in the process of being worked out. It can be seen that Ben Sira has recast the story of wisdom's origin and quest with a particular objective in mind. That objective is to identify Second Temple Judaism as the flowering of all God's works of wisdom in creation and history. The constitutive elements may now be named that play some specific role in the discovery, articulation, codification, and manifestation of wisdom's presence in that society. For Ben Sira, these are the Temple (24:10); the Book (24:23); the system of jurisprudence and ethic; the intellectual achievements of the scholar-priest (39:1–11), his poems, hymns, and ethical instructions; the piety to the faithful (the "fear of the Lord"); and the manifestation of the Creator's glory in the office and ritual occasion of the high priest. This is a fairly comprehensive grasp of the religious structure of the society and a daring claim. Ben Sira has apparently found it possible to bless this religious order as an arena within which wisdom can be learned and taught again. He may in fact have seen aspects of this social order as especially compatible with the implicit needs and desires of a wisdom view of things. The nature of authority; the privilege granted to repetition, ritual, and typicality; conventional binary ethical categories—these and other aspects of the religious mentality of a temple society could have been found worthy of wisdom's blessing. But the assertion that wisdom was to be found here was made without recourse to such considerations, because as a name for a means and way of creating order, wisdom really had no content until it had an occasion to identify and to be identified with the society itself.

Theoretically, any number of human social orders could be claimed for wisdom, so the heightened sense of claim that Ben Sira's rehistoricizing necessitates must be noted. Ben Sira must say, to say anything at all about the wisdom of a social order, that this manifestation of wisdom is nothing less than the Creator's intention from the beginning. The various orders in need of correlation (creation, society, human beings) have been unified narratively, therefore, by ascribing the myth to divine purpose and relating it to Israel's history as intentional. The identifications among the orders were made quite simply at the narrative level by using wisdom as a major metaphor to valorize and unify the Jewish order and history. Ben Sira's assertion was made at first merely on the basis of a mythic claim. This claim would have to be validated, however, by considerations from a philosophical assessment of the world. Only so could the logic of the narrative claim be recognized and rationalized, only so could it persuade. This explains, of course, the great attraction of Hellenistic thought for Ben Sira. It provided the conceptual categories to rationalize the myth.

Ben Sira has not provided a full account of a correlation of the wisdom myth with Hellenistic philosophic systems, as in fact occurred in subsequent reflections (e.g., Wisdom of Solomon, Philo). But he sensed the need to do so and began the process in a number of telling ways. For one, he set up the two readings of the myth in such a way as to create the dialectic between potentiality and actuality (wisdom available to Adam in creation, wisdom available to Israel in her history). This is a logical relationship. It corresponds also with the contrast between the universal or generic and the particular or ethnic classifications of the human, also a firmly entrenched application of Hellenic logic; and it is grounded in the schema of creation/culture, a Jewish version of a basic and longstanding Greek philosophical exploration (*physis/nomos*). The very creation of these dialectic and diaeretic sehemata is significant as an indication that Ben Sira sought a logic of correlation. When, then, the concept of totality occurs in the context of a creation hymn (*kōl, to pan* [43:27]) or the idea of an original endowment for perception occurs in the context of a midrash on the creation of Adam (17:7; cf. 17:5: *nous*), he is marshalling Hellenistic philosophical categories for the explication and conceptualization of the various schemata of correlation.

Middendorp and others have shown that Ben Sira was acquainted with and influenced by Hellenistic philosophical commonplaces. He "equated" sin and hybris, wisdom and *aretē*, and regarded the passions as the cause of unseemly behavior, for instance. More difficult to document, but more important for our thesis, is the possibility of seeing the various schemata by which Ben Sira articulates correspondences among the several orders of reality as Hellenistic as well. If the schema *cosmos-polis-anthropos* or *physis-nomos* stood behind and gave structure to Ben Sira's mythology of creation and culture, a possibility given with the influence of Hellenistic thought itself, the logics of classification and correspondence inherent to these systems would have been at work as well. To the degree that they were, a Hellenistic philosophical foundation would have been gained as a thought and discourse capable of providing external validation for Ben Sira's primary narrative claim that the Second Temple institutions were anchored in a creation order governed by gracious and philanthropic design. The correlation with Hellenistic philosophical categories would allow that claim to be translated as follows: the Jewish *polis* is based upon a *nomos* identical to the natural order (*physis*) of the world (*cosmos*). To see the logic (*logos*) of this arrangement (*taxis*) of the orders of reality is wisdom (*sophia*), the perception of things that makes possible the achievement of human excellence (*aretē*)—an imitation (*mimēsis*) of the correlation of *nomos* and *physis*—in human life (*anthropos, bios*).

Such a translation could shore up the wisdom myth and imagery against the threat of emptiness by providing another, reasonable perspective on the narrative categories. The very discovery that the translation was possible would have provided the primary power and impulse for Ben Sira's claim and may have been the basic reason for the cross-cultural intellectual adventure in the first place. The mere fact that a given notion (e.g., a "wisdom order in creation") might be renamed (as *cosmos*) would strongly suggest that the referential reality intended was assured. More important, however, is that the new name came with the force of that logic inherent in the Hellenistic system of philosophical thought. As concepts won in the intellectual endeavors of definition, classification, and quest for the ground and interrelationships of phenomena, the Hellenistic categories served to rationalize the imagery with which wisdom had been expressed. The process may be understood as making explicit in discursive terms what was implicitly intended via narrative and metaphor. The translation would, in itself, have been a significant step in conceptual resignification. But we should not overlook the important factor of the additional perspective that was won in this translation process, the sense that the thing named actually was something. This notion came with the new name as a philosophical concept belonging to a system of conceptuality that offered a reasonable account of the world.

With Ben Sira, the correlation of wisdom imagery and categories with Hellenistic philosophical conceptions has not been carried out systematically, at least not at the level of philosophical terminology. He wrote, after all, in Hebrew and continued to work with proverbial and poetic genres. But the evidence is that he was broadly conversant with and deeply influenced by Hellenistic learning. That he continued to express his reflections, wisdom, and literary achievements for the most part in terms of recognizable wisdom metaphor reveals both the limits of his Hellenization and the seriousness of his creativity. No simple identification or accommodation of the two systems was being made. The moments of translatability have not occurred arbitrarily, nor by merely speculative interests, nor as playful experimentation. For Ben Sira, wisdom was the language of truth and its correlation with Hellenistic philosophy was intended to serve its own claims, not to recommend Hellenistic learning and culture as a superior option.

JEWISH WISDOM AND HELLENIC PAIDEIA

It is important now to see that the point at which Jewish culture could begin a conversation with Hellenism was given with the phenomenon of wisdom itself. Among scholars, the customary approach to the question of Jewish-Hellenistic syncretism has been to discuss cultural identities in terms of particularizing theologies, pieties, and practices, to set up a pattern of competition, then to note the degree to which any acceptance of the other's cultural constructs accommodated the traditions. It is, however, not insignificant that the major translations in the Hellenization of Jewish religious and cultural traditions, those at least intended to be constructive, were made precisely at the level of an exchange of wisdom. This of course is hardly a surprising discovery, indicating as it does that a process of thought, a linguistic translation, was required as the basis for understanding another culture's conventions in any respect at all. What we have not understood, though, is the degree to which it was Jewish wisdom that provided the intellectual fabric of Jewish culture and so could be the vehicle for such an exchange.

By intellectual fabric, more must be meant than that implied in the usual study on intellectual and philosophical ideas. It has been customary, for instance, to make a comparison between Jewish *ḥokmah* (as a term for theological knowledge) and Hellenic *sophia* (as a term for philosophical knowledge). To stay at this level of investigation confines the study to an exchange among elites and treats Jewish wisdom as a subcultural phenomenon, that is, as a distinct tradition cultivated by a class of intellectuals. What must now be considered is the extent to which wisdom gave Judaism its own cultural coherence on terms equal to the challenge of cross-cultural dialogue and competition in the Hellenistic period. Of far more significance than the correlation with the *sophia* of the philosophers was undoubtedly that with *paideia* as a system of learning itself.[9] Here it must have been that the basis was found, not only for the cross-cultural conversation in the first place, but for the consciousness within Judaism of the institution that must carry the day in the new time. We are not able yet to trace the history of education in Israel and early postexilic Judaism, and much of what eventually surfaces for us to see already is stamped heavily by Hellenistic modes of learning. But the basis for this receptivity surely was already given with the materials and conventions called wisdom. Here in quite recognizable forms was to be found the Jewish analogue to a whole range of elements constitutive for the Hellenistic culture of *paideia*: the proverbial wisdom of the sages as the first texts for learning reading, then writing; the use of such material to inculcate the virtues and values of the cultural tradition; the methods of teaching and learning (rote memorization, the authority of the rod, the promise of eventual success in society); the schema of the sequence work-reward to motivate learning and rationalize socialization via education; the comfortable combination of religious and humanistic ethics—all pedagogical conventions easily assimilated by wisdom thought and practice.

Here, then, must have been the matrix for endeavors in teaching and in learning that could take up the values of the Jewish legacy in a self-conscious way under the question of their transmissability, translatability, coherence, and competitive status. Here it would have been understood that Jewish

wisdom could assume a prominent role in the conceptual organization and rationalization of the constitutive elements of
Jewish tradition. The Book and the books could be read now
in a different light, as we have seen. So could the religious cult,
the system of ethics, its anthropology, and so forth, as we have
also seen. Here, too, whether subtly or more self-consciously,
the Hellenic patterns of logic and rationalization assumed in
the enterprise of *paideia* would have been learned most naturally.

One of these logics would have been the pedagogical and
rhetorical (logical, argumentative, persuasive) values of historical examples—exactly what we have found to determine the
composition of the hymn.[10] We need not argue that Ben Sira
had read Aristotle on the paradigm, or even that he had pursued Hellenistic *paideia* to the level of specifically rhetorical
training or theory. The paradigmatic principle was embedded
in the Hellenistic texts and their readings from the earliest
encounters with them. A Jewish sage would have been a perceptive reader indeed of those materials set forth as containing
the way and wisdom of the Greeks. That it would have occurred to him to read his own history paradigmatically too is,
not only possible, but probable.

It thus seems likely that, should the hymn in praise of the
hasidim turn out to be structured and textured by wisdom
myth and metaphor, the wisdom myth is the text and texture
that can account for the Jewish-Hellenic intertextuality of the
hymn. Wisdom as educational and intellectual enterprise
would have been the bridge across which the exchange of
those ideas occurred that can account for the hymn as a syncretistic phenomenon. As a Jewish sage, Ben Sira would have
learned more than philosophical options to Jewish ideas of
God and creation from the wisdom of the Greeks. He would
have learned about texts and poetics and rhetoric, discovered
the humanistic assumptions within his own intellectual system,
and gained the power of Hellenic skills and consciousness to
read (i.e., to rewrite) his own texts with a certain rhetorical
goal in mind. That goal had to do with the affirmation, elucidation, and memorialization of the Jewish ethos as a culture with

an originary moment, a complete history, a glorious anthropology, and a humane approach to social and religious
ethics. The logic that underlay this program was a creative
combination of Hellenistic learning and Jewish wisdom.
Wisdom is not mentioned in the hymn expressly as a major
theme. But, as will now be argued, it would have been Ben
Sira's thoughts about wisdom in a Hellenistic frame of reference that made it possible to conceive of the hymn. Because it
trades in Hellenistic forms of rhetoric, one might even say that
with the hymn a logic was given for the wisdom myth itself.

THE HYMN AS A WISDOM TEXT

The hymn is placed at the end of Ben Sira's book of wisdom.
Its procm promises to list the great hasidim in their generations
to whom, as the reader has just been told in the final distich of
the preceding hymn on the creation, the Creator has given
wisdom. Since the question of the presence of wisdom in the
world has been a major concern throughout the book and the
quest for and discovery of wisdom has been a recurring theme,
the promise to praise those who have been granted wisdom does
not strike the reader as strange. But in the reading, it becomes
clear that the theme of wisdom itself is missing. The hasidim are
characterized without reference to the quest for wisdom and, as
it turns out, are depicted in sequence as carriers of a history
within which a primal cultic intentionality is narrated. The
problem for the reader is not that the didactic expectation has
not been met. Indeed, the "instruction" that unfolds is much
more profound and powerful than one might have expected.
But the terms in which the expectations have been met are, as
we now know, not those for which the reader thought to be
prepared. Our question has been whether in the hymn Ben Sira
has introduced categories and considerations extraneous and
irrelevant to his enterprise of instruction in wisdom. We have
argued that with the hymn, those anthropological and so-
ciological assumptions basic to the structure and concern of
wisdom thinking have in fact achieved an articulation. The
articulation is worked out in relation to a specific social system
as the arena for the concrete manifestation of wisdom. This

claim is arbitrary in a sense, and that accounts for the particular conception of office along Jewish institutional lines, the peculiar form of virtue depicted, the general lack of recognizable manifestations of conventional forms of wisdom. But the way in which the study unfolds—its patterns, structures, and development of themes and plot—may indeed be, not only a product of wisdom thought, but an expression of its logos as a realized myth.

We may begin by noting that certain aspects of the hymn reflect a perspectival reading of Israel's history of which a sage would have been capable. The expressly anthropological focus is the first and perhaps most obvious of these. The human situation and the typicalities of human behavior stood at the center of a wisdom view of the world. If now the typical is cast in high-mimetic characterization and placed at the center of a mythic reading of history, the level and scope of the picture have changed, but not the way it is organized around the human figure. This figure is, moreover, still being depicted through devices reflecting categories of wisdom thought: classification by opposites, single-case exemplifications, rhetorical use of praise and blame (or shame), attribution of virtue (character) on the basis of behavior (deeds), and so on. Because each of these conventions has obvious analogues in the Hellenistic rhetoric and literature of anthropological depiction, it would have been the sage's training in wisdom that enabled their employment.

The expansion of vision to include the social order, a thematic and constitutive moment of the hymn, is also indicative of the structure of wisdom thinking. At first assumed, then seen as necessary frame for the continuing viability of a wisdom anthropology, the social order must be affirmed. The problem for traditional wisdom thought, which worked inductively from individual cases to the typical, is that without opportunity and method for a comparative sociology, the category of the typical cannot be used in this case. The solution was to seek an even larger frame of reference, namely, that of the world itself, within which to place the social order. Stability now could be affirmed on the basis of regularity in the world order and any correlations or associations that might be seen between the creation order and the social order. To achieve a higher level of argumentation, the problem of the several social orders possible (*nomos*) and the nature (*physis*) of the cosmos would have to be addressed, as indeed it was among the Greeks. Within the limits of wisdom thinking itself, this was not possible, but Ben Sira sensed the problem and addressed it along Hellenistic lines. The items used to designate the social order in the hymnic depictions are those moments of legislation that create the legal fabric of the community (covenant, law, and office). The claim is that these are established by God, an intellectual appeal to tradition that implicitly addresses and solves the question of correlation between *nomos* and *physis,* if, that is, the God in question is also understood to be the creator of the natural order.

That he is has been made clear in the hymn to creation (42:15–43:33), which is intended as the preface or first section of the hymn. By reading it with the hymn, the schema wisdom-in-creation/wisdom-in-the-social-order can be discerned. This schema belongs to the wisdom myth and, used here to suggest the correlation of creation and society, indicates that wisdom thought has been at work. If the wisdom myth itself is structured narratively in a way similar to the mythic history in the hymn, then the narrative categories of wisdom thought provided the intellectual matrix for the merger of Jewish and Hellenistic textualities in the hymn. The problem of the rationalization and defence of the contemporary Jewish religious society would have been understood primarily in wisdom terms.

This would account for the otherwise surprising presence in Ben Sira's book of wisdom of a whole range of topics having to do with Jewish social history not normally understood to fall within the provenance of wisdom interests and poetry. The example most frequently cited is the so-called identification of the mythic figure of wisdom with the law. This phenomenon has been called since Rylaarsdam the "nationalization" of wisdom. But it may have been the other way around. Wisdom thought may have been used to conceptualize the basis and structure of the religious society. Again, wisdom thinking would have been the bridge for the exploration of Hellenistic categories helpful for this task. It is not improbable that the conception of Torah as law, for instance, a truly foundational moment for Judaism, took place in just this exchange between Jewish wisdom thought and Hellenistic *paideia*. It was in any case the Hebrew epic as the Book of the Covenant that Ben Sira invested with wisdom in order to begin his hymnic history. This also can be explained as a logical move on the part of a Jewish sage in touch with Hellenistic learning.

One of the great discoveries of the wisdom-*paideia* exchange was that a nation's history could be read in order to disclose its logos. With this discovery, the sage could take up the history as paradigmatic and understand it as elucidation of the principle that constituted and ordered the social structure itself. This Ben Sira has done, using for his own purposes—for wisdom concerns—the rhetorically effective forms of encomiastic historiography. If, then, the paradigmatic history turns out to have a plot that can be recognized as that of the wisdom myth, we will have found the precursor text we seek.

THE HYMN AS WISDOM MYTH

Ben Sira's reading of the wisdom myth is given in chapter 24.[11] It is sung as a hymn by and to wisdom, whose destiny is recounted from the beginning of creation to its full incarnation in the temple cult of Jerusalem. The hymn falls easily into three sections, which can be taken as strophes, and includes both an invitation to accept wisdom's story and the instruction that it is available in Moses' Book of the Covenant, the Torah. The Torah is said to be wisdom's "memorial" (24:20; the entire section is 24:19–27).

In the first strophe (24:3–7), wisdom tells of her origin from the mouth of the Most High, how she "covered" the earth, described the great circles of order in creation, and thus achieved sovereignty over all that she had created. At the end, however, a theme is announced that will impel the narrative forward. This theme is of wisdom's quest for a place to dwell among a people. If the strophe had ended with an assertion instead of a question about wisdom's location, it would have agreed with the basic plot of the wisdom myth as seen in Proverbs 8 and the Egyptian prototypes of wisdom mythology in general. This plot is simply the narrative form of the sequence wisdom-in-creation/wisdom-in-the-social-order noted on other occasions. That the final lines invert the moment of wisdom's establishment in the social order, making of it a question, reflects the postcrisis sense of wisdom's absence, that is, "homelessness." The human quest for wisdom has, however, been taken up into the myth itself as a part of wisdom's own quest for dwelling and is thus made part of the mythic answer to the social problematic. As a narrative theme, the quest sets up the story for a series of events in which resolution is to be expected.

The second strophe (24:8–12) relates that the "Creator of all things" created wisdom before the world and commanded her to take up her dwelling in Israel. Wisdom did this, took root among an honored people, and ministered in the sanctuary at Jerusalem. Between this and the first strophe, there is a significant bit of narrative slippage. Instead of merely taking up the story at the point of wisdom's quest, the author has chosen to recast the first episode, that is, the creation of the world, as an act of Yahweh. Wisdom now becomes a creature too and can be told what to do. The commandment of strophe 2 does answer wisdom's question at the end of strophe 1 and thus provides its sequel. But because strophe 2 recasts the creation episode, it ends up containing all the major moments of the myth as well.

The third strophe (24:13–17) finds wisdom singing a song of exultation. Her "rootage" in Israel has gone well. She has "flourished" to the point of producing all she could have expected. As a result, she can now invite all those who desire her to come to her (24:19–23). She is, she says, there, available, and ready to be possessed.

If we understand wisdom's question in the first strophe and Yahweh's commandment in the second to belong to a single moment, that is, the quest, the narrative as a whole consists of four moves: creation, quest, location, and exaltation. In table 4, these have been given as the narrative outline underlying the

TABLE 4. THE STRUCTURE OF THE HYMN AS WISDOM MYTH

The Wisdom Myth (Sir. 24: 3–17)	Strophe 1 (3–7)	Strophe 2 (8–12)	Strophe 3 (13–17)	*The Hymn (Sir. 44–50)*
1. *Creation*	Wisdom is enthroned in creation.	Yahweh creates wisdom.		1. *Establishment* — The order of the covenants is designed in a primeval age.
2. *Quest*	Wisdom seeks a dwelling among a people.	Yahweh commands a dwelling in Israel.		2. *Conquest and History* — The quest is to actualize the order in Israel.
3. *Location*		Wisdom takes root among an honored people; she ministers in the temple in Jerusalem.		3. *Restoration* — The order is actualized in the temple cult.
4. *Exaltation*			Wisdom glories in her exaltation in Jerusalem.	4. *Climax* — Simon is exalted and glorified.

hymn in chapter 24, with which the mythic history of the hymn in 44–50 may now be compared.

In the hymn, the design for the covenantal order is established in the account of the first seven figures. Its place as "preland," and therefore "prehistory," has been noted as a mythic moment that casts the order thus established as archetypal, ideal, and perhaps transcendent. It is also here that the foundational activity of God is most manifest in the hymn, suggesting that the epoch is originary and creative. It corresponds to the moment of creation in the wisdom myth, the covenantal order itself taking the place of wisdom as the manifestation of the order of things that the Creator intends to be actualized in human society.

The second major section of the hymn, the history of the prophets and kings, corresponds to wisdom's quest and Yahweh's commandment. We have noted the quest aspect of this section as having to do with the actualization of the design in the specific place of the temple in Jerusalem. In the wisdom hymn, Yahweh commands wisdom to make her dwelling in Jacob (Israel), in the tabernacle (Zion), in the Holy City (Jerusalem). In the final section of the hymn, which praises Simon, the actualization of the design has been achieved and the high priest is exalted. This corresponds both to the location of wisdom in the Jerusalem temple and to her exaltation there. The imagery used to describe the flourishing is identical: the magnificence of the (cosmic) tree and the glory of the (temple) incense. The combination of metaphors makes the point: the integration of the natural and social religious orders.

Thus the structure of the hymn in praise of the hasidim does correspond to that of the wisdom myth. We may be justified, then, in reading it as a composition enabled by the wisdom text. The process of reflection and creative conceptualization necessary to move from the myth to the hymnic history is extremely complex, necessitating the conscious correlation of wisdom imagery with Hellenistic conceptualities in order to take up the Jewish social history in just this way. But the imaginative, intellectual process can be accounted for in terms of our thesis, and the power the composition gains from its intertextual correlation of precursors can be imagined.

One aspect of this literary achievement should be noted in passing. It is the way in which the post-Pentateuchal history has been read, especially in relation to the Pentateuch itself. The wisdom myth provided a narrative structure for a reading of the history as a whole. But the correlation of its episodes with the biblical materials resulted in their classification according to distinctively valorized readings. The Pentateuch has been read to correspond with the first episode of the myth, that of the establishment of order in the presocial world at large. It is important to see that this reading was not at all a matter of arbitrary superimposition of the mythic valence on resistent materials. The priestly redaction and reading of the epic was quite congenial to this new construction, and the Hellenistic notion of an archaic period at the beginning of a national or universal history added its support. One suspects Hellenistic influence, also, in the tightly knit development of the covenants with the first seven figures as a sort of genealogy of the order of things that was to determine human history. But that this reading of the Pentateuch could then be joined systematically to a reading of the sequel history was a major achievement attributable mainly to the mythic text that has guided the whole. This sequel history, the entire history from Joshua's to Ben Sira's time, has been read as a single "moment" of the myth. Valorized as "quest" and rationalized by Hellenistic concepts of history, paradigm, and testing, Jewish history has been assigned a function quite compatible with wisdom thought. It is a remarkable achievement, making sense of the whole by seeking out a logic capable of bridging the times from the Pentateuchal accounts to the present. The sense that is made of it is, of course, wisdom's own. There is no development at all, neither of ideas, nor of social history, nor of great acts that redirect the course of history itself. The great design is predetermined, and "history" is now the lesson about how important it is to see the design and to structure the social order accordingly. History has been structured systematically as a moment in a myth about structure itself.

Glory as the Presence of Wisdom

We hope now to have discovered the text that can account for the hymn's overall structure. With that text comes also a particular context of thought, sensibility, and concern. Assuming this as the literary and intellectual matrix of the hymn, we are able to see more clearly the several rationales for the complex literary combinations from which the hymn has been composed. What we have not seen yet is the presence of any reference to wisdom itself within the hymn capable of providing a recognizable texture. There is perhaps no reason to expect any sign of wisdom's presence in Israel's history at the surface level of the text. The purpose of the hymn would have been achieved for the sage in its account of the covenant order itself. The shift in ethos from the wisdom myth to the mythic history of the covenantal order may in fact preclude references to conventional wisdom in that account. But the question persists precisely because the sensibility of the sage seems to invite it. May there not be, the question goes, some aspect of the covenantal order, its offices, and especially of the character of its pious leaders throughout history that can serve as a sign for wisdom's presence? I would suggest that the repeated mention of glory throughout the hymn has as one of its functions the evocation of the sense of wisdom's presence in the history from the beginning.

The use of the term "glory" (*kābôd*) is, in any case, one of the most startling features of the hymn. Its affinities to religious concepts of the holy and the transcendent mark its attribution to the hasidim as bordering on profanity. Yet it is used, emphatically and repeatedly, to claim for them a surpassing excellence. This excellence, it is said, could not but be recognized by the people. It is this usage of this term that gives the history its continuity and the hymn its texture.

The preceding hymn to creation has as its theme the "glory of Yahweh," which is "over all His works" (42:17). This glory is visible in the created order and indeed is celebrated in the hymn. Yahweh himself cannot be seen, but he can be praised because of the manifestation of his glory. Then the hymn in praise of the hasidim is introduced. Again the theme is glory, the glory that they had as the Most High's portion (44:2). It is visible in these men both to their generations and to the readers of the hymn. Glory, honor, dignity, memorial, exaltation, blessing—these are the notes sounded throughout. Moses is made "glorious as God" (45:2); Aaron is blessed with majesty and glory (45:7, 12); Phineas was glorious (45:23); and Joshua, "How glorious he was" (46:2). The litany ebbs and flows throughout the history of the prophets and the kings and comes to climax in the portrayal of Simon: "How glorious he was when he looked forth from the Tent. . . . When he went up to the altar of majesty, and made glorious the court of the sanctuary" (50:5, 11). Ben Sira's choice of this term to give his poem brilliance and the sense of holy presence offers us a precious chance to see the sage at work with words. The term itself is capable of being read in relation to the fundamental concerns and purposes of each of the hymn's precursor texts. Thus it is able in itself to organize and integrate them round a common theme.

The temple cult as that social order toward which the mythic history moves is the primary source and locus for the term "glory," of course. In this context, glory refers to the presence of God in the sanctuary. This connotation of the divine presence is clearly in evidence throughout the hymn, but especially so in the final scene. But even here, the term is not used expressly of the presence of God, but of a quality of the presence of the human figure who performs perfectly his high office. It is this usage that at first profanes the term, but it is precisely the profane sense that is appropriate to the other set of texts read into the hymn from the Hellenistic tradition. Glory is the purpose of the encomium and the encomiastic history. It too is being acknowledged and evoked. We may understand the Greek and Syriac translations of 44:2, that the glory of the hasidim was "created for" or "alloted to" them by the Most High, as an attempt to mediate the tension this creates between the contrasting views of the human and divine.[12] This sense of the matter would be right, for as we have seen, the pattern of characterization contains no moment of human aspiration or achievement, and the great deeds are carefully balanced by the countertheme of divine purpose and will. But the tension remains nonetheless, and it is created and held in tension mainly by the term "glory."

We must be careful, however, not to cast the dialectic entirely in cross-cultural terms. The reason for this is that the term has the capacity to evoke yet another arena of discourse, that of the myth of wisdom itself. Respect, honor, and glory are deeply rooted in traditional wisdom and mark a major value and motivation for the teaching-learning enterprise. Glory also becomes the sage, and wisdom coming to speech is said to praise herself and receive honor both among the people and in the presence of the Most High (24:1).

The term, then, belongs as well to the linguistic field of wisdom discourse and thus alludes to wisdom itself throughout the hymn at those junctures where the intertextuality is thickest and the syncretistic purposes most complex. Its usage is the primary device by which the precursor texts and their perspectives on the human scene are brought to focus in a new vision. The vision is tensive and dialectical with respect to exactly whose glory is manifest or on what basis the human figures actually may be said to be worthy of glorification. The mediation between the glory of the radically transcendent God on the one hand and that of the man of superior achievement on the other, a mediation made possible by the wisdom anthropology of the sage, leaves little room for questions about the conditions and possibilities of glory. Glory is simply posited and allowed to draw upon all of its significations in older contexts for the newly textured manifestation. This layeredness is the genius of the new image and perspective and provides the hymn as a whole with the texture and tone that distinguish it from all precursors.

The term "glory" is peculiarly capable of receiving and containing diverse and tensive manifestations of excellence because, like the term "wisdom," it really has no content of its own, depending for that upon its context. This is most strange, because as a term for presence, it is energized by the notion that it creates its own context—as aura, as manifestation. This redundancy charges the term with the radicality of presence. It is the full manifestation of itself. Nothing really is revealed in a moment of glory except glory itself. It becomes a hyperbole for presence, at the same time so highly charged with fullness that one cannot bring to it any other thought or consideration and so empty of any specific content that it can be filled with anything.[13] It marks that space in the human imagination where terms can be substituted for one another or conjoined, transformed, or destroyed. In the glory of the final scene of the hymn, not only are such specific and contrasting terms as "God" and "human" combined, but basic categories of differentiation are transcended and entire and diverse schemata for the organization of human experience are merged. It is a powerful word, used to open out each of the linguistic traditions onto the others. It does create for the reader the sense of climax and fulfillment. Wisdom is present here as the manifestation of divine intention (wisdom), what one has seen of creation's glory, known of history's rhyme and reason, and considered the height of human piety, excellence, and achievement. It is there in the social order, the religious blessing, and the high moment of community enactment and celebration that stops the flow of time in the *kairos* of the present.

This of course was the goal toward which the sage was moving all along. It was an audacious thought and claim, but one that was apparently required if a solution was to be found for the postcrisis dilemma of wisdom itself. Ben Sira at least understood that it was the actual social-religious structure that needed blessing, that this blessing had to be gained by a process of mythic rationalization. He realized this in his wisdom poetry, drawing upon texts that could be helpful for these ends. For his time, the presence of wisdom could be seen, then, and his work as teacher and scribe secured. It was a marvelous achievement in imagination and words. The poetry was strong and good enough to last. Alas, it was not to be so for the temple and the priest. The poetic vision Ben Sira achieved in the quest for a humanizing social order had to travel free and disembodied, seeking other homes. But those are other stories for other times. We conclude here with the thought of Ben Sira's own glory, for the glory seen in the high priest's moment is really there only because of Ben Sira's own glorious act of giving praise.

Conclusion

This study has followed a certain course and arrived at the sense of an ending. That sense is related to the discovery of the wisdom myth as one of the hymn's precursors, indeed the most important one because by exploring its patterns and logic, the many structural components of the hymn can be imagined as a system, and its many signs and symbols can be integrated in a coherent, conceptual image. The hymn makes sense structurally and thematically, the logic of its purpose can be seen, and its composition can be regarded as the product of an intellectual who knew what he was doing.

This sense of conclusion is illusory in a way. All of the precursor texts in Ben Sira's library have not been identified and explored. The Psalms are a case in point. Neither have all of the traits, themes, and conceptualities belonging to the poem been seen or discussed. Our examination of its intertextual relationships has only touched the surface of things, moving along quickly to sketch in the main outlines of the picture. Nevertheless, enough has been noticed to get the picture straight, demonstrate the relationship of the poem to its precursors, catch sight of the author at work in its composition, and identify the essential thrust of its rhetorical intention and power. An understandable reading has been proposed.

Discretion requires the admission that this understanding is our own. Considerable labor has been invested in the attempt to imagine the composition and reading of the hymn in its own social setting, effected by its own salient history. But the notion of a structural system, which has allowed us to delimit what would otherwise become an unending series of observations on textual relationships, belongs to our own mental machinery. The same is true for the sense of a center, some theme or image or concept around which the system of signs revolves. Then there is the question of the capacity of that centered system of signs to "reflect" upon what is known of the world in other ways and to suggest a way to see it all together through its lens. Each of these intellectual sensibilities is evoked in the proposal that we now understand the poem and need not continue to press the search further. Our study has certainly relied on the way in which we make sense of things ourselves.

No injustice has been done to the poem. We may not have seen all there is to see about it, but what we have seen is really there. Ben Sira also worked with structures, systems, centers, essential themes. He strove to encompass all the knowledge there was about all the worlds known in a single poetic reflection. It was the possibility of demonstrating this aspect of Ben Sira's labor that has enabled our study to unfold as it has. For him also it was important to touch upon and bring together all of the orders of perceived reality in an integrative vision—creation and history, social order and human life. By evoking Hellenic logic about the orders of things (*cosmos, polis, anthropos*), he rationalized his wisdom myth and focused a reading of Israel's history in a single, glorious image. The image centered on a figure and an enactment, but it reflected, and reflected upon, all of the orders of things imaginable. So in the case of Ben Sira, we were lucky. Our categories for making sense of things were apparently much like his as well, and his book was big enough, and rich enough, to let us discover what they were.

But now that the study has come to an ending, one wonders about the difference it might make. This is another kind of question, to be sure, a nagging kind that frequently leads to the chasing of chimeras. But the question is important nevertheless and should at least be acknowledged. One wonders, on the one hand, whether the writing of such a poem made any difference in Ben Sira's time, and on the other, whether the reading we have managed makes any difference now. These two questions are interrelated in a very strange way.

Whether Ben Sira was justified in glorifying Simon's reign and whether his glorification of it was an effective factor in subsequent social history are simply unanswerable questions. But there are two things about the relation of Ben Sira's poem to its social circumstances that can be noted. The first is that the poem was written while the political situation was still relatively stable. The other is that the picture Ben Sira painted of Simon's glorious moment did survive both Simon and Ben Sira himself. The poem was strong enough to last. It is still here for the reading, having been tucked away in that collection of hidden texts known now as the Apocrypha. It was primarily its inclusion in the larger set of texts that determined a certain history of its readings, and it was that history of its readings, mainly, that brought it to modern scholars' desks. Taking it up now for another reading is to take up the entire history of its readings.

This history has been bumpy. It was treasured by the Jewish sages of the next two or three centuries; as the many additions, changes, and versions of Sirach show, it spawned a very fertile manuscript tradition. But it did not make the rabbis' selection of Hebrew texts for normative reading, though they did cite Sirach frequently, at least until the medieval period, when it looks as if Ben Sira was forgotten for a while. The Greek translation has another story. Included in the Septuagint by the Jewish scholars in Alexandria, Sirach popped up in the Catholic canon, where it has since been cherished as a book for Christian devotion, ethical instruction, and theology. The Protestants were the ones who decided against it again, because they couldn't find it in the Hebrew Bible. But it has been

read by Protestant theologs as well, on occasion, as all forbid-
den books are read—with a sense of trespass, daring, caution,
and titillation. Its readings have been varied, determined for
the most part by those prior judgments about the status of the
book among the several collections of books.

It is difficult to say if Ben Sira would be pleased. He wanted
to be read, and he wanted to be remembered. He understood
something about texts, too, and about the fuzziness there always is between the acts of reading and writing. He thought
his poems were able, as he said, to "increase wisdom." So in a
sense he shouldn't mind. But wisdom for him was one thing
and wisdom for the fathers of the church has been another.
Reading Ben Sira through a Christian lens has repeatedly dis-
torted the pictures he painted in ways he would not recognize.
An entirely other set of interests and concerns phrased the
questions with which those readers took his poems up. Now
another reading has been done, with yet another set of questions as its guide. But there is no claim to wisdom here, neither
an increase of Ben Sira's wisdom nor an extraction from it of
the wisdom theologians seek. To account for the sense of the
poem in its own time, to enlarge our picture of its human
scene, to catch sight of a poet reading and writing his world—
that has been our goal.

But the history of the other readings has not been lost sight
of. These readings come with the text, a kind of patina, or an
invitation to certain attitudes as one handles it again. Ben Sira's
heroes, times, and text belong to our cultural history, it seems,
from a period we call formative. We don't know how to talk
about the way in which it still affects us, to be sure, or why.
But the Greco-Roman age is still important to us. We do keep
trying to get the history straight. It was then that certain constructions were put upon things, certain patterns of thought
were worked out, and certain social notions established—all
of which set some courses for the ensueing history of the
West. Rabbinic Judaism and Christianity both were born then.
The inquisitive ones among us have always wondered how
each came to be.

In the tradition of Christian readings, Ben Sira's hymn has

been thought important mainly for one reason, that is, the way in which the figures of the Hebrew epic were recast as heroes of religious faith and of the destiny of Israel. It has been re- garded as a very early instance of what was to become an intense preoccupation with heroes, ideal figures, and mytho- logical imagery during the next three hundred years. Much of the scholarly energy devoted to exploring this phenomenon has been generated by the question of the origins of Chris- tianity, especially the origins of the Christ myth. All of the many mythic configurations in Jewish texts of the period have been studied largely with this question in mind. The favorite figures, those that have been classed as "messianic," tend to be singular depictions of mediation, at first displaced from social history, about which patterns of destiny and salvation seem to accrue. Ben Sira's heroes have therefore not been counted among them, appearing too mundane for comparison with the grand pattern of cosmic destiny imagined for the Christ. But the poem has always been in the peripheral vision of Christian scholars, lying on the early fringes of the significant period. If not immediately helpful for the Christological question, then, perhaps the poem relates to the phenomenon of the "heroes of the faith," a correlate notion of ideal types, understood to function by calling for imitation. Thus the alternative in- terpretation has been posed.

Uneasy about that retrospective lens, I thought to have an- other look. I chose Ben Sira's hymn because it seemed a man- ageable text, a text whose author was known and about which something of literary, cultural, and social setting had been de- termined. The questions I have asked of it, and the nature of the understanding sought, have been critical in the sense that any human sciences approach to religion, literature, and soci- ety is critical. And they have been implicitly critical of the history of the theological readings. I tried to set aside that history with its theological concerns, and the study unfolded as it did. But now it appears that an assessment of what we may have learned about the text requires comparison with that history of its readings. Certain assumptions about ideal figures appear to have guided the interpretations of those readings.

My reading does not bear them out, so something should be said about the novelties that surface in this study.

Several proposals have been made about the composition of the text that are new to the public discourse on Sirach. Some of these may appear strange, and all will require testing by others. The thesis about a pattern of characterization is one example. It has not been customary to make so much of a compositional outline, much less infer from it an author's employment of a set of techniques fully articulated and rationalized in a rhetorical theory of literature. To discover such a pattern is to see the author at his craft.

The discernment of an architechtonic structure to the hymn is also new, as is the thesis that this structure intended a complete reading of the epic history. Ben Sira would not have called this hymnic history a mythic etiology for Second Temple Judaism, as we must do in order to understand its function, but the intention I have theorized would have been recognized by him in his own terms. That reading of the history and Ben Sira's view of Second Temple society belonged together in his mind. To propose this is to suggest that Ben Sira's poetic construction was ultimately that of an ideal social history and world. That he achieved this correlation by imaginative manipulation of the myth of wisdom is also a new thesis, one that scholars of the wisdom traditions in Israel and Judaism may find farfetched. It is proposed, however, with utmost seriousness. Only by means of some such thesis can we imagine Ben Sira as a sage, thinking things through clearly and courageously, in the interest of making sense of his society.

Novelties such as these should be amenable to debate, however, given the resources available to scholars in the traditions of literary criticism. Conventional notions about "traditions history" need not be given up entirely when the set of precursor texts is expanded as I have pursued them. Certain assumptions about the history of ideas and the monolinear development of genres will have to go, to be sure. But that shift has already happened in the scholarly guild, and the phenomenon of multiple relations with other "texts" should come as no surprise. The problem now for the literary critic is, not to find enough texts for comparison, but to limit the number of comparable texts and argue for their sufficiency. Sufficient would be a set of texts complex enough to reflect upon a human social setting and its labors.

But what about the characterizations achieved by this poetic means? In the course of our study, the terms "hasidim" and "heroes" have been used to refer to the figures Ben Sira created. But neither term is adequate as a generic designation, especially not in the connotations each possesses in contemporary usage. Ben Sira's figures are certainly not heroes of achievement. Neither are they heroes of faith, nor ideal types of personal piety or righteousness.[1] They are not saviors. They have not been invested with any ontological or soteriological significance, as if the act of praising them might border on awe or veneration. They are to be remembered, and their glory noted under a single aspect only. They are ideal figures of official functions, the very functions requisite to a social construction of Israel's history.

We should pause here in order to explore more fully the significance of this finding. The proposal is that history was understood in just the way it was in order to erect a mythic foundation for a social construction. The mythic claims inherent in the poem therefore do not apply to the heroes as individuals or as types, but to the structure of the society itself. Not even Simon can be said to be invested with glorious being in any sense. He is merely an officiant in the line of officials who center the picture of the essential nature of Israel. This ideal picture, moreover, was imagined, reasoned out, and crafted in order to make a statement about a very real society in the author's own time, his own society. The claim is astonishing. The lack of fit between the idealization and the reality should be kept in mind, but that disjunction only casts into higher relief the tremendous investment Ben Sira was willing to make in the society in which he lived. Thus the hymn is marked, not by any interest in the idealization or glorification of the human conceived as individual persons, but by what might be called a studied investment in a social anthropology.

It is important to see that the investment of intellectual and poetic energy and skill was called for by the desire to make social sense of, to see the wisdom in, that social system. Its idealization was not a product of whimsy, fantasizing, mystic vision, or wishful thinking. The scholarly labor required to craft such a poem is evidence that this cannot be the case. But because the social sense of the society required rationalization, could not be won by mere description, the social notions that were involved in its organization needed to be probed and assessed. The result was a conservative assessment, in spite of the liberal learning used to achieve it. It called for the continuance of the system even as it claimed to have discovered in the past the reasons for that continuance. This call to see the structure centered in the office of Simon was celebrative. But by only slight shifts in the social contexts of its reading, the poem could serve as polemic as well, polemic against other interests and other views that threatened to tarnish Ben Sira's picture. It could become the basis for a political program, an ideology.

We cannot tell whether Ben Sira's poem was used that way, or whether it made any difference of the kind for which he may have hoped. But we can note that a change in social circumstances forced other kinds of reading. Already in the Greek translation rendered by Ben Sira's grandson, Simon's name was deleted in the final blessing of the hymn, and there is no longer any trace there of the petition that "no one ever be cut off from the covenant of Phineas" (50:24). In chapter 36, a petitionary poem was added to Ben Sira's book by a later hand. It contains still the vision of "all the tribes of Jacob" gathered in Jerusalem at the temple where God's glory is, but the petition is now born of despair, and the projection is eschatological. Now the vision can only be imagined in another time and place, though the guarantors for it are still the prophets and the promises of the past (36:11–17). Thus another time brought another circumstance, and with it a radical displacement of Ben Sira's mythic vision. With names erased, and the lines no longer drawn down and out into an actual society, the ideal image floated free. The question is whether such freefloating images, the poetic visions that burgeoned in the cen-

turies after Ben Sira, can still be understood as intellectual
achievements. Did the difficult history force an abandonment
of the kind of social labor we have found to be true of Ben
Sira's reflections?

There is the possibility, to be sure, that another, more mimetic reading accompanied some of these ideal depictions. Even
Ben Sira's vision could have been taken as a charter for what
had to be done in more difficult times. Though we cannot be
sure, popular leaders may have wanted to start over again with
Ben Sira's Joshua somehow in mind. The Hasmonean leaders
may have sought to claim his high priest's glory. Others still,
worried about the lack of fit between the glorious vision and
the world, may have tried to take the vision with them, away
from the city, to build a model in the desert on its lines and
prepare for another restoration. For all of these, in any case,
the model of the Second Temple society was the way to think
Israel. Something like Ben Sira's poem may have furnished the
rationale.

But the times were tough on Second Temple models. The
social history was marked by tremendous efforts to establish a
stable sovereignty in Judaea in the face of foreign powers. Internal conflicts over how that sovereignty was conceived and
how best to go about achieving it errupted and took their toll.
Alternative social formations both in Judaea and in the Diaspora were created as well. It was a period that, eventually,
did not succeed in its designs for Jerusalem. The literatures
reflect the agony of all of this for the sages. No poet after Ben
Sira's time could afford to make the claim he made, write
another poem like his. But others did step into his shoes, taking up the poet's task, to write yet other poems. Was the
imaginative labor of the same kind?

My suspicion is that many of the poems in the subsequent
period, poems depicting ideal figures, were born of the same
concerns that produced the hymn in praise of the fathers. The
so-called messianic figures, the ideal types and mythological
configurations in the wisdom literatures, the various figures of
the apocalyptic visions, the mythic elaborations of the epic
heroes—all might be seen as scholarly labors in the interest of

rethinking Israel. They would be the poet's way of probing the grounds for legitimation, reflecting on the social structures, and seeking the locus of Israel's authorities. The intellectual investments would be the same as Ben Sira's. The poetic idealization would have occurred similarly. The revisioning of the history would have been achieved by the same methods. The focus on official figures would have been for the same reasons. The difference would be that no claim to actualization in the present would have been possible. The separation of the ideal from the realities of history would be painfully acknowledged in the very fact of the ideal's placement in imagined time and order. But that displacement need not consign the mythic visions to fantasy. They may have reflected a very astute and serious assessment of the social realities under review as inadequate.

That a singular figure of high office—a priest, a scribe, a warrior, or a king—could be used to concentrate a reflection on the ideal social structure of Israel as a whole is now plausible, given the evidence from Ben Sira. We might note that, in general, these mythic figures of the period represented the functions and qualities essential for the social formation of Israel. This can be seen in the selection of endowments and functions attributed to these figures. They are exactly and only those that were under discussion throughout this period as problematic. Piety, power, place among the nations, guarantee of social justice, system of governance, legal basis or constitution, and what to do about internal diversity were all issues needing resolution in the struggles to conceptualize, actualize, and defend the notion of Israel in the many forms of Judaism that were attempted during this time.

For these imaginary figures, also, a formal pattern of characterization seems to have been used, much like that used by Ben Sira. The pattern was filled in by selecting the combination of carefully nuanced features that could be integrated in a single configuration. This configuration solved imaginatively certain political issues of consequence. A particular slant to the definition of office, a careful selection from among the many notions of legitimation, the mode of power proposed and its con-

straints, perspectives on piety, definitions of justice, and stance
toward conflict, enemies, and the law or traditions reflected
decisions made about Judaism and its constitution in Greco-
Roman times. Each ideal figure put the pieces together in a
particular way, working out the troublesome issues in a singular image. They appear to have been organizing centers for
reflection on social construction, studies in the intersection of
the forces in play in social formation. In the absence of a single
comprehensive and acceptable social system, they could serve
as Archimedean points of intellectual leverage for gaining perspective on the situation. Thus they could be used to solve
certain problems theoretically that some group was struggling
to rationalize. They appear to have been imaginative labors in
the interest of analyzing, understanding, recommending, and
facilitating particular social modes of being in the world. We
would do wrong to think that an ontology of the ideal was
intended.

But our suspicion requires testing. The texts are many, and
the configurations diverse. That placement of each text must
be found that determined its contexts, that intersection of social and cultural history where it was composed. Only by finding that point and then exploring the texts used in composition will it be possible to ask in each case about intention. As
the circumstances changed throughout the history of this period, texts and traditions and interests other than those available
to Ben Sira entered the intellectual arena. These have to be
identified as well.

There were, however, some constants in the contextual
equations throughout the period for Jewish writers, and these
deserve special attention. Torah and wisdom and Hellenic
paideia continued to describe the volatile cultural mix in general for the next three centuries. And it was the social history of
the Second Temple state that was constantly under review.
Taking a clue from Ben Sira, then, for whom these texts and
concerns were basic too, the methods employed by the scholarly poets might have run somewhat as follows. A judgment
would have been made on the state of affairs in keeping with
traditions held dear. Many of these judgments appear to have

been critical. The need to assess the reasons for the lack of
social sense then turned the scholar to the texts. The common
texts of most importance were the Hebrew epic and the ancient histories. Researching them as charter documents, Israel's wisdom could again be seen, idealized as foundational
pattern. The ancient models settled upon could then be juxtaposed to the times. Ideal images could be used to assess just
where it was that things went wrong and to suggest what must
happen to set them right again. They could also be used as
charters for polemic or programs. The rule might be that the
greater the displacement of an image from the times (whether
in the cosmos, in the future, or in the realm of ideas), the
harsher the assessment of the actual state of affairs in Jerusalem.

Such poetic madness would not have been without its logic.
To reread the past as critique of the present and propose an
ideal for reflection upon it, that would be to call for most
serious discussion. A certain remythologization of history
would be involved, as would be the logics of narrative, rhetoric, and philosophy. The narrative would simply be the tri-
partite sequence of archaic promises, failure, and the road to
resolution. In contrast to Ben Sira's narrative, the present
would still be perceived as the period of struggle, forced to
look back and ahead to models and ideals quite different from
itself. The rhetoric would simply marshal the commonly
agreed upon traditions for a proposal in keeping with their
intent. Philosophical logic would involve the reasonableness
with which, in the ideal image as configuration, the set of
complex factors requisite to social functioning were arranged,
interrelated, and positioned with regard to the world scene.
Wisdom and *paideia* would also have participated in most of
these efforts, and with them the literatures that made those
intellectual traditions available to the sages. Ben Sira would not
have been, then, the only wise, scholarly poet of the times
using poetry to think big thoughts. His ideal figures would not
have been the only mythologies generated in the matrix of
social conflict and formation.

Our reading comes around to the point at which we began.
I hope the new questions have formed a set, have represented

adequately current scholarly desires to combine critical and historical approaches to the interpretation of literature, and have been asked rigorously enough to enable a strong alternative to the traditional reading of Sirach. The difference this analysis might make for other studies has been suggested now, mainly in regard to a long-standing scholarly discourse on the origins of the Christ myth. If my reading of Ben Sira is right, that quest has assumed some things about the nature and function of mythological figures in Jewish literatures of the period that are very misleading. I hope to have suggested another and better way to understand them.

I do not consider the question about the value of the study exhausted with these thoughts, however. There are other literary phenomena of the period for which Ben Sira's way with texts may provide some fresh approaches as well. A brief mention may be made of two of these in closing, two that occur quite frequently in a very wide range of early Jewish and Christian literatures. One is known as a series of examples. Ben Sira's hymn has often been classed with this genre. It is, in fact, just this literary form with which it has been compared with greatest regularity by scholars, as the numerous instances of the citation of parallel texts show.[2] Whether all of the parallels usually cited belong to the class is questionable, but some of these texts do appear to be based on Hellenistic prototypes.[3] In our study, however, Ben Sira's hymn has not been found to function paradigmatically, as the Greek series do. This means that his poem may be helpful in the attempt to understand these other texts, but mainly as a contrastive example. An investigation of the Greek genre itself is required, and each instance of its apparent usage in Jewish and Christian literature needs to be looked at carefully in regard to its intention. This would not be an insignificant investigation, for it probably would involve clarifying the notions of repetition and imitation, notions that would put the Jewish and Christian texts in question much closer to Greek ways of thinking than we have found to be the case with Ben Sira.[4] The difference this would make for social reconstructions might be very important to understand.

The second type of serialization that also needs to be better

understood appears to unify a relatively small number of figures in genealogical relation to form an "epoch." A clear example of the type is found in chapter 10 of the Wisdom of
Solomon. The names of the seven great figures from Adam to
Moses have been erased and a singular typology has been superimposed. Seven times it happens that "the righteous one"
is "saved" by wisdom. The epic history in Genesis was obviously understood to be an account of the primeval age. This
aspect of the text reminds one of Ben Sira's view of the epic as
primeval history with its seven figures related to the covenants. In the Wisdom of Solomon, however, history is not
rehearsed down to the present time. Once the primal epoch
has been imagined, it becomes a model for the significance of
saving events in all times. The midrash on the Exodus story in
Wisdom 11–19 has added a climactic moment to the primeval
epoch, interpreted the Exodus in terms of eschatological imagery, and transformed it into a timeless event of salvation itself.
One suspects that the effacement of individual characteristics
such as proper names has been called for by this move. One
suspects, also, that a wisdom mode of reading the Pentateuch
as primal and archetypal history has enabled the modeling.
This would be the same as Ben Sira's reading of the Pentateuch
and his construction of the first seven figures of the hymn as
constituting a foundational epoch. With Ben Sira, however, it
was the election-covenant theme that predominated; in the
Wisdom of Solomon, it is the figure of wisdom herself that
provides the genealogical connections. That the figure of
wisdom has been introduced expressly into a reading of the
epic history must be seen as another daring and audacious
moment. With it, the way is prepared for a fully allegorical
interpretation of the scriptures that searches out those textual
signs (e.g., Sarah) with which the figure of wisdom may be
identified.

Finally, a suggestion about the possible significance of Ben
Sira's awareness of what it meant to be an author should be
given. This is certainly one of the more remarkable traits about
him. In contrast to the authorship of Jewish works before his
time and to the pseudonymity of much of the literature after
his time, Ben Sira's consciousness and acknowledgment of

being an author is a strange and wonderful anomaly. It was no doubt the result of his learning about texts, education, and authorship on the model of the Greeks. This conception of authorship expected that the author be responsible for his utterances, and it rewarded him for their sagacity. The author knew, also, that the texts of others belonged to them, their product and property. The potential for competition was real, both with regard to precursors and with regard to contemporaries. Ben Sira probably had not confronted the problem of his relationship to the authority of Moses, the author whose text he rewrote. But once the conception of authorship was there, combined as it was for Ben Sira with an extremely high view of Moses' place in the hierarchical structure of Israel's mythic paradigm, the tension between the two authorities could hardly have been avoided.

If, as the evidence indicates, Moses' position in this and other respects became a widely pervasive notion in the late Hellenistic and early Roman periods in Judaism and Christianity, it may well be that his authority simply was found to be overpowering. Readers of his texts, unable to claim peerage in authorship as Ben Sira implicitly did, would have to offer some disclaimer in order to write anything new at all. There seem to have been three options. The exegete could acknowledge the superiority of the scriptural texts by offering his own views as commentary upon them. The author of pseudonymous works could compose without these constraints, but at the cost of self-effacement and the attribution of his writings to figures of the past. Or one might yield at the point of poetic claims to special authority and be content, not to write an inspired piece, but to set forth reasoned and prosaic history, as for instance, Josephus did.

But now the discourse has really taken us too far afield. With Moses on the rise, acknowledged author of the foundational texts, another age dawns and another authority comes to take Ben Sira's place. It is best to return, then, for our last remarking, to Ben Sira's own time and to conclude with his own glory in mind. I trust that my reading has not tarnished its brilliance.

Appendix A
The Proem
and the Hymn
to Creation

Several scholars have drawn attention to the introduction of the theme of praise in 42:15 and noted the appropriateness of the hymn in praise of the Creator (42:15–43:35) as an introduction to the hymn in praise of the fathers. But the relationship has not been thoroughly explored, and most have focused their attention upon chapters 44–50 as a literary unit in itself, taking 44:1 as the introduction of a new theme.[1] I would argue that the two hymns of praise are meant to be taken together, and that the thematic development that results provides a significant perspective on the purpose of the hymn in praise of the fathers.

There are some obvious indications of a literary nature that the two hymn sections were composed as a unit. The first is the striking similarity of the first lines: "Now I will remember God's works"; "Now I will praise pious men." The differences between them are easily accounted for in terms of the respective themes. That each is introduced by an announcement of the poet's intention in the first person, however, is a signal to the reader of their close relationship. One may wonder, too, whether there may not be an element of intentional juxtaposition in the slight degree of linguistic inversion in the choice of the verbs. Either of the two words (remember, *zākar;* praise, *hillēl*) could be used in either of the two announcements, of course. But one might have expected the term for praise to be a bit more appropriate for the hymn to the Creator's works, and the term for remember to be more appropriate for the "deeds" of the fathers (where the memory of their name becomes an obvious theme). By interchanging these terms a subtle nuance is created that allows the subject matter of the two hymnic sections to be taken together. The "recital" (*zikkārôn*) begins with the hymn to the Creator.

The transition from the first section to the second also shows literary continuity. Following the description of the glorious works of God in the creation (43:1–26), the themes of human inability to comprehend God's works and of God's unfathomable majesty are combined in an exhortation for a heightened form of praise (43:27–32). This is on the one hand a return to the inability of the "holy ones" themselves to recount the Lord's wonders fully (42:16), and thus forms a period of the first hymnic section (cf. also 42:15, "What I have seen I will recount," and 43:32, "But few of his works have I seen"). But it is also a preparation for the following hymnic section (44–50) and sets the stage for the final distich: "It is the Lord who has made all things, and he gives wisdom to the pious" (43:33). This is a fitting conclusion to the hymn in praise of God's works, resolving as it does the tension that has been created between the manifestation and hiddenness of God's glory by means of the gift of wisdom to the pious. But it is clear that the statement functions as a transition as well, the movement being now to a consideration of these pious ones: "Now I will praise pious men" (44:1).

Little mention has been made of the fact that each hymnic section begins with a proem of approximately equal length, nor of the fact that the proems exhibit comparable features and perform similar functions in relation to the subsequent hymnic descriptions. The similarity in the pattern of theme development may be seen in the outline in table 5.

Each proem forms a nice period, with the concluding line returning to a mention of the intention announced at the first,

Table 5. The Two Proems

Sir. 42:15–25	Sir. 44:1–15
Announcement of Hymnic Theme:	
To remember God's works (42:15)	To praise the hasidim (44:1)
The Divine Origination:	
Formed by God's word, decree (42:15)	The Most High's portion (44:2)
Brief Summary Classification of Works/Hasidim:	
The sun, all his works (42:16)	The types of the hasidim worthy of praise (44:3–7)
The Human Limitation:	
Only God knows the mystery fully (42:17–20)	Some men have left no memorial (44:8–9)
Affirmation Nonetheless of Abiding Glory:	
God's creative power and works abide forever (42:21–25)	The glory of the hasidim abides forever (44:10–14)
Mention of the Appropriate Response:	
To behold the beauty of creation (42:25)	To praise the memory of the hasidim (44:15)

thus providing a fresh point of departure for the descriptions that follow (cf. 42:25, "Who can see enough of their splendor," with 42:15, "What I have seen I will recount"; and 44:15, "And the assembly proclaims their praise," with 44:1, "Now I will praise"). Each forecasts briefly the content of the hymn to follow. In the first case, the list of God's works is an onomasticon of natural phenomena from the heavens down to the waters.[2] In the second case, the list of the hasidim is based upon a selective chronological reading of the great men of Israel's history. In both proems, the hymnic intention to render praise is heightened by reference to some difficulty having to do with the recognition or acquisition of glory.[3] But in each instance this is overcome by a strong affirmation of the abiding reality of the glory that comes from God. As summary statements that introduce the hymns proper, each proem provides the reader with a theological lens through which the subsequent descriptions are to be viewed. The common theme is the

manifestation of God's glory; the intention is to affirm its manifestation both in creation and in history.

This movement from reflection on creation to a consideration of the human situation occurs frequently in Sirach. The
sequence and manner of reflection in this movement is a theological schema traceable to wisdom thought. The occurrence
of this schema in the sequence of the two hymns is therefore a
further and telling argument for taking them together as a
compositional unity. It may be helpful to note that although
wisdom itself is not a theme in either of the two hymns, each
proem does contain express mention of wisdom themes. The
problems of the limits of wisdom and death-without-memory,
for instance, have been used to set the scene for the great
affirmations of those things that endure. This reflects Ben
Sira's grappling with the basic issues of wisdom theology of his
time, that is, the possibility of the knowledge of God and the
problem of theodicy.[4] Ben Sira's position both here and in the
book as a whole is affirmative in the question of the knowledge
of God, and he makes a brave attempt to resolve the problem
of theodicy on its terms. He does so by affirming the wisdom
of God by which the world was created and claiming the institutions of Israel's religion (Torah, Temple, Jurisprudence,
Piety) as loci for its manifestation. This is intended to undergird an optimism about Jewish piety—its basis in divine and
cosmic structures—that can answer the questions of theodicy
and cynicism. If in these concluding hymns the locus of
wisdom in Jewish ethos is to be celebrated in a review of the
glorious saints of Israel's history, the novelty is that the "human situation"—a category congenial to wisdom thought—is
now being understood in terms of its past history. This means
that Ben Sira had found a way to unite a wisdom view of the
pious one with the category of Israel's sacred history. The
hymn's place at the conclusion of the book may indicate something of a climax both for the literary composition of the book
and for the development of wisdom categories it achieves.

There is one additional observation to be made in support of
the unity of the two hymnic sections in question. Some of the
psalms in praise of Yahweh's deeds in Israel's history have been

noted as examples of possible literary precursors for Ben Sira's hymn in praise of the fathers (Psalms 78, 105, 106, 135, 136).[5] Such a recital of God's deeds need not include mention of the human agents of the history, as Psalms 135, 136, and other oracular and narrative examples show (Ezekiel 20, Nehemiah 9, Judith 5). But in Psalms 78, 105, and 106, one sees that mention can be made, for example, of Abraham, Moses, and David, in the course of the recital of the great events in Israel's history. In Psalms 135 and 136, the praise of Yahweh's creative works precedes the recital of his actions in history. While none of these examples depicts the great figures of Israel's history as subjects worthy of the praise appropriate to the hymnic form, it is helpful to see the extent to which Sirach 44–50 may be a development of this type of psalm. Its transformation would have occurred because of the glorification of the great figures, but it may not have ceased entirely to be a celebration of Yahweh's deeds as well. This would mean that the divine aretalogical aspect of the hymn in 44–50 is quite compatible as a sequel to the hymn in praise of God's works in creation in 42:15–43:33. The scheme of wisdom-in-creation/wisdom-in-human-ethos may be suspected to have enabled the correlation.

Appendix B
The Conclusion
in Praise of
Simon

A curiosity of the scholarship on Sirach 44–50 is that a discussion of the final section in praise of Simon has been avoided rather consistently. It has even been said expressly that this hymn cannot belong to the hymnic series in praise of the fathers.[1] Two reasons have been articulated and two others probably play a role in this judgment. The reasons given are (1) that Simon cannot have been understood to have belonged to "the fathers" of Israel and (2) that the section on Enoch, Joseph, Shem, Seth, Enos, and Adam (49:14–16) forms a conclusion to the hymn proper. I suspect the two unarticulated assumptions are (3) that as a contemporary figure Simon must have been distinguished from all the others for whom there were memorials in written traditions and (4) a certain lack of scholarly appreciation of, and understanding for, the obvious cultic interests that the hymn in praise of Simon exhibits. Because Ben Sira engaged in an ethical "critique" of certain forms of the cult elsewhere, his glorification of a ritual scene in chapter 50 has been difficult for some to understand. I would argue that these reasons are not convincing and that the praise of Simon, not only belongs to the series as a whole, but in fact is intended to conclude that series as its climax.[2]

The argument that Simon cannot have been included in a listing of "the fathers" is based upon the mention of the fathers in 44:1 (or perhaps on the assumption that the heading "Praise of the Fathers" was original). Because the listing has been taken as a generic designation that limits the classification of those to be praised, it has been found difficult to see how Simon could have been included. There are two problems with this. The first is whether Ben Sira has intended a generic designation as a technical definition at all. The second is whether such a designation can be shown to have provided a principle of classification appropriate for all of the descriptions that follow. A closer look at the proem shows that while the idea of ancestry is certainly involved, the concern is rather to establish other categories of characterization, categories that will be the basis for the fathers' praise. There are three such categories given in addition to their identification as ancestors. The first is that they were men of piety (44:1, 10); the second is that they were men of great power, wisdom, and achievement (twelve classifications are given, 44:3–6); the third is that a certain "covenant" and "prosperity" that belongs to them continues to be effective now and forever among their descendents. It has frequently been noted that the listing of the twelve statements about great men is difficult to correlate with the subsequent descriptions of those praised.[3] The designation ḥāsîd is only infrequently found in subsequent characterizations. The idea of covenant does become thematic in the descriptions, including that of Simon (50:24), and is certainly appropriate for certain figures, but it can hardly be understood as a classification in the tehnical sense for all of the figures praised (including prophets and postexilic statesmen). Thus it appears that the characterizations presented in the proem are serving some other literary function than that of delimiting the selection of figures to be praised. This does not mean that the designation "fathers" is without significance for the collection. Indeed, the conception of ancestry is basic to the composition.

But it should be clear from our study that the reason for memorializing the ancestors would not have precluded similar praise to a contemporary high priest. Indeed, it may just be the case that it was the glorification of the high priest that resulted in the glorification of the fathers themselves.

The argument that 49:14–16 forms a conclusion to the hymn in praise of the fathers, to which the praise of Simon has been added as an appendix, cannot be convincing precisely because the relation of this section to the original composition raises several very difficult questions. It is argued in appendix C that it was probably a later addition. If it is deleted, the transition from Nehemiah to Simon would be quite understandable and no more difficult than other transitions between literary units in the hymn. The contemporaneity of Simon has been noted as a problem at the level of generic classification of these figures. But at another level, it raises the question of Ben Sira's view of the scriptural traditions from which the descriptions of all but Simon have been taken. Can Ben Sira have dared to add to his review of heroes memorialized in the scriptures his own hymn in praise of a contemporary? The answer seems to be yes.

The movement from wisdom research to wisdom composition—a movement that does acknowledge a kind of hiatus of inspiration—when combined with the express mention of the wide range of resources from which wisdom is to be won, provides an exceptionally clear and coherent rationale for the kind of creativity involved in the composition of the hymn in praise of the fathers. In accordance with this rationale, Ben Sira would have seen no problem in the transition from writing hymns in praise of the ancients based on wisdom research to the composition of a hymn in praise of a contemporary who manifested the same glory.

The suspicion that a certain embarrassment about the express interest in living cult in Sirach 50 has been a factor in the lack of scholarly discussion about this section need only be mentioned here. In our analysis, it becomes clear that it is precisely the priestly covenant and its manifestations in Simon

as the high priest that interest Ben Sira, provide a significant
theme of continuity in the series of praised men, and allow us
to see the setting within which the intention of the hymn of
praise as a whole can be understood. Without the inclusion of
the praise of Simon, this would hardly be possible.

Appendix C
Later
Additions to
the Hymn

One of the problems in the study of the hymn's literary structure has to do with the scope and arrangement of its subsections. There are three places where serious questions have been raised about the inclusion of material in the original hymn on the basis of textual and exegetical considerations. Significantly, two of these loci are also of critical importance for the question of the hymn's beginning and conclusion, and all three are of importance for the question of the development of themes. They are the mention of Enoch in 44:16; the description of Elijah in 48:9–11; and the section on Enoch, Joseph, Shem, Seth, Enos, and Adam in 49:14–16. In my opinion, all three of these passages are additions to the original hymn that occurred in the course of the exceedingly rich and complex history of the manuscript tradition.

The brief mention of Enoch in 44:16 is fraught with exegetical difficulties. Not only do the Hebrew (B) and Greek texts not agree in substance, they reflect independent midrashic traditions. The only thing they have in common is that Enoch is mentioned here in both texts, and that can be explained on the basis of a later redaction of one in terms of the

other. Which manuscript tradition introduced the figure of
Enoch to the other is difficult to ascertain. Telling, however, is
that neither the Masada text nor the Syriac version contains a
reference to Enoch here. We are therefore justified in concluding that the original hymn did not begin with Enoch, but
with Noah,[1]

In 48:9–12, Elijah's translation and eschatological function
is mentioned. Middendorp has argued that this is a later em-
bellishment of the Elijah-Elisha section of the hymn.[2] A judgment here is not crucial to the question of whether Elijah was
included at all in the roster of those praised, of course, but it
does have some bearing upon the questions of characterization
and theme. Middendorp's argument has to do with the view of
eschatology expressed in 48:9–12, which is difficult to recon-
cile with Ben Sira's optimistic views of creation, history, and
cult. There is only one other passage in the whole book that
expresses a similar eschatology (36:1–17), and Middendorp argues convincingly on textual and philological grounds that it
too is a later addition to Ben Sira's book of wisdom.[3]

It should be mentioned that Ben Sira certainly has offered
clear points of departure for a later apocalyptic reading and
redaction of his work. His interest in the prophets is clear, as is
his understanding of prophecy as privileged information about
the future. But it is questionable whether Ben Sira understood
such wisdom to be of apocalpytic content. Not only does he
name as "prophecy" inspired wisdom-instruction (24:31), he
also uses the ascription of the knowledge of the future to God,
to support his contention of God's eternal unchangeableness as
creator of a good universe (42:18–25). That Ben Sira has reflected about the problem of Israel's future is clear, but to
conclude that he sought to resolve it in terms even of a pro-
toapocalypse is to short-circuit a quest for his overall understanding of history. Three of the five studies that have addressed the hymn in 44–50 directly have been sidetracked by
raising the eschatological question of Ben Sira's messianology.[4]
Our study makes clear that the figures of Israel's past are understood to exercise still a powerful and determining influence
in Ben Sira's time, but not at all in an apocalyptic sense.

The section in Sir. 49:14–16 is the most troublesome of all the disputed sections. We do not have, unfortunately, a text from Masada after 49:17 to help us with a judgment in this case, and though there are significant variations among the Hebrew, Greek, Syriac, and Latin manuscripts, they all do agree in placing a mention of Enoch, Joseph, Shem, Seth, Enos, and Adam here. The argument for excluding it from the original hymn is thus based on considerations of its lack of appropriateness to the themes and structure of the hymn as a whole.[5]

It will be noted that with the exception of Joseph, these are all antediluvian figures. There is at first glance no particular reason why Ben Sira could not have included them in his roster of heroes. But the reasons given for their glorification, combined with the observation that this would be the only instance in which the author has broken from historical chronology, begin to make one suspicious. Adam is the only figure of the five with which Ben Sira has worked elsewhere in the book.[6] There it is clear that for Ben Sira, Adam symbolizes universal humanity. Adam does have a potential capacity for wisdom, to be sure, but this capacity is only to be actualized by means of a decision to accept God's will (wisdom as the law of life) in obedience. There is in each of the three descriptions of Adam a rapid movement from his mention as the first man to a discussion of the human situation in general, and there is no evidence of interest in Adam's chronological priority or any privileged position he may have had. This being the case, it is very difficult to understand the significance of the statement in 49:16 that "the splendor of Adam was above that of every living thing" as coming from Ben Sira himself.

One must also question whether the heightened glorification of the other figures in this section is compatible with Ben Sira's pattern of characterization and intentions in the hymn as a whole. It appears that in each case, interests in these figures are manifest that Ben Sira did not share. Enoch is ascribed exceptional status because of his special destiny. We have already discussed the mention of Enoch in 44:16 as secondary on the basis of textual evidence. Here it is the literary location and the reason for his glory that are telling. Ben Sira reveals no interest in the question of the destiny (much less special destiny) of any of his heroes. This is fully in keeping with the fact that he does not ascribe to any idea of postmortem destiny in the rest of the book. The inclusion of Joseph in this section also appears to reflect some interest in the motif of special destiny, since his uniqueness has to do with the transportation of his body from Egypt to Palestine after death as a "visitation." Nothing else is mentioned in the Hebrew text and the statement is otherwise curiously out of place.

Shem and Seth and Enos are merely mentioned with no reason given for their glory. But it is clear from other midrashic traditions that they were important as genealogical successors who guaranteed the continuity of certain blessings from their fathers (Adam, Noah) to subsequent generations. Ben Sira was not uninterested in questions of succession and the historical continuity of blessings. But it is very doubtful that he would have found the parochial and slightly esoteric aspects of even the earlier forms of those traditions congenial. Certainly he had no need of a Sethian principle, given his understanding of Adam, and in the case of Noah, it is Noah himself who is the "continuator," or "renewer" (44:17). The purpose of this for Ben Sira, however, is the survival of all flesh, and it is posited on the basis of Noah's righteousness and God's covenant with him. There is no mention of Shem in the hymn at the chronologically appropriate place (44:17–18), nor is there any reason to mention him. The next named is Abraham, whose importance is also related to a covenant concluded with him. This indicates a scheme for succession and historical continuity that would have no need for glorification of Shem or Seth. Reasons for the mention of Enos in 49:16 are less clear. As Seth's son, he was important in certain midrashic traditions for the construction of the genealogy of election from Adam to Noah, of course; and as a figure about which the scriptural account did include a curious bit of information ("At that time men began to call upon the name of the Lord"), his mention provided later interpreters with occasion for reflection and debate. But nothing of this is indicated in Sir. 49:16.

It thus appears that all of the figures in this section were important for reasons other than those in which Ben Sira otherwise shows interest. Their inclusion here appears to reflect midrashic concerns with remarkable origins and destinies, especially of the antediluvians, and in keeping with some genealogical scheme that ran from Adam through Seth, Enos, and Enoch to Noah and Shem. Their insertion into Ben Sira's hymn at just this point would not be difficult to understand. After the mention of Nehemiah and before the praise of Simon would have been a covenient place to add a brief mention of biblical figures of interest not found in the rest of the hymn. Because it reflects genealogical interest and in some respect moves backward from Enoch to Adam (Joseph, Shem, and Enos disrupt this order however), the illusion of periodizing, a return to the beginning, is created. This can hardly reflect Ben Sira's purpose, however, and without it, the conclusion of the series becomes more appropriately the praise of the high priest Simon.

Appendix D
The Pattern of
Characterization

The express mention of a figure's office occurs in one half of the cases.[1] It is not included in descriptions of the kings, but it is clearly implied, as 49:4 shows. Of the three prophets not so designated (Nathan, Elisha, and Ezekiel), it is clearly implied as well. The office of priesthood is mentioned for all priestly figures except Jeshua, who is listed as one of the three leaders of the restoration without official designations. The office that we have called "the fathers" is the least clearly expressed of them all. This may have to do with the function of these figures as pre-Mosaic founders of the covenants upon which the later spectrum of offices in the narrower sense comes into being. Nevertheless, Abraham is called "the father of a multitude of nations" (44:19); Noah "the renewer" of the human race (44:17); and Jacob "the firstborn," that is, Israel (44:23)—all designations of their function as "fathers" of certain generic classifications of and within the human race. Moses is not given an office, presumably because his function is sui generis. But his office could be designated as the "seer-teacher," and all subsequent offices are derived from him in some way.

The designation of office for Joshua, Caleb, Zerubbabel,

Jeshua, and Nehemiah is problematic. Joshua is assigned by Ben Sira to the prophetic office (46:1), and he does share in the attributes ascribed to the prophets. But he is cast also as a warrior and ruler and thus may be understood as a composite figure who, along with Caleb and the judges, is appropriate to the period of conquest. The three figures of the restoration are described chiefly in terms of functions that Ben Sira has attributed to the earlier kings, building, defense, and restoration of the city and the temple. But these functions are also associated with the priest Simon (50:1–4), indicating that Ben Sira understands certain aspects of the royal office to have been performed in the restoration and Second Temple periods by leaders other than kings. It seems best, therefore, to correlate the three figures of the restoration (Zerubbabel, Jeshua, and Nehemiah) with the earlier figures of the judges as leaders of composite functions appropriate to the two periods of transition in the architectonic movement of the history.

The idea of election or selection for office is clearly expressed for figures in all categories and may therefore be included in the pattern of characterization. Nevertheless, the terminology differs appropriately from office to office; and with the exception of the prophets, three of whom are said to have been "formed" ("from the womb"), the ascription is limited to founding figures with whom covenants were established. Thus Noah was *māṣa'*, "found," blameless (44:17), and Abraham was "found" faithful (44:20). Of Moses it is said that God *bāḥar*, "chose," him out of all flesh (45:4), and of Aaron that God "chose" him out of all living (45:16). David was *mûram*, "separated," out from Israel (47:2). For the prophets Joshua, Samuel, and Jeremiah, some form of the idea "formed from the mother's womb" is used (46:1; 46:13; 49:6). It is significant that the idea of election is not used for kings succeeding David, nor priests succeeding Aaron.

Covenants are expressly mentioned in relation to founding figures in each category of office except that of the prophets. Each of the several covenants is clearly defined and distinguished from the others. The covenant with Noah was "not to destroy [again] all flesh" (44:18).[2] To Abraham, with whom the covenant of circumcision was established, the promise of the blessings upon his seed and the nations was given (44:20–21). To Moses the law was given (45:5), and for Aaron the priestly ministry became "an eternal covenant" (45:15). The covenant with Phineas was that the office of the high priesthood would belong to him and his descendents forever (45:24). The covenant with David was the kingship (47:11; cf. 45:25).

Religious virtues are ascribed to many of the figures spanning all categories of office. We are therefore justified in concluding that a designation of religious virtue belongs to the pattern of characterization. But ethical virtues having to do with wisdom, obedience, and righteousness do not predominate. The only figure characterized as "wise" is Solomon (47:12), and he turns out to be an ambiguous figure whose sins offset his wisdom and introduce the sorry history of the divided kingdom. The only figure called "righteous" is Noah,[3] and that is taken from the scriptural account, as is the designation "blameless" (tāmîm, 44:17; cf. Gen. 6:9). Obedience is mentioned expressly only once, in regard to Abraham (44:20), but the context shows that the reference is to circumcision as a sign of the covenant made with him.

The majority of the designations of character are midrashic, that is, taken directly from the scriptural accounts of the figures. This is so for Moses' meekness (45:4; cf. Num. 12:3) and Aaron's holiness (45:6; cf. Num. 16:3–7). Scripture is also the source for the ascriptions of zeal to Phineas (45:23; cf. Num. 25:10–13) and Elijah (48:2; cf. 1 Kings 19:10, 14). In all of these cases, therefore, it is extremely difficult to discern any specific contour of a pattern of virtue to which Ben Sira may have intended to give expression.

In regard to the ascriptions of faithfulness, strength, and piety, we are in a somewhat better position to make an assessment of Ben Sira's concerns. Not only does he use these designations repeatedly and in relation to several of the figures, but the midrashic process involved is also a bit more complex, thus reflecting a special interest. "Faithful" ('āmôn) is used to describe Abraham (44:20), Moses (45:4), Samuel (46:15), and Isaiah (48:22). There is a very natural scriptural point of departure for the ascription of faithfulness to Moses (Num. 12:7: "He is *entrusted* with all my house"). This occurs, too, in close proximity to Num. 12:3, from which the designation "meek" is taken. Both are mentioned together in Sir. 45:4.

One wonders whether the terminology of "faithfulness' in the hymn indicates a movement in the direction of characterization in terms of virtuous qualities instead of in terms of office or performance. The same consideration could apply to the ascription of faithfulness (reliability) to Samuel, which may be based on the statement in 1 Sam. 9:6 that "all that he says comes true." Isaiah, however, is said to have been "faithful *in his vision*" (48:22), and Abraham was "found faithful *in trial*" (a reference to the binding of Isaac in Genesis 22). Here the ascription of faithfulness is clearly Ben Sira's contribution, but the aspect of performance or narrative context that is retained shows that the designation does not emphasize a quality of character descriptive of the person as an individual. It is not mainly that these men were trustworthy; it is that their performance was true or reliable. Their faithfulness is manifest in events that are of significance for the office. In all four cases, there is an element of election to agency in the divine activity by which Israel's history is understood to be directed, and the term "faithful" is therefore understood to be important only in this context.

The same seems to be true of Ben Sira's ascription of strength to several of the figures: Moses (45:2), Phineas (45:23), Joshua (46:1, 7), Caleb (46:7), and Hezekiah (48:22). Even though various Hebrew terms are employed, the idea of strength is clearly of interest to Ben Sira, an added emphasis to the scriptural accounts. Moses is said to have been made strong by God in his "awe-inspiring deeds"; Phineas was strong in his act of slaying the Israelite who had taken a Midianite woman, that is, in "making atonement for the children of Israel" (Sir. 45:23; cf. Num. 25:7–8); Joshua was strong as a warrior and, with Caleb, as one who "stood firm" in recommending an entrance into the land; and Hezekiah was "strong in the ways of David," that is, performed properly as a king. In each case, strength has to do with the quality of performance of deeds in keeping with the offices held. The reiteration of the idea does produce the effect of making strength a noteworthy quality of Israel's leaders, however, and combined with the idea of faithfulness, it begins to give some shape to Ben Sira's notion of virtue.

Under the rubric "piety," several ascriptions of excellence may be classed together that appear to be of some significance for Ben Sira's conception of leadership. Of Joshua it is said that "he fully followed after God, and did an act of piety in the days of Moses" (46:6). The designation "following God" is taken from the account in Num. 14:24 and Josh. 14:8, 9, 14. But the mention of an act of piety is added. This is noteworthy in that the proem has announced that the figures to be praised were "pious men" (Sir. 44:1, 10). In the hymn, no one is expressly described as a pious one, but there is this mention of Joshua's act of piety, and it is said of Josiah that he "gave his heart wholly to God, and . . . he practiced piety" (49:3).

The association of practicing piety with the ideas of "following God" and "giving one's heart wholly to God" alerts one to the significance of two other ascriptions of religious devotion. Of some of the judges, it is said that their "hearts were not beguiled" and they did not turn back from "following after God" (46:11). Of David it is said that he "loved his Maker with his whole heart" (47:8). We see here a set of descriptions of religious piety that have been brought together by association. In the case of the ascription to David, it is difficult not to think that Deut. 6:5 or Deut. 10:12 has not been influential. If so, the same may be true for the statement about Josiah giving his "heart wholly to God." In Deut. 10:12, the metaphor of walking in God's way is also employed, providing a link to the "following" metaphor used of Joshua and then of the judges. The cluster as a whole indicates at first a type of piety that reminds one of the religious loyalty called for in the Deuteronomic tradition. It is probably significant that it is attributed to Josiah and David, kings who are praised as defenders of the religious institutions and whose piety is disclosed in those deeds of defence. Joshua's act of piety refers to his exhortation to the people to enter the land. Loyalty to the religious codes of Israel is also the point of praise with the judges. If Hezekiah were added to this list, the roster of pre-exilic rulers who are commended would be complete. Of him it is said that he "did that which was good and was strong in the ways of David." This is hardly a clear description of Hezekiah's "piety," but it is a statement of commendable performance in keeping with the kind of piety ascribed to the other rulers.

In summary, it may be said that there is a clear tendency in the hymn to praise and characterize various figures in terms of traits or qualities of religious significance. Especially important appear to be "faithfulness," "strength," "zeal," and "piety" (= loyalty). They are easily combined in a coherent picture of religious virtues. They are strikingly conservative and, used as they are to express approval for religious leaders in the performance of their offices, serve primarily to characterize the quality of their leadership.

As one might expect, the hymn in praise of the pious men is replete with accounts of grand and glorious deeds. They can be classified according to types, and there is some correlation between the types of deeds and the offices or functions of the leaders to whom they are ascribed. All are taken from the scriptural accounts, of course, so that the ascription of deeds appropriate to the various figures and their offices is at first glance simply given by the tradition and determined by the "archaic" distinctions. But the selection of material is Ben Sira's own, and there is considerable evidence of a strong interest in developing a rather consistent typology of deeds and leadership functions.

Before moving to a discussion of those deeds that are especially appropriate to the performance of a specific office, mention should be made of what might be called "deeds of piety." It is noteworthy that references to actions of religious and ethical piety in general are so few. If these are found to be placed judiciously, it may be that Ben Sira has succeeded to some extent in combining two paradigmatic functions, of "obedience" and of "office." It has already been pointed out that there is only one reference to keeping the law in the entire hymn, and that is to Abraham's act of circumcision. This reference is doubly noteworthy because he is also the only father for whom any deed is recounted at all. The function of the fathers as founders of the covenants of promise is primarily the reception of the blessings. But in the figure of Abraham, Ben Sira relates the promise of these blessings to his act of obedience by combining it with a reference to the binding of Isaac (which is the occasion in the Genesis account for the blessings, as Ben Sira knew [44:20b–21]). Since circumcision would be an appropriate act and symbol of obedience to the law for all, Abraham is an appropriate figure to combine models both of obedience and of office. Of him it is also said that "he did not tarnish his glory" (44:19). Since Solomon did "tarnish his glory," reference to his taking of many foreign wives (47:19–20), it is probable that in this regard, too, Abraham is intended to serve as a model of obedience for Jewish religious ethic in general.

There is only one other deed ascribed to any of the figures that might be taken as a model for general religious piety. It is the reference to prayer. "Calling upon God" is ascribed to Joshua (46:5), Samuel (46:16, 19), and, interestingly enough, to the people under attack by Sennacherib during Hezekiah's reign (48:20). David is said to have "given thanks in all that he did" (47:8). It is quite possible to see here a reflection of religious piety appropriate to all the people. This would be in keeping with the few other instances in the hymn of reference to performance by the people themselves. Usually, however, the response of the people is shown to be determined by the quality of their leaders. There is reference to the daughters singing David's praise (47:6), the progeny of Solomon distressed over his sins (47:20), Israel's sins caused by the evil kings (47:23–24), the people's failure to repent at the message of Elijah and Elisha (48:15–16), and the people gladly receiving the blessing from Simon (50:17–21).

In contrast to the paucity of references to deeds of obedience and piety in general, deeds appropriate to the offices of the leaders are recounted in number. We may distinguish five

types: (1) the miracles and prophecies that belong to the prophetic office, (2) the work of building the temple and the
restoration and defense of the city that belong to kings, (3) the
teaching ministry that begins with Moses, (4) the ministry of
the priestly office, and (5) the conquest of enemies that belongs to the warrior-ruler.

Miracles are ascribed to Moses (45:2–3), Joshua (46:4),
Samuel (46:20), Elijah (48:3–5), Elisha (48:12–14), and Isaiah
(48:23). All of the miracles mentioned are ascribed in one way
or another to the prophets as agents of God. Some are miracles
of healing (Isaiah) and deliverance (Moses), others of victory
over enemies (Joshua, Elijah). Some are merely "signs" (Elisha), and two are miracles of continuing to prophesy after death
(Samuel, Elisha). These miracles serve in general to image the
power of the prophets in their work as agents of the judgments
and restorations by which the history of Israel has moved.
Their prophecies had the power "to destroy" and "to establish" the kings and their kingdoms (Jeremiah, 49:6; Joshua,
46:6; Samuel, 46:13c, 18; Elijah, 48:2, 8). Although Samuel is
called "seer" (46:15) and Ezekiel is praised for his vision of the
chariot (49:8), Isaiah is the only one of whom it is said that he
had a vision of the future (48:24–25).

The deeds for which the kings and ruler are praised, on the
other hand, consistently have to do with constructive acts related to the city, temple, and institutions of the cult. David
ordered the calendar and ordained the musical forms of liturgy
(47:9–10), Solomon built the temple (47:13), Hezekiah fortified and defended the city (48:17), Josiah cleansed the cult
(49:2), Zerubbabel and Jeshua built the temple (49:12), and
Nehemiah restored the city walls (49:13).

With Moses and Aaron, the functions of teaching and
priestly ministry are understood to have begun. Teaching
draws its glory from the "law of life and discernment" that is
its content (45:5). Moses' glory as teacher is described in
terms, not of what he did, but of what happened to him, what
was revealed to him. He was given the law "that he might
teach" (45:5). Aaron, too, really performs no deed. He is
chosen, invested, exalted "to minister" (45:15) and given the

commandments "that he might teach" (45:17). Here the idea
of "great deeds" has been transformed into the idea of the
grandeur of religious office itself.

It is important to note the extent to which the descriptions
of these figures do include explicit reference to setting. Not all
do, to be sure. Isaac and Jacob are not placed in any context.
Of Moses it is said only that God made him bold "in the
presence of the king" (45:3). The judges are mentioned as a
class without narrative or historical context, as are the twelve
prophets (46:11–12; 49:10). Ezekiel also is not placed (49:8–
9). But for all the rest, there is express mention of some context in relation to which deeds or office derive significance.

Noah became the renewer "in the season of destruction"
(44:17), and Abraham was found faithful "in trial" (44:20).
There is no reflection about the cause or nature of these
threatening situations, and they appear at first merely to be
descriptive background. But with the descriptions of Aaron
and Phineas, it is clear the "jealousy" and sin among the people establish the context for their office, and with Joshua, it is
a "hostile people" without (46:6). Tracing references to setting
throughout the hymn from this point on, one can determine
that it is given repeatedly in terms of these two threats—sins
within, enemies without. With these threats, a background or
context is given that belongs to the pattern of characterization.
It is the social-historical setting within which the leaders and
their deeds have meaning and against which they are seen to
be glorious.

The question of reward is raised by statements that indicate
certain bestowals of covenants, status, and inheritance on the
basis of virtue. After the statement that Abraham was found
faithful in trial, for example, it is said "therefore ('al kēn) he
promised him with an oath to bless the nations in his seed"
(44:21). Of Jacob it is said that God "gave him his inheritance,
and set him in tribes" (44:23). Moses "found favor . . . and
He made him glorious as God" (45:1–2). After Aaron's office
was threatened by Korah, God "increased his glory and gave
him his inheritance" (45:19–20). Because Phineas demonstrated his zeal, "therefore (lākēn) for him, too, He established

an ordinance, a covenant" (45:24). Caleb was "given strength" and cause "to tread upon the high places of the land" because he stood firm (46:8–9).

Office and ministry belong together conceptually, and in the descriptions of the hasidim who founded and fulfill these offices, there is repeated mention of the effects of their ministry both upon their descendents or successors and upon the people they serve. Noah is the renewer of a remnant, the survivors, and the occasion of a promise that affects all humankind. The promise to Abraham becomes a blessing passed on to the twelve tribes of Israel. Moses' ministry is to teach the statutes, testimonies, and judgments of the law to Israel. Aaron is to minister to God and "to bless His people in His name" (45:15). Phineas' great deed is that he "made atonement for the children of Israel" (45:23). Joshua and Caleb "turned away wrath from the assembly" (46:7). None of the entire roster of these illustrious men is praised for personal achievements. All are great because of effective ministry to and for the people.

Notes

1. A date of ca. 180 B.C.E. can be established for Sirach. For this and other introductory matters, see the recent summaries in Nickelsburg, *Jewish Literature*, 55–69; Crenshaw, *Old Testament Wisdom*, 149–73, 283.

2. Maertens, *L'éloge des pères;* Jacob, "L'histoire"; Siebeneck, "Sirach's Praise"; and te Stroete, "Van Henoch tot Simon"; Lee, "Studies."

3. The monographs by Haspecker, Marböck, Middendorp, and Rickenbacher are examples.

4. The hymn as a rewriting of Israel's history has been emphasized by Maertens, Jacob, Siebeneck, Noack, and Janssen. Siebeneck contrasts the new view with those of the Yawhist, Elohist, priestly writer, and Deuteronomist ("Sirach's Praise," 415). In the scholarship, frequent reference is made to Psalms 78, 105, 106, 135, 136, Nehemiah 9, and Ezekial 20 as precursor texts to Sirach 44–50. The most recent discussion is found in Lee, "Studies," 21–26, where, however, the dissimilarities are emphasized. On the hymn's reflection of cultic interests, see especially Jacob; Middendorp, *Stellung*, 162–174; Hengel, *Judaism*, 1:133; Lee, "Studies," 9–19.

Since Maertens references to the genre *De virus illustribus* have been customary (*L'éloge des pères*, 11). Thus Siebeneck, "Sirach's

Praise," 414; Pautrel, "Ben Sira," 541; Hengel, *Judaism,* 1:136. The earliest extant text of this genre is from Cornelius Nepos (94–24 B.C.E.) and is a development of the Hellenistic biographical tradition. Lee argues that comparison of Ben Sira with the earlier Hellenistic "lives" by Hermippus, Satyrus, and Sotion would be of more value than with the later Roman development of the genre ("Studies," 52–55). We shall discuss this question in chapter 5.

5. On the value of the Greek version (G1), see Vattioni, *Ecclesiastico,* xxiii; Middendorp, *Stellung,* 2, 100–112; and the introduction to Patteson, "Study." For the Hebrew text, see Yadin, *Masada;* Levi, *Hebrew Text;* Rüger, *Text und Textform;* and *The Book of Ben Sira* (Jerusalem, 1973). There is now a concordance to the Hebrew text by Barthélemy and Rickenbacker.

CHAPTER ONE

1. There are five occurrences of the sequence wisdom-in-creation/wisdom-in-human-history: (a) 1:1–8/1:9–18; (b) 16:24–30/17:1–11; (c) 24:1–7/24:8–21; (d) 39:12–35/40:1–11; (e) 42:15–43:35/44–50. The sequence is given with the wisdom myth, but its theological significance is based on a logic seen in the narrative. This borders on systematic concern. See Mack, *Logos,* 31–32, 150–53; Marböck, *Weisheit,* 68–74, 131–33. The wisdom theme is discussed at length in chapter 6. For an exegetical demonstration that the two hymns have literary links, see appendix A.

2. See Box and Oesterley "Book of Sirach," 479–81; Snaith, *Ecclesiasticus,* 216. The twelve descriptive statements might be reduced to six types if one takes the parallelisms together. But one is then left with composite characterizations such as warrior-king (44:3) and prophet-sage (44:3), which while reflective of some persons described in the hymn, do not appear to have been developed there as types per se. The next six statements (44:4–5) are even more difficult to combine typologically, each having to do with aspects of the leader-sage as instructor and author. No one in the hymn is expressly described in these terms, although aspects of Moses' office and Solomon's activity are partially comparable. The final distich (44:6) about "men of resource . . . living at ease" is curiously inappropriate as a type characterization, especially for those praised in the hymn. It is best, then, to regard this list of statements, not as a typology itself, but as a series of commendable leadership qualities and functions worthy of praise. It does provide the reader with a kind of lens through which to interpret what follows, but it is sin-

gularly deficient as a comprehensive statement about the types or offices of those men to appear in the hymn. Particularly telling is the omission of any reference to the cultic functions of the priests. For the opposing view, that 44:3–6 does intend a typology of those to be praised in the hymn, see Lee, "Studies," 267–68. A very suggestive study by Skehan, "Staves and Nails," shows that most of the phrases used here are poetic and metaphoric descriptions that draw upon scriptural language, and that they were apparently at home in a postexilic scribal ethos in which the connection had been made between "leaders" and "scholars." He shows that a later *pesher* from Qumran (CD. vi. 3–11) made explicit many of the allusions still implicit in Sirach. His study lends support to our thesis in chapter 4 that Sir. 44:3–6 is heavily weighted with allusions to the ideal scholar-scribe and is not intended as a comprehensive typology of ideal leaders as such.

3. A distinguishing characteristic of the hymn is the regularity of its meter (4 + 4). Sirach 3–43 does not reveal such a regular pattern, following the proverbial model instead. Cf. Stanislav, "Vorarbeiten"; Rickenbacher, *Weisheitsperikopen*, 67–68.

4. Ben Sira's anthological and interpretive use of scripture has been noted and studied by a number of scholars, including Koole, Snaith, Middendorp, and Sheppard.

5. See Middendorp, *Stellung*, 35–91.

6. I used the following procedure to determine the pattern. First, I made detailed lists of the significant items in the description of each figure named. I then arranged the lists as a set and compared them. Seven features emerged as common characteristics in a recurring pattern. Some figures are not fully described according to this pattern, but most are. Where figures are not fully described, the details of their descriptions still seem to fall within the list of the seven common features.

7. The units of description range from thirty-six distichs to a single distich. Using this as a scale of interest, it can be seen that attention has been focused upon Simon (with 36) and Aaron (with 32). The kings follow: David (17), Solomon (16), Hezekiah (10). Others granted extensive description are Joshua and Caleb (together 18), Samuel (13), Elijah (12), Phineas (10), Moses (9), Elisha (9), and Abraham (6). These are in fact the figures of greatest significance for Ben Sira's view of the history he has developed.

8. This is because, though the fathers represent the divisions of humanity into nations, "the people" as a technical component of the

social structure cannot be mentioned until the offices have been established. It is the office itself that determines the concept of the congregation in the hymn. This is indicated clearly in the depiction of Moses, with whom the structure of office emerges, as "issuing from Israel" and having "charge of His people" (44:22, 45:3).

9. Anointing is mentioned for Moses (45:15), Samuel (46:13), and Elijah (48:8).

10. Jaubert does not think that this reflects any position-taking with regard to competitive genealogical traditions among priestly classes or parties during this period (*La notion d'alliance*, 38–39). On this question see de Vaux, *Ancient Israel*, 394–403.

11. Since this line is partially destroyed in MS. B, there have been several attempts to reconstruct it, but all retain the mention of "the third" in keeping with the Greek (*tritos eis doxan*). Lee agrees that "the reference here seems to be to the trinity of Moses, Aaron, and Phineas" ("Studies," 249–50).

CHAPTER TWO

1. The mention of David in 45:25 is the only instance of a deviation from chronological arrangement. It is to be accounted for in terms of the covenant theme that governs the sequence only of the first seven figures and requires that the covenant with David be mentioned here if at all.

2. There has been very little work done on the structure of the hymn. Baumgärtner could find no principle of continuity in it ("Gattungen," 174). Jacob, "L'histoire," finds neither a chronological plan nor any apologetic system that gives the hymn structure. Maertens, *L'éloge des pères*, divided it into three "cycles": (a) patriarchal, (b) paschal, (c) royal. His insight has not been followed up, but there are remarkable points of similarity with my thesis. Maertens did not develop his division of the hymn as a literary moment of significance, and a curiosity of his work is the failure to include the poem in praise of Simon in the hymn. Haspecker divides the hymn into two parts: (a) 44:1–45:26 with its theme of covenant; (b) 46:1–50:24 with its theme of piety (*Gottesfurcht*, 85, n. 94). The most recent attempt to assess the hymn's compositional structure is that of Lee, to be discussed in chapter 5.

3. Haspecker has also noted the covenant theme that governs the first section of the hymn and makes of it a unit (*Gottesfurcht*, 85, n. 94). Maertens first groups the patriarchs together as a set then dis-

cusses the figures from Moses through the judges as "le cycle pascal." There is neither thematic nor literary justification for these groupings. Lee sees 44:15–49:16 as a single unit corresponding to the *genos* of the Hellenistic encomium, and he thus does not investigate its subunits ("Studies," 265).

4. See also Jaubert, *La notion d'alliance*, 39. Priest sees this verse as evidence for the idea of a dual authority in the community analogous to the two messiahs in Qumran ("Ben Sira 45:25"). I have not found his arguments convincing. See below chapter 3.

5. Hengel (*Judaism*, 1:136) singles out this term as special evidence for a "principle of succession" in the hymn, which he sees as a Hellenistic notion. Lee argues against this because its usage in the hymn reveals several notions at work, each of which may be accounted for as midrashic ("Studies," 72–78). Lee is correct in seeing that a singular "principle of succession" is not in evidence as program in the hymn, but he has overstated the case with regard to midrashic derivation as a sufficient basis for its repeated occurrence. His point is that the Hellenistic genre to which Hengel refers (Sotion's *Diadochē tōn philosophōn*) is not the model upon which the hymn has been constructed. My own position is more pliable. See chapter 5.

6. The notion of a succession of the prophets is of course attested for later writers. Cf. Eupolemos in Jacoby, *FGr Hist*, 3C.723.F2b,F5; Josephus, *Contra Apionem*, 1.41.

7. On this correlation of primal pattern and ordered history from a history of religions point of view, see especially Eliade's *Cosmos and History*.

CHAPTER THREE

1. Haspecker has seen clearly that the hymn does not address the individual in the same way as do the earlier portions of Ben Sira's book: "Tatsächlich weicht Kp 44–50 in zweifacher Richtung vom Hauptteil des Buches ab. Formal verlässt es ganz den Raum der Individualparänese und wendet sich einem Kollektiv zu . . . Wichtiger ist, dass in diesen Kapiteln als Hauptthema der Gottesbund behandelt wird, der sich seinem Wesen nach an ein Kollektiv (Bundesempfänger und seine Nachkommen) richtet" (*Gottesfurcht*, 85, n. 94).

2. For the term "good fortune," I have retained the reading of MS. B as given by Vattioni, but it should be noted that the Masada

text contains another reading. The manuscript is damaged beyond the first two letters, but these are *wṣ* instead of *wt*. Vattioni reconstructs to *ṣ[dqtm]*, which is apparently what the Greek (*dikaiosynai*) and the Syriac read, that is, "righteous deeds." It is probable, therefore, that *ṣidqātām* stood in the original text. If so, the distich 44:10 presents a separate idea, namely, that the righteous deeds of the hasidim themselves "shall not come to an end." This would be fully appropriate as proem to the hymn, where deeds are recounted in number, but the manner in which these deeds continue to be effective is not yet clear. In a private conversation I had with Richard Weis of the Ancient Biblical Manuscript Center at the School of Theology at Claremont, he noted that the scribe responsible for the reading in MS. B had apparently understood the context of these verses to have to do with memory (*zākar*, 44:9, 13). Weis pointed to Sir. 38:21 (B) where memory (*zākar*) and "hope" or "good fortune" (*tiqwāh*) occur together in the advice about grief: "Remember him not, for he has no hope." In 44:8–10, the hasidim are being contrasted with those "who have no memorial, so that there was an end of them where they came to their end." The word field *tiqwāh* = *zākar* is thus in play, and it is this that has apparently influenced the change from *ṣidqātām* to *tiqwātām*. The new meaning ("their good fortune") correlates nicely with "prosperity" and "heritage" in the next distich (44:11) and thus is not obtrusive. If we take this scribe's lead as to the importance of the memory theme in this section of the proem, a significant clue will have been won for our question about the manner in which the legacy of these men in all of its aspects ultimately becomes effective. This will be discussed below.

3. The Greek encourages the more literal connotation by translating *ṭûbām* with *agathē* (as modifying *klēronomia*) and *nāḥālātām* with *klēronomia*. It is possible, of course, that Ben Sira intended a more metaphorical nuance in keeping with notions of covenant theology. In that case, the "good portion," "lot," or "legacy" these men received and passed on would be that which accrues by being included in the covenant community itself. It is difficult, however, to avoid completely the thought that this heritage is understood to include contemporary social and empirical realities in some sense.

4. On *ta agatha* as theme in the encomiastic speech, see *Rhetorica Alexandrum* 35.1440b.15; Theon, *Progymnasmata* (Walz, *Rhetores,* 1.227); Hermogenes, *Progymnasmata* (Rabe, *Hermogenis,* 16.12–13).

5. A discussion is available in Rist, *Stoic Philosophy,* 1–21. One wonders whether the Greek translator may not have been troubled

by this problem and thus transformed the noun *ṭûbām* into an adjectival modifier of the term for inheritance: *agathē klēronomia.*

6. Jaubert, *La notion d'alliance,* emphasizes throughout the "sacerdotal" ingredient in the idea of covenant for our period.

7. Middendorp, *Stellung,* 155–62.

8. Ibid., 155–56, 159.

9. See Hengel, "Proseuche and Synagoge." He demonstrates that *proseuchē* is the earlier and normal designation for a Jewish place of worship in the Diaspora. The term *synagōgē* does not occur in this sense until around the first century C.E.

10. Of the twenty verses in which these terms occur, only two clearly refer to the assembly as a place where legal judgments are rendered (Sir. 7:7 and 23:24; in Sir. 1:30 the Lord may "cast down" in the assembly). There are three references to Israel of the biblical period as an assembly (Sir. 24:23; 46:7; 46:14). In four cases, the term is used to refer to a godless company, presumably not within Israel (Sir. 16:6; 21:9; 41:18; 45:18). The assembly gathered for ritual occasions is mentioned two times (Sir. 50:13, 20). Caution in the assembly is advised twice, presumably having to do with a wisdom ethic of speech (Sir. 4:7; 7:14). The remaining six occurrences have to do with some form of wisdom speech in the assembly (Sir. 15:5; 24:2; 31:11; 33:19; 39:10; 44:15). This spectrum of usages hardly supports Middendorp's thesis.

11. See Liebreich, "Impact of Neh. 9:5–37"; Hengel, "Proseuche and Synagoge," 165, n. 30, with further references. In Hoenig's fascinating article "The Ancient City-Square," there are references to appropriate scriptural readings on ritual occasions in certain cities with designated "stations" (*maamadot*) for lay assembly. Those were occasions during which the local "priestly watch" was on duty in the temple and served, apparently, as services of worship by means of which those at a distance from the temple could participate in its cult. This is helpful as an indication of the public reading of the scriptures during the Second Temple period. But the scriptures read appear to have been only those related to the ritual-festival occasions, and the cities with *maamadot* appear to have been only in Galilee or the Diaspora, not in Judea.

12. Middendorp, *Stellung,* 162–64.

13. Note that the praise offered by the congregation (44:15) corresponds to the author's intention to write a hymn of praise (44:1) and forms in fact the *inclusio* for the proem. If the author's intention to praise connotes more the Hellenistic element, the congregation's

act reflects more the Jewish and liturgical components. The correlation of encomiastic and liturgical praise is thus achieved artfully for
the reader before the hymn itself actually begins.

14. Middendorp, *Stellung*, 167–69.

15. This reading of Ben Sira's political stance and openness to
Hellenism sees him as decidedly less polemical than is true of the
reconstruction offered by Hengel, *Judaism*, 1:131–53. Nickelsburg is
in agreement with my position (see *Jewish Literature*, 64).

16. Middendorp, *Stellung*, 137–74, especially 142–43, 149, 158–
59, 164, 166.

17. For a list of references see ibid., 140–54.

18. Sir. 10:2–3.

CHAPTER FOUR

1. Hengel reviews the evidence for "the development of the Jewish school" and notes that Sirach marks a new development under
Hellenistic influence (*Judaism*, 1:78–83). Both Segal, *Sepēr Ben Sîra*,
and Roth, "Gnomic-Discursive Wisdom," find that the organization
of the book reflects systematic concerns appropriate to a school-
instructional setting.

2. On Ben Sira's knowledge and usage of Theognis, see Middendorp, *Stellung*, 7–34 (with summary statement at 24–25). On Cynic-
Stoic philosophical commonplaces in Sirach, see Pautrel, "Ben Sira
et le Stoicisme"; Hengel, *Judaism*, 1:146–50, 159–62; Marböck,
Weisheit, 143–45; Middendorp, *Stellung*, 7–34.

3. The collection of maxims in blocks or literary units according
to theme, a characteristic of Sirach accented by the insertion of
appropriate theme titles in the later manuscript traditions (Marböck,
Weisheit, 168), reflects a common Hellenistic practice. On Sirach 24
as a Hellenistic hymn, see Conzelmann, "The Mother of Wisdom";
Hengel, *Judiasm*, 1:158–59; Marböck, *Weisheit*, 48–54; Mack, *Logos*,
40–42. On Sirach 44–50 as encomium, see Lee, "Studies," and the
discussion below in chapter 5.

4. On Sirach 24 and the Isis aretalogies, see Conzelmann, "The
Mother of Wisdom"; Marböck, *Weisheit*, 49–54; Mack, *Logos*, 38–49.
One of the more significant theses put forth by Middendorp is that
Ben Sira crafted maxims that could allude to both Jewish and
Hellenic gnomological traditions (*Stellung*, 78–84). This is a particularly skillful technique, a special case of literary finesse in the overall
syncretism that marks his work. On the relation of wisdom mythology and Hebrew scriptures, see chapter 6; cf. Sheppard, *Wisdom
as a Hermeneutical Construct.*

5. Theme units were recognized early on in the manuscript and translation traditions, as is shown by the addition of chapter headings in B and especially in the Greek version (cf. Marböck, *Weisheit,* 168). Several scholars have seen the wisdom hymn in chapter 24 to mark either the ending of the first half or the beginning of the second half of the book. A discussion is given in Marböck, *Weisheit,* 41–44. Building upon this notion, Nickelsburg is able to trace themes and associations in chapters 1–23 that may be governed by the two large poems about wisdom in chapters 1, 2, and 24 (*Jewish Literature,* 56–59). A suggestion by Middendorp is that the wisdom poems in chapters 1, 2, 4, 6, 14, 24, and 51:13ff. may be related to successive compilation of school materials (*Stellung,* 141, n.2). The alternative would be to see these poems as providing the organizational principle of the book by introducing themes around which blocks of ethical maxims have been collected. Marböck has seen this possibility (*Weisheit,* 15–16). See also the excellent studies by Segal (*Seper Ben Sîra*) and Roth ("Gnomic-Discursive Wisdom") on the arrangement of the book according to themes for instructional purposes. Roth suggests that section 24–51 is composed of three additions by Ben Sira himself to the earlier handbook of wisdom in 1–23. The later additions are marked by authorial consciousness and offer the creative contributions of the mature scholar.

6. On the place of religious hymns in the Hellenistic curriculum, see Marrou, *History of Education,* 164, 189–92. On the relation of the Hellenistic school to the religious calendar and life of a city, cf. Nilsson, *Hellenistische Schule,* 61–75. An example of an anthology for use in instruction is found in Gueraud and Jouguet, *Un livre d'écolier.* It includes an encomium. On Meleager of Gadara as the creator of the Greek anthology, see Hengel, *Judaism,* 1:84–85. Advice to the teacher of rhetoric at the *progymnasmata* level on composing one's own anthology of instructional materials from classical texts is given by Theon (Walz, *Rhetores,* 1:158–72). Middendorp has argued that Sirach is a school textbook for instruction at an advanced level (*Stellung,* 32–33). It should be noted, though, that its high degree of literary creativity and compositional organization set it apart from the teachers' handbooks in the primary and secondary schools, as well as from the handbooks of the higher rhetorical and technical schools. A better analogy may be the *protreptic* or introductory lectures customary in the higher schools of philosophy in combination with thematic collections of the school's own philosophical writing (see Marrou, *History of Education,* 283, 284–85). If so, Ben Sira combined aspects of several literary forms customary in the Hellenistic

tradition of education in order to achieve a creative and programmatic book. Its value as an instructional vehicle would still be recognizable, but its status as authored work would enhance its value as a
literature in its own right. The manuscript traditions, with their
additions, emendations, glosses, and versions, show the degree to
which Sirach was used in ways that reflect this anomaly—a prized
text to be interpreted itself, as well as a compendium of traditional
wisdom ethic.

7. See Mack, *Logos,* 21–29, 31–32.

8. In Sirach, cf. 4:11–19; 6:19–31; 14:20–15:8; 51:13–30. Crenshaw gives some good examples of exhortations to wisdom and suggests that they are a definitive characteristic of the sapiential
tradition (*Old Testament Wisdom,* 58–65).

9. So, for instance, Box and Oesterley, "Book of Sirach," 455;
Spicq, *Ecclésiastique,* 767; Lebram, "Aspecte der Kanon bildung,"
182–83; Koole, "Bible"; Marböck, *Weisheit,* 89. Other scholars have
avoided this difficult question (e.g., Haspecker, *Gottesfurcht,* 328) or
expressed themselves more cautiously (e.g., Lee, "Studies," 47:
"That Sirach had before him the materials which would become
those of the Hebrew canon."). The more cautious position is certainly called for, especially in light of the exceedingly wide range of
reference Ben Sira gives to the term "Torah" itself (cf. the survey by
Marböck, *Weisheit,* 86–96). Given the range of nuances for Torah,
which in its connotation as wisdom is understood to be present in
the creation order from the beginning, the references in Sir. 39:1 to
the "Torah of the Most High" and in 24:23 to the "Book of the
Covenant" are clearly special cases in which specific scriptures are
taken up under a broader rubric. It is in this sense that von Rad's
thesis about the relationship of wisdom and Torah in Ben Sira can be
helpful: "It is not that wisdom is overshadowed by the superior
power of the Torah, but, *vice versa,* that we see Sirach endeavoring to
legitimatize and to interpret Torah from the realm of understanding
characteristic of wisdom" (*Wisdom in Israel,* 245). Sheppard discusses
the problem of postulating a "closed" canon of scriptures according
to the later threefold division for Ben Sira's period but decides then
in favor of the value of the term "canon" to indicate both "the
Torah" and "the Prophets" as already being "authoritative books"
and "canonical divisions" by this time (*Wisdom as a Hermeneutical
Construct,* 14–15, n. 61). He does this, apparently, in the interest of
his thesis about wisdom hermeneutics as scriptural interpretation.
Later he argues that the reference to the Book of the Covenant in

Sir. 24:23 is a canonical expression that refers to the Torah as "the five books of Moses" (p. 62).

I wish to proceed without making these assumptions. Thus the notion of canon that informs my usage of this term is taken, not from its later technical sense in Jewish and Christian views of the scriptures, but from its much more fluid connotation in current literary criticism. In literary-critical discourse, canon refers to those precursor texts that have influenced greatly a given author or literary tradition and are acknowledged as "strong" or "classic" texts. By introducing this perspective, I do not intend a resolution of the complex question of Jewish scriptural canon formation and function. The suspicion is that factors other than those involved in the formation of literary canons must also come into play. These probably have to do with the value of the writings for the religious community as a whole as it seeks to determine its identity against other cultures. There can be no question about the existence of the literatures later to be canonized as Torah, Prophets, and Writings during Ben Sira's time. His own reading and usage of them is well attested. The question is whether he took them up because he understood them to be "authoritative" for reasons similar to those later to be articulated.

It is possible to use the term "canon" in its literary-critical connotation because Ben Sira's own reading of the Jewish writings takes place as a literary event in his work as a scholar and author. Only by assessing how he has read all of his precursor texts, including Hellenistic texts, can we even begin to press the question about the special nature of the authority of Torah for him or for others in his time. Our study will not be able to resolve this question fully. But clues will emerge in subsequent chapters. Anticipating the conclusions in chapter 5 and 6, it may be suggested that the authority of the Jewish scriptures for Ben Sira is a function of their capacity to be read as wisdom texts. I cannot find that Ben Sira has reflected on the question of what it is about them that results in this capacity. This means that the question about canon that theologians wish to ask may not find a satisfactory answer here.

10. Cf. the programmatic statement in Sir. 1:14.

11. One of the more important ideational developments in Sirach is the resignification of the notion of prophet and prophecy. Biblical scholars will know that the concept of the prophet in the subsequent period is quite different from that of the Hebraic period, and that following the so-called prophetic tradition into this later period is

fraught with difficulties. The evidence from Ben Sira is thus of considerable value, documenting as it does a reinterpretation of "inspired wisdom" as the provenance of the scholar-sage. The motivations for this correlation of prophet and sage have not been studied and are extremely complex. One factor that must be considered, however, is the recognition of the prophets as those who came to speech by name, that is, as authors. This alone would have marked them and their writings as distinctive among the traditional scriptures and would have evinced appreciation for them along the lines of Hellenistic views of authorship. A second consideration might be the extent to which the Jewish notion of prophetic inspiration was analogous to the Hellenistic view of poetic inspiration. The idea of the hiddenness of wisdom that prevailed at this time required some such view for anyone who aspired to knowledge. I suspect that Ben Sira understood the sage on the model of his view of the Old Testament prophets. In Sir. 24:33, he himself comes to speech in the statement "Yet again will I pour forth teaching as prophecy, and leave it to all future generations." Other evidences of prophetic genres and roles in Sirach are discussed in a fine section in Hengel, *Judaism*, 1:134–38.

12. This is something of an oversimplification, even as an interpretation of Ben Sira's views. The "vision" of the prophets is repeatedly emphasized in the hymn, as we have seen, and functions as a "text" on the basis of which their judgments are given. But the "textuality" of their vision is not elucidated in Ben Sira, and he would not have understood it in any case as modern scholars now do. We know that the prophets were well read in the sacred traditions known as Mosaic or Zionistic, and that they "read" the human situation against these. See the study by Sanders, "Hermeneutics in True and False Prophecy." Ben Sira has perhaps equated the prophets' inspiration (vision as experience, audience) with their view (vision as content) of the theocratic ideal, an approach formally comparable to modern views of the prophets' use of sacred traditions. When Ben Sira evokes the prophetic model for the sage, then, a new "content" is given to the vision itself. It is being understood as "wisdom," that is, the religious-ethical ordering of creation and history according to the wisdom myth. We shall see in chapter 6 that this myth can be used to "visualize" a "sacred tradition" too, in this case, the priestly tradition of a covenantal community with cultic history.

It is important to note that it is the power of the word that has fascinated Ben Sira about the prophets. This is closely related to the notion of authorship that emerges in Sirach, one correlate of which is the recognition of the rhetoricity of composed speech. If Ben Sira no longer understands the prophet-sage to be an overt agent of change in the political arena, it does not mean that he has resigned before the task of influencing cultural configurations. We have already noted the rhetoricity of the hymn as mythic creation in support of an institutional position. We have now to see that the arena of the scholars' influence is in literary instruction and creation, a setting that may account in part for the prophetic displacement and effacement in Ben Sira's vocation. The "power of the word" was a Hellenic theme articulated clearly already by Gorgias (*Helena*, 8–14). There is a fine discussion of the question of the effectiveness of speech when combined with various philosophies, lifestyles, and vocations (i.e., praxis) in Cicero, *De oratore*, 3.56–71.

13. See Fletcher, *Prophetic Moment*.

14. Bloom, *Anxiety of Influence*, 15. Bloom's concept of "belatedness" is given expression in Sir. 33:16–18: "I indeed came last of all, as one that gleans after the grape-gatherers." This verse is noted by Crenshaw as of significance for Ben Sira's self-understanding (*Old Testament Wisdom*, 159–60).

15. The references to Torah in Ben Sira are collected and discussed by Marböck, *Weisheit*, 88–92. See also above note 9.

16. Hengel notes that canon formation in Ben Sira's time would have been impelled by an anti-Hellenistic polemic (*Judaism*, 1:135). The corollary is that a consciousness of a corpus as literary canon was itself a Hellenistic idea. The establishment of the Hellenic "classics" no doubt took place within the Hellenistic schools. See Marrou, *History of Education*, 224–28. An important aspect of the Hellenistic formation was apparently a selection of texts understood to be manifestations of traditional (cultural) aesthetic and ethical values (cf. ibid., 234–35). This corresponds to the somewhat later idea about caution in selecting authors to be read because of the mimetic influence of their words. Cf. Theon, *Progymnasmata*, in Walz, *Rhetores*, 1.151.11–152.1; Seneca, *Epistle*, 11.8, 52.8, 71.7, 94.40; Plutarch, *How the Young Man Should Study Poetry*.

17. Cf. Epictetus 3.22, "On Cynicism," 23–25, 69–72, 77. These are late reflections on the Cynics from a Stoic point of view, but they do correspond to Cynic practice as documented in the Cynic epistles for the last century B.C.E. and the first of the next era. Cf. Malherbe, *Cynic Epistles*, also Plutarch, *Moralia*, 1.70C–D.

18. A fine historical survey of this tradition is given by Lee, "Studies," 128–244.

19. The classic study is Jaeger's *Paideia*. The move from warrior culture to scribal culture is a basic theme as well in Marrou's *History of Education*. The subsequent manifestations include the emergence of biography as a literary genre with its dependence upon *chreiai* as telling characterizations, the Stoic ideal of the sage, and the social prominence of poets, teachers, and rhetors. A recent article by Lefkowitz, "The Poet as Hero," traces the beginnings of this shift to a "pattern of autobiographical fiction" employed by fifth-century poets in the interest of a new heroic morality critical of the Homeric tradition. This autobiographical fiction became the source for subsequent biographies of the poets themselves. It is significant that the earlier poets, for example, Pindar, developed their new heroic morality as sages in the context of literary competition with other poets and especially with precursors. It is significant, also, that this occurred with the emergence of the polis and the demands that created for facility in rhetoric and the "democratization" of *aretē*. With this move, the stage was set for the culture of *paideia* as the system of values, conventions, and literary achievements that fostered and carried the Hellenic anthropology into the Hellenistic period. On the encomia, see Lee, "Studies," 172–73. He notes that Philiscus of Miletus wrote an encomium on the orator Lycurgos; Speusippus and Clearchus wrote encomia on Plato; and Demetrius of Phaleron wrote one on Socrates.

20. Self-references in Sirach: 24:30–34; 33:16–18; 34:11–12; 39:13, 32; 42:15, 27, 32; 41:1; 50:27; 51:13–30. On this topic see Roth, "Gnomic-Discursive Wisdom."

21. Consciousness of authorship has been noted as a clear mark of Ben Siras' Hellenistic learning: for instance, Hengel, *Judaism*, 1:78–79, 112; Crenshaw, *Old Testament Wisdom*, 159–60; Roth, "Gnomic-Discursive Wisdom."

CHAPTER FIVE

1. Marböck, *Weisheit*, 85–92.

2. Sir. 45:14 (Lev. 22:12); Sir. 45:16 (Lev. 16:34); Sir. 50:9a (Lev. 16:34); Lev. 19:19 (Sir. 31:15; cf. Sir. 6:10; 37:2). See Middendorp, *Stellung*, 60.

3. References by Middendorp, *Stellung*, 51–60.

4. On Homer as the classic text of Hellenistic education, see Marrou, *History of Education*, 226–27. One of the first sentences used

in the writing lesson was "Homer was not a man, but a god," and in the later exercises on selected passages the incipit *epē* (epic verse) is given. The phenomenon of allegorization is closely related to the study of Homer. See Heinemann, *Allegoristik;* Pepin, *Mythe et allegorie,* 85–124. The Stoics were particularly interested in using allegorization to correlate philosophical and ethical ideas with the writings of Homer. See Pepin, *Mythe et allegorie,* 125–72.

5. See below, pp. 121–22, and note 15.

6. Cf. the intriguing suggestion made by Hengel that "a kind of priestly historical writing . . . can be demonstrated from the Priestly Writer, the works of the Chronicler, Eupolemos, I Maccabees and the anti-Herodian source of Josephus himself" (*Judaism,* 1:99). It is possible now to place Ben Sira within this tradition.

7. Koch, *Priesterschrift,* 99–100.

8. The references to Sir. 46:1; 47:9–11; 48:17; 50:17 may be found in Box and Oesterley, "Book of Sirach." Smend bases a similar judgment upon Sir. 47:8ff (*Weisheit,* 414). Middendorp does not discuss Ben Sira's use of Chronicles, but references given in his index show that with only one or two possible exceptions elsewhere, the use of Chronicles is limited to the inauthentic section in Sirach 36 or to the level of Greek translation (*Stellung,* 130–31, 176).

9. See Momigliano, "Tradition," 171. The reference is not to the older practice of keeping archives in local institutions or royal houses in the Orient (and in Rome), but to the composition of a local history based upon such archives and other lore. He distinguishes this Hellenistic genre from the classical "historians of change."

10. See Höffken, "Sirach über Ezra," who comes to the same conclusion about Ben Sira's aversion to the Levitical-Ezra tradition.

11. Steck, *Israel,* 146–47.

12. Cf. Marböck, *Weisheit,* 73, 95–96, 176–77. See also Sheppard, *Wisdom as a Hermeneutical Construct,* 63–71. Sheppard's thesis is that Sirach 24 reflects significant allusions to the book of Deuteronomy and may be considered an interpretation of it. This is possible and does not disagree with Steck's finding that the later Deuteronomistic theology of history is not present in Sirach.

13. Steck, *Israel,* 146–47.

14. Most older studies recognized that Sirach 44–50 presented a new view of Israel's history but compared it only with other forms of earlier Jewish historiography. See above Introduction, n. 4. But Hengel places the hymn in the context of his fine discussion of

Greek and Jewish historiography of the Hellenistic period as an early example of Hellenistic influence (*Judaism*, 1:88–106). On the hymn as biography, see above, Introduction, n. 4. On the encomium, see Lee, "Studies."

15. A brief discussion of this component of the encomium from Pindar on is given in ibid., 138–41. As a component of Hellenistic historiography, cf. Hengel, *Judaism*, 1:88–90. The Anonymous Samaritan, a contemporary of Ben Sira, rewrote the Genesis account of primal history by combining with it motifs from Hesiod (the Titans), Berossus (the foundation of Babylon by the god Bel), and Babylonian cosmogonies. A comparison of Ben Sira's view of history with the *Babyloniaka* of Berossus might prove to be of some interest. Jonathan Z. Smith argues for the inclusion of the astrological material attributed to Berossus as the final section of his history:"taken together they reveal an overall pattern that closely approaches the apocalyptic: a history of a cosmos and a people from creation to final catastrophe dominated by astrological determinism. . . . the *Babyloniaka* appears to have described the history of the world from its creation to its final destruction and offers a periodization of the history of Babylonia which stretches in between" ("A Pearl of Great Price," 10). We may outline this history as follows: (1) Archaic Period, (2) History of Babylonia, (3) Final Catastrophe. Ben Sira's hymn may then be outlined as (1) Archaic Period, (2) History of Israel, (3) Final Actualization. Do we have here an early instance of a wisdom alternative to apocalyptic? Instead of astrological determinism, a wisdom interpretation of the covenants provides the rationale.

16. See Momigliano, "Tradition," 168.

17. Cf. Momigliano, "Eastern Elements," 29–30, 33. In his article on tradition and the classical historian, Momigliano distinguishes clearly between the chronicles of local traditions with their antiquarianism and the histories of the great historians of the fifth and fourth centuries. The latter focused upon recent events of conflict between peoples and were dominated by a sense of change. They had no sense of being "in the grip of the past" ("Tradition," 173). According to Momigliano's distinction, Ben Sira's hymn shares more with the tradition of chronicles than with the purposes of the "historians of change."

18. A survey of this early biographic literature is found in Lee, "Studies," 52–78.

19. See Momigliano, "Tradition," 166.

20. Middendorp suggests an allusion to the political concept of

diadochē (*Stellung,* 54). This connotation was certainly familiar during Ben Sira's time and may have played a role in its usage by him. This may also be true for the notion of a succession of kings and prophets in Eupolemos and Josephus. See below n. 22. But the more interesting possibility is the one we have referred to. The problem that Ben Sira may have had in its application to a series of prophet-sages may have to do precisely with the tension between prophetic inspiration and the transmission of tradition, a tension that would not have been resolved easily. The Hellenistic notion is illustrated by Diogenes Laertius, who uses the image of a prize passed from sage to sage (*Lives of Eminent Philosophers,* 1.28). (See below n. 23 for further documentation.) Ben Sira would not have been able to work out a resolution between prophetic (individual) inspiration and the notion of tradition at this early a time. But the subsequent developments that eventually produced the program in the Pirke Aboth can hardly be understood without it.

21. That I have not misread the singular importance of Moses in Ben Sira's hymn, nor overstated the potential for an extremely high characterization that lurks there beneath the surface, is shown by the quasi-mythological depictions of Moses in Eupolemos ("the first wise man") and Artapanus (the precursor-founder of Egyptian and Greek wisdom and religion). See Hengel, *Judaism,* 1:92–93.

22. Eupolemos records the "succession" of kings and prophets (Jacoby, *FGr Hist,* 3C. 723.F2b = Eusebius, *Prep. Ev.,* 9.30, 1ff.; and F5 = *Prep. Ev.* 9.39, 2). Josephus also knows about the "succession of the prophets" (*Contra Apionem,* 1.41).

23. Bickermann, "La chaîne de la tradition," traces the tradition of this notion in philosophical and biographic literature. Cf. also Fuhrmann, *Systematisches Lehrbuch,* 149.

24. It is unfortunate that a scholarly monograph on the encomium is not available. There is, however, a fine historical survey in Lee, "Studies," 126–243. He includes examples of encomia and discussions of rhetorical theory on the epideictic speech from the technical handbooks. Documentation for much of what follows in my own discussion can be found in Lee, even if many of my observations and emphases interpret the data in other ways. In the Bibliography, a brief selection of scholarly studies in classical rhetoric is included to which reference may be made also concerning epideictic theory and practice in the context of speech theory in general (cf. Clark, Kennedy, Lausberg, Martin, Perelman, Volkmann.) The task of mining this scholarship for specific knowledge about encomia, however,

is difficult, both because of the nature of the organization of the classical discussions and because of the organization and interests of the scholarly studies themselves. The summary discussion given here is based upon a reading of this literature, but specific documentation of details has been rejected as requiring an argumentation out of proportion to the needs of the study.

25. Our outline is a condensed synthesis of those given in the *progymnasmata* of Theon (Walz, *Rhetores,* 1. 227–31), Hermogenes (Rabe, *Hermogenis Opera,* 14–18), and Aphthonius (Rabe, *Aphthonii Progymnasmata,* 21–27). But the lineaments can be traced back through the rhetorical handbooks to the *Rhetorica ad Alexandrum* (3 and 35). See Cicero, *De inventione,* 2. 177–78; *De Oratore,* 2. 341–48; *Ad Herennium,* 3.6.10–3.7.15; *Quintilian,* 3.7, 8.4.

26. One example may be given. The *topos* on the defense of the city (Sir. 50:1–4) as encomiastic motif finds an exceptionally fine parallel in Isocrates' *Evagoras:* "Evagoras remedied all these defects . . . acquired much additional territory, surrounded it with new walls and built tiremes, and with other construction so increased the city that it was inferior to none of the cities of Greece" (47).

27. One example is Ben Sira's statement not to count anyone happy before his death (Sir. 11:28). This is attributed to Solon by Herodotus (1. 32. 86) and occurs also in Sophocles, *Oedipus Rex,* 1528.

28. Lee, "Studies," 262.

CHAPTER SIX

1. Though an interpretation of the "wisdom tradition" will be offered here, discussion with the views of other scholars will be minimal. The reader is referred to a selected number of references in the Bibliography as works to which I am indebted and that may be recommended as introductions to the exceedingly rich scholarship in this area. See Collins, "Cosmos and Salvation"; Crenshaw, *Old Testament Wisdom;* Mack and Murphy, "Wisdom Literature"; von Rad, *Wisdom in Israel;* and Schmid, *Wesen und Geschichte.* The scholarship has rightly and repeatedly emphasized the lack of overt concern for religious institutional history in this literature. A noteworthy exception which lends support to the thesis presented here is the study by Leo Perdue, *Wisdom and Cult.*

2. Sheppard gives an excellent review of the problem of defining a tradition of wisdom (*Wisdom as a Hermeneutical Construct,* 1–11). See

also Whybray, *Intellectual Tradition;* and Crenshaw, "Prolegomenon," 22. Crenshaw presents a more optimistic position with regard to "a professional class" of sages and the sapiential tradition (*Old Testament Wisdom,* 28–36, 42–65). It is put forth cautiously and argued extensively, indicating that he has seen the problems clearly. I am not convinced that Crenshaw has made the case, but there are a number of fine observations and several helpful compromises that make of his study an excellent summary statement. In some ways, it may function as a comparison piece to my attempt here to elucidate a wisdom mode of thinking without accepting traditional assumptions about "the wisdom tradition."

3. A point seen by Crenshaw, *Old Testament Wisdom,* 36.

4. This classification is taken from the article on wisdom by Fohrer in *The Theological Dictionary of the New Testament.* The curiosity is that scholarship, oriented as it has been to questions about the place of wisdom within Israel's ethical and religious life and thought, has tended to treat this data merely as philological background and thus has lost track of the variety of connotations that probably continued to exist within the culture even after the term had been personified and theologized. A similar phenomenon in classical scholarship has now been remedied by an exceptionally important study by Detienne and Vernant, *Cunning Intelligence.* With this work, a conception of "wisdom" deeply imbedded in Hellenic culture emerges, a wisdom whose function was quite the opposite of the philosopher's *sophia.* A companion study for Jewish wisdom would mean a reevaluation of a long list of religious, social, literary, and rhetorical-logical phenomena of the tradition. Collins, "Court Tales," has recently used the distinction between "mantic" wisdom and "proverbial" wisdom in a very helpful way in order to be more precise about the kind of wisdom intended in an apocalyptic book. This approach is most commendable and should give guidance to studies in other "wisdom" literatures.

5. Helpful studies here are found in von Rad, *Wisdom in Israel;* Schmid, *Wesen und Geschichte;* and Crenshaw, *Old Testament Wisdom.*

6. Social and cultural crisis as a crisis for wisdom thinking has been noted by Crenshaw in several of his articles. See his "Prolegomenon" as a place to begin. Jim Sanders has called my attention to the scathing attacks on "the wise" in Jeremiah as a related phenomenon. Thus the prophets may also be better understood as spokesmen during times of social crisis. Both their indebtedness to wisdom thinking and their criticisms of it might be functions of the

attempt to see again the fundamental religious structures of the community and call for their acknowledgment and actualization. An interesting study would be a comparison of Amos, Jeremiah, and Ben Sira from this point of view.

7. That the notion of order, especially the order of creation (cosmos, world), is basic to a wisdom view of things has become a commonplace in the scholarship. Zimmerli ("Struktur der Weisheit"; "Place and Limit of Wisdom") may be credited with its discovery as a theologumenon. The studies of von Rad and Kayatz explore it as a wisdom assumption and relate it to the conception of Maat in Egyptian wisdom literature. Its function for wisdom speech and ethic as an order-to-be-actualized has been investigated by Gese and Schmid (*Wesen und Geschichte*) among others. In *Gerechtigkeit als Weltordnung,* Schmid has expanded the discussion by showing that the term for "righteousness" in all of its arenas of application (social, ethical, legal, and religious) derives its power ultimately from the assumption of world order itself. The point I wish to make here is that this assumption is at first (in the precrisis situation) not explicit, not articulated, and therefore unreflected.

8. The traditional view on the "development" of wisdom "thought" includes the emergence of skepticism and cynicism in Job and Qohelet as a "stage" in the history of the tradition. This view of a developmental history was articulated clearly by Rylaarsdam in 1946. Von Rad's *Wisdom in Israel* may be seen as a study in the evolution of the structure of wisdom thinking along the lines of this developmental schema. Crenshaw's *Old Testament Wisdom* is organized also along these lines.

9. This suggestion is intended as a serious alternative to traditional scholarly assumptions about a tradition of theological wisdom. In the context of the present study, it can be no more than a suggestion. But it is hoped that the nature of the study as a whole may lend support to its plausibility and that its implications for the scholarly assessment of the wisdom literature may be provocative. I suspect that the bridge between Judaism and Hellenism was not struck at such lofty heights of theological-philosophical discourse as has frequently been assumed by scholarly orientation to the history of ideas.

10. There is a large literature on the example (paradigm, *exemplum*) in Greco-Roman literature, rhetoric, and logic. Its persuasive power (rhetorical logic) assigned it a firm place in the relatively

small list of "proofs" given repeatedly in the technical handbooks of rhetorical theory. Its logical power was derived from the Hellenic valorization of correspondence and identity, but its rhetorical power had to do with the notion of actualization in a "historical" person or case. I have not explored the rhetoricity of Ben Sira's use of characterization as paradigmatic, choosing rather to emphasize the function of the high mimetic for the construction of a mythic system. But an investigation of the rhetorical function of the "paradigms" in the hymn, in comparison to Greek usage, would be possible. A place to begin is Perelman and Albrechts–Tyteca, *New Rhetoric,* 350–410.

11. On the structure and thematic development of Sirach 24, see Conzelmann, "The Mother of Wisdom"; Hengel, *Judaism,* 1:153–62; Marböck, *Weisheit,* 34–95; Rickenbacher, *Weisheitsperikopen,* 111–72; Gilbert, "L'éloge de la Sagesse"; Skehan, "Structures in Poems on Wisdom." The earlier view of Smend (followed by Rickenbacher), that the poem consists of six strophes of six lines each, has been superseded in the studies of Marböck, Gilbert, and Skehan. Skehan offers a reconstruction of the Hebrew text and argues convincingly for the following outline on the basis of poetic and syntactical observations: 1–2 (introduction, 2 lines); 3–7 (strophe 1, 5 lines); 8–12 (strophe 2, 6 lines); 13–15 (strophe 3, 5 lines); 16–22 (strophe 4, 6 lines). Gilbert's study is concerned to follow the development of the themes of space (location) and time (history) throughout the poem and thus breaks the poem up into somewhat smaller units. But he agrees that 1–2 are introductory, he sees 3–8 as a unit (theme of space), and he notes that 16–17 are bridging verses to the invitation that follows in 19–22. There is no difficulty in agreeing with both Skehan and Gilbert if one sees that the introduction and development of themes is not limited by the strophic structure. Gilbert's discussion of the smaller units (9, 10–12, 13–14, 15, 16–17) can be organized easily in recombinations of materials that break conveniently at just those junctures suggested by Skehan's strophic outline. The one disagreement is the placement of verse 8, and it is noteworthy that it is precisely verse 8 where we can see that a "narrative slippage" of significance has occurred. My own outline agrees with Skehan's but was based upon considerations of the narrative flow of the myth as Conzelmann reconstructs it. I am delighted to learn that it falls into poem units of syntactic coherence as demonstrated by Skehan. I have included verses 16 and 17 in strophe 3, in the interest of my narrative reading of the poem (as does Marböck), but I would

not argue on this basis against the poetics demonstrated by Skehan. The recent study by Sheppard takes another tack entirely (*Wisdom as a Hermeneutical Construct*, 19–71). He is concerned to trace the allusions in the hymn to the five books of Moses in order to demonstrate his thesis about a wisdom hermeneutic as the interpretation of a canonical literature. He can show that the language and flow of the hymn evoke associations with, and in some cases actually refer to, significant moments in the epic. But in order to sustain his thesis, which appears to be the priority status of the Torah, he must reject other structuring aspects of the hymn, specifically, its intertextuality and poetic composition. The disappointment in Sheppard's book is that he intends in this way, but fails, to arrive at a definition of "wisdom" itself. I can accept Sheppard's findings about the hymn as a reading of the Hebrew epic. But that reading is enabled by a rich intertextuality that includes an Isis aretalogy as well as a poetic articulation of the wisdom myth. Sheppard avoids a discussion of the Isis aretalogy (p. 35) and does not account for the emergence of a wisdom figure and mythology in the context of wisdom thought and composition at all. He cannot say why a reading of the Torah epic has resulted in just such a hymn, that is, a wisdom myth.

12. I read the Hebrew, Greek, and Syriac of 44:2 with Skehan, "Staves and Nails."

13. This is an appropriate place to refer to the recent work by Terrien, *The Elusive Presence*. His thesis is that the notion of presence is a theme uniting the literatures of the Old and New Testaments, that it is tensive and dialectic in respect to human experience in time, and that its celebration requires cultic liturgy. He also knows about the "absence" that the liturgy of presence cannot overcome. My own use of the terms "presence" and "absence," by contrast, derives from current literary criticism.

CONCLUSION

1. It has been customary to speak about "the righteous one" in the literature of the Second Temple period as if it were a commonplace requiring no further discussion. Actually the case is just the reverse. We do not know the range of incidence, the derivation traditions, the norms for recognition, the capacity for intertextual translatability, nor the rhetorical powers of this linguistic sign. In this study, we have encountered the problem essentially in terms of

the relationship between *ḥāsîd* and *ṣaddîq*. But the relationship of both of these to *ho dikaios* is the larger issue. The notion of the "righteous one" appears as a significant datum in martyrological (Maccabees), apocalyptic (Enoch), wisdom (Wisdom of Solomon, Philo), and eschatological (New Testament) texts subsequent to Ben Sira. Why? What new vision of the world or anthropological understanding can account for its emergence? With what intention is it employed? One suspects that some refinement of Jewish understanding of the logic of the Hellenic schema of *nomos-polis-anthropos* is involved. But in order to be precise, the social system in need of being rationalized must be determined for each case.

2. The list of parallels frequently cited, often as additions to the list of psalms and other possible precursors from Jewish literature (see above Introduction, n.4), includes Jud. 5:5–21, 16:1–17; 1 Macc. 2:51 60; 3 Macc. 2:3–8, 6:2–8; 4 Macc. 16:20–23, 18:11–24; Cairo Damascus Document 2:17–3:12; Wisd. of Solomon 10; Pirke Aboth; Acts 7:2–53; Heb. 11; 1 Clement 4–19. The list could be expanded.

3. A discussion is given by Lee that includes references to Hellenistic literature, "Studies," 26–46.

4. The move away from Sirach 44–50 is marked by (a) a focus upon individuals; (b) the naming of virtues and vices exemplified; (c) emphasis upon rewards and punishments (which may include destiny patterns); and (d) final exhortation to heed or imitate.

APPENDIX A

1. The following scholars have argued for the close relationship of Sir. 42:15–43:35 with Sirach 44–50: Pfeiffer, *History,* 362; Hamp, *Das Buch Sirach,* 685; Siebeneck, "Sirach's Praise," 413; Born, *Wijheid van Sirach,* 206–7; Fransen, "Sirach 42"; Marböck, *Weisheit,* 68, 147–48; Schökel, *Proverbios y Eclesiastico,* 299. Those who have expressed reservations, argued against the literary relationship, or treated Sirach 44–50 as an independent composition include Baumgärtner, *Die literische Gattungen,* 169–73; Maertens, "L'éloge des pères"; Jansen, *Psalmendichtung,* 71; Noack, *Spätjudentum,* 41; te Stroete, "Van Henoch tot Simon," 123; Lee, "Studies," 3–9. Lee's argument is that the two units were composed independently and joined later by a redactional device (especially verse 43:33). He considers this argumentation necessary in order to establish his thesis about the encomiastic structure of Sirach 44–50. It is unfortunate that he has found it

necessary to play down many of the ensuing literary relationships between the two units, which are rich in signification even if viewed as "merely" redactional.

2. This ordering of natural phenomena has been seen as a wisdom topos. Cf. von Rad, "Job 38."

3. Marböck has seen the significance of the term "glory" as a theme of continuity between the two literary units (*Weisheit*, 148).

4. Reference may be made here to Crenshaw's discussion of theodicy in Sirach ("The Problem of Theodicy").

5. See above Introduction, n. 4.

APPENDIX B

1. The following scholars are those who regard chapter 50 as an appendix not integrally related to the hymn and probably added later: Smend, *Weisheit des Sirach,* 412; Box and Oesterley, "Book of Sirach," 479, cf. 506; Maertens, *L'éloge des pères,* 195–96 (49:14–16 is discussed as the "conclusion" of the hymn); Jacob, "L'histoire," 290; Hamp, *Das Buch Sirach,* 708; Haspecker, *Gottesfurcht,* 85, n. 94; Lamparter, *Jesus Sirach,* 211 (in *Die Apokryphen*).

2. Those who include chapter 50 within the hymnic unit are Siebeneck, "Sirach's Praise," 415; Noack, *Spätjudentum,* 42–43; Janssen, *Gottesvolk,* 16–33; te Stroete, "Von Henoch tot Simon"; Lee, "Studies", 9–19. Lee's study makes the strongest case yet for the inclusion of chapter 50. His thesis is that the hymn as a whole is an encomium on Simon himself.

3. See above chap. 1, n. 2.

APPENDIX C

1. The argumentation of Middendorp for excluding 44:16 from the original text is convincing (*Stellung,* 53–54, 109, 112, 134). See also Yadin, who agrees that 44:16 was not original, but who then reconstructs 49:14–16 to include it (*Ben Sira Scroll,* 38).

2. Middendorp, *Stellung,* 134–35.

3. Ibid., 113, 125.

4. This is especially true of Siebeneck but governs the interests of Maertens and Jacob as well. It is Middendorp's study as a whole, and especially in relation to the question of locating later additions in a different provenance, that should settle the question of Ben Sira's participation in any apocalyptic eschatology (see ibid., 113–36).

5. On Sir. 49:14–16 as a gloss, see ibid., 135; Galling, *Studien zur*

Geschichte Israels, 129, n. 3; Snaith, *Ecclesiasticus,* 248. Lee argues for the inclusion of 49:14–16 on the basis that a mention of Adam would be appropriate in an encomium ("Studies," 10–11, 272–76). He is convinced by Yadin's reconstruction of these verses to include 44:16bc, which according to Yadin, was moved to its earlier placement in subsequent manuscript redaction (*Ben Sira Scroll,* 38). Lee accounts for the list of pre-Noah figures by analogy to the practice of Hellenistic encomia that compared their subjects with "the gods from whom the subjects were said to have descended" ("Studies," 276). This thesis does have merit, but it could be used to account for a later addition of the pericope just as well. My own reflections on the significance of Adam for Ben Sira elsewhere in the book, and the special destiny characterizations for the others mentioned here, make it difficult to align this unit with the concerns that control the hymn.

6. Sir. 15:14–20; 17:1–18; 24:28; 33:10–15; 40:1.

APPENDIX D

1. Designations of office occur at 44:19 (Abraham as father); 45:15 (Aaron as priest); 45:25 (Phineas as high priest); 45:25 (David as king); 46:1 (Joshua as prophet); 46:11 (the judges); 46:13 (Samuel as prophet, judge, and priest); 48:1 (Elijah as prophet); 48:22 (Isaiah as prophet); 48:23 (Hezekiah as king); 49:4 (kings of Judah); 49:7 (Jeremiah as prophet); 49:10 (the twelve prophets); 50:1 (Simon as priest).

2. It may be significant that Ben Sira refers here to the Yahwist's account of the blessing on Noah (Gen. 8:21) rather than to the priestly writer's account of the covenant with him (Gen. 6:18–21). In our study, it has been seen that Ben Sira ranked the series of covenants in such a way as to subsume them all in the covenant of the priesthood itself. Noah functions for Ben Sira as a pre-Israel, prepriestly figure who represents the divine promise to all humankind.

3. The lack of any evidence for a wisdom or Torah piety in the hymnic characterizations is one of the more startling findings of this study. Most scholars have assumed that Jewish piety at this time would have been oriented primarily to some form of Torah righteousness. In Ben Sira's book as a whole, it is clear that the relationship between wisdom and Torah is being addressed in some constructive way. But in the hymn there is no reflection of this.

Haspecker has seen this clearly (*Gottesfurcht,* 85, n. 94); Lee has not. Lee argues that Ben Sira cited "only those specific events . . . through which the subject demonstrated his piety or fidelity to the law," and that he offered his depictions "as examples to be emulated" ("Studies," 71). This is clearly not the case. In view of these reflections about the lack of the theme of Torah righteousness in the hymn, it is of some significance that Noah is the only one for whom the designation "righteousness" is used at all. When one notices that Noah functions as a representation of all humankind, an additional and telling consideration is given. It is that the universalistic anthropological horizon in Sirach, a commonplace observation in the scholarship, is capable of combination with the ethical concept of righteousness. In the light of this usage, Ben Sira's views on righteousness and piety need to be complemented by a consideration of his views on the distinctiveness of Jewish identity. That this distinctiveness is not based upon a claim to an exclusive capacity for righteousness with its corollary division of humanity into "righteous" and "godless" peoples is the important point to remember.

Bibliography

Barthélemy, Jean Dominique, and Rickenbacher, Otto. *Konkordance zum hebräischen Sirach mit syrisch-hebräischen Index*. Göttingen: Vandenhoeck und Ruprecht, 1973.

Baumgärtner, Walter. "Die literarische Gattungen in der Weisheit des Jesus Sirach." *ZAW* 34 (1914): 161–98.

Bickermann, Elias J. "La chaîne de la tradition pharisienne," *RB* 59 (1952): 44–55.

———. *From Ezra to the Last of the Maccabees*. New York: Schocken, 1962.

Bloom, Harold. *The Anxiety of Influence: A Theory of Poetry*. Oxford: Oxford University Press, 1973.

The Book of Ben Sira: Text, Concordance, and an Analysis of the Vocabulary (in Hebrew, with an Introduction in English). Jerusalem: Academy of the Hebrew Language and the Shrine of the Book, 1973.

Born, Adrianus van den. *Wijsheid van Jesus Sirach*. Roermond: Romen en Zonen, 1968.

Box, G. H., and Oesterley, W. O. E. "The Book of Sirach." In *The Apocrypha and Pseudepigrapha of the Old Testament in English*, edited by R. H. Charles, 268–517. 1913. Reprint. London: Oxford University Press, 1971.

Burke, Kenneth. *A Grammar of Motives*. Englewood Cliffs, N.J.: Prentice-Hall, 1945 (paperback editions in 1962 by World and 1969 by University of California Press).

———. *A Rhetoric of Motives.* Engelwood Cliffs, N.J.: Prentice-Hall, 1950 (paperback editions in 1962 by World and 1969 by University of California Press).

Clark, Donald L. *Rhetoric in Greco-Roman Education.* New York: Columbia University Press, 1957.

Collins, John J. "Cosmos and Salvation: Jewish Wisdom and Apocalyptic in the Hellenistic Age." *History of Religion* 17 (1977): 121–42.

———. "The Court Tales in Daniel and the Development of Apocalyptic." *JBL* 94 (1975): 218–34.

Conzelmann, Hans. "The Mother of Wisdom." In *The Future of Our Religious Past,* edited by J. M. Robinson, 230–43. New York: Harper and Row, 1971.

Crenshaw, James L. *Old Testament Wisdom: An Introduction.* Atlanta: John Knox, 1981.

———. "The Problem of Theodicy in Sirach: On Human Bondage." *JBL* 94 (1975): 47–64.

———. "Prolegomenon." In *Studies in Ancient Israelite Wisdom,* edited by J. L. Crenshaw, 1–60. New York: KTAV, 1976.

———. "Wisdom." In *Old Testament Form Criticism,* edited by J. H. Hayes, 225–64. Trinity University Monograph Series in Religion 2. Hartford: Trinity University, 1974.

Derrida, Jacques. *Of Grammatology.* Baltimore: Johns Hopkins University Press, 1978.

Detienne, Marcel, and Vernant, Jean-Pierre. *Cunning Intelligence in Greek Culture and Society,* translated by Janet Lloyd. Atlantic Highlands, N.J.: Humanities Press, 1978.

De Vaux, Roland. *Ancient Israel: Its Life and Institutions.* 2 vols. Translated by John McHugh. 1961. Reprint. New York: McGraw-Hill, 1965.

Doran, Robert. "The Martyr: A Synoptic View of the Mother and her Seven Sons." In *Ideal Figures in Ancient Judaism,* edited by George W. E. Nickelsburg and John S. Collins, 189–221. Chico, Cal.: Scholars Press, 1980.

Döring, Klaus. *Exemplum Socratis: Studien zur Sokratesnachwirkung in der kynisch-stoischen Popularphilosophie der frühen Kaiserzeit und in frühen*

Christentum. Hermes Einzelschriften 42. Wiesbaden: Steiner, 1979.

Eberharter, Andreas. *Der Kanon des Alten Testaments zur Zeit des Ben Sira.* Münster: Aschendorf, 1911.

Eliade, Mircea. *The Myth of the Eternal Return; or, Cosmos and History.* Bollingen Series 46. Princeton: Princeton University Press, 1954 (Reprints 1965, 1971, 1974; published by Harper Torchbooks as *Cosmos and History* in 1959).

Fletcher, Angus. *The Prophetic Moment: An Essay on Spenser.* Chicago: University of Chicago Press, 1971.

Fohrer, Georg. "Sophia (B. Old Testament)." In *Theological Dictionary of the New Testament,* edited by Gerhard Kittel and Gerhard Friedrich, translated and edited by Geoffrey W. Bromiley, 7:476–96. 1971. Reprint. Grand Rapids, Mich.: Eerdmans, 1977.

Fransen, Irénée. "Cahier de bible: les oeuvres de Dieu, Sirach 42:1–50:20." *Bible et vie chrétienne* 79 (1968): 26–35.

Frye, Northrup. *Anatomy of Criticism.* Princeton: Princeton University Press, 1957.

Fuhrmann, Manfred. *Das systematische Lehrbuch.* Göttingen: Vandenhoeck und Ruprecht, 1960.

Galling, Kurt. *Studien zur Geschichte Israels in persischen Zeitalter.* Tübingen: Mohr, 1964.

Gese, Hartmut. *Lehre and Wirklichkeit in der alten Weisheit.* Tübingen: Mohr, 1958.

Gilbert, Maurice. "L'éloge de la Sagesse (Siracide 24)." *RTL* (1974): 326–48.

Gueraud, O., and Jouguet, P. *Un livre d'écolier.* Textes et documents 2. Cairo: Publications de la Société Royale Égyptienne de Papyrologie, 1938.

Hamp, Vinzenz. "Das Buch Sirach oder Ecclesiasticus." In *Echter-Bibel: Altes Testament 4,* 571–717. Wurzburg: Echter Verlag, 1959.

Haspecker, Josef. *Gottesfurcht bei Jesus Sirach.* Analecta Biblica 30. Rome: Biblical Institute, 1967.

Heinemann, Isaak. *Altjüdische Allegoristik.* Breslau: Marcus, 1935.

Hengel, Martin. *Judaism and Hellenism,* translated from the 2d German edition of 1973 by John Bowden. 2 vols. Philadelphia: Fortress, 1974.

————. "Proseuche and Synagoge." In *Tradition and Glaube: Festschrift Karl G. Kuhn,* edited by Gert Jeremias, H. W. Kuhn, J. Stegemann, 157–84. Göttingen: Vandenhoeck and Ruprecht, 1971.

Hoenig, Sidney B. "The Ancient City-Square: The Forerunner of the Synagogue." In *Aufstieg und Niedergang der römischen Welt,* edited by Wolfgang Haase, 2: 448–76. Berlin: de Gruyter, 1979.

Höffken, Peter. "Warum schwieg Jesus Sirach über Ezra." *ZAW* 87 (1975):184–202.

Jacob, Edmond. "L'histoire d'Israel vue par Sira." In *Mélanges bibliques André Robert,* 288–94. Paris: Bloud et Gay, 1957.

Jacoby, Felix. *Die Fragmente der griechischen Historiker (FGr Hist).* Leiden: Brill, 1950–62.

Jaeger, Werner. *Paideia.* Vol. 1 of *The Ideals of Greek Culture,* translated from the second German edition by Gilbert Highet. 2d ed. Oxford: Blackwell, 1954.

Jansen, H. Ludin. *Die spätjüdische Psalmendichtung: Ihr Entstehungskreis und ihr 'Sitz im Leben.'* SNVAO 2: Hist.-filos., Klasse 3. Olso: Jacob Dybwad, 1937.

Janssen, Enno. *Das Gottesvolk und seine Geschichte: Geschichtsbild und Selbstverständnis im palästinischen Schrifttum von Jesus Sirach bis Jehuda ha-Nasi.* Neukirchen-Vluyn: Neukirchener, 1971.

Jaubert, Annie. *La notion d'alliance dans le Judaisme aux abords de l'ère chrétienne.* Patristica Sorbonensia 6. Paris: Éditions du Seuil, 1963.

Kayatz, Christa. *Studien zur Proverbien 1–9.* WMANT 22. Neukirchen-Vluyn: Neukirchener, 1966.

Kennedy, George A. *The Art of Persuasion in Greece.* Princeton: Princeton University Press, 1963.

————. *The Art of Rhetoric in the Roman World.* Princeton: Princeton University Press, 1972.

————. *Classical Rhetoric.* Chapel Hill: University of North Carolina Press, 1980.

Koch, Klaus. *Die Priesterschrift.* FRLANT 71. Göttingen: Vandenhoeck und Ruprecht, 1959.

Koole, J. L. "Die Bibel des Ben Sira." In *Oudtestamentische Studien* 14: 374–96. Leiden: Brill, 1965.

Lamparter, Helmut. *Die Apokryphen I: Das Buch Jesus Sirach.* Die Botschaft des Alten Testaments 25:1. Stuttgart: Calwer, 1972.

Lausberg, Heinrich. *Handbuch der literarischen Rhetorik 1–2: Eine Grundlegung der Literaturwissenschaft.* Munich: Hüber, 1960.

Lebram, Jürgen. "Aspekte der alttestamentlichen Kanonbildung." *VT* 18 (1968):173–89.

Lee, Thomas Robert. "Studies in the Form of Sirach (Ecclesiasticus) 44–50." Ph.D. diss.: University of California, Berkeley, 1979.

Lefkowitz, Mary R. "The Poet as Hero: Fifth-Century Autobiography and Subsequent Biographical Fiction." *Classical Quarterly* 28 (1978): 459–69.

Lentricchia, Frank. *After the New Criticism.* Chicago: University of Chicago Press, 1980.

Levi, Israel, ed. *The Hebrew Text of the Book of Ecclesiasticus.* 3d ed. Semitic Studies Series 3. Leiden: Brill, 1969.

Liebreich, L. J. "The Impact of Neh. 9:5–37 on the Liturgy of the Synagogue." *HUCA* 32 (1961): 227–37.

Mack, Burton L. *Logos und Sophia: Untersuchungen zur Weisheitstheologie im hellenistischen Judentum.* SUNT 10. Göttingen: Vandenhoeck und Ruprecht, 1973.

_____. "Under the Shadow of Moses: Authorship and Authority in Hellenistic Judaism." In *SBL Seminar Papers,* 299–318. Chico, Cal.: Scholars Press, 1982.

Mack, Burton L., and Murphy, Roland. "Wisdom Literature." In *Early Post-Biblical Judaism and its Modern Interpreters,* edited by Bob Kraft and George Nickelsburg. In press.

Maertens, Dom Thierry. *L'éloge des pères.* Collection Lumiere et vie 5. Bruges: Abbaye de Saint-André, 1956.

Malherbe, Abraham. *The Cynic Epistels: A Study Edition.* Missoula, Mont.: Scholars Press, 1977.

Marböck, Johann. *Weisheit im Wandel: Untersuchungen zur Weisheitstheologie bei Ben Sira.* Bonner Biblische Beiträge 37. Bonn: Peter Hanstein Verlag, 1971.

Marrou, Henri I. *A History of Education in Antiquity,* translated from the third French edition by George Lamb. New York: Sheed and Ward, 1956.

Martin, Josef. *Antike Rhetorik: Technik und Methode.* Munich: Beck, 1974.

Middendorp, Theophil. *Die Stellung Jesu ben Siras zwischen Judentum und Hellenismus.* Leiden: Brill, 1973.

Momigliano, Arnoldo. *Alien Wisdom: The Limits of Hellenization.* Cambridge: Cambridge University Press, 1975.

———. *The Development of Greek Biography.* Cambridge: Harvard University Press, 1971.

———. "Eastern Elements in Post-Exilic Jewish and Greek Historiography." In *Essays in Ancient and Modern Historiography,* 25–35. Middletown, Conn.: *Wesleyan University Press,* 1977.

———. "The Fault of the Greeks." In *Essays in Ancient and Modern Historiography,* 9–23. Middletown, Conn.: Wesleyan University Press, 1977.

———. "Tradition and the Classical Historian." In *Essays in Ancient and Modern Historiography,* 161–177. Middletown, Conn.: Wesleyan University Press, 1977.

Nickelsburg, George W. E. *Resurrection, Immortality, and Eternal Life in Intertestamental Judaism.* Harvard Theological Studies 26. Cambridge: Harvard University Press, 1972.

———. "The Wisdom of Jesus the Son of Sirach." In *Jewish Literature between the Bible and the Mishiah,* 55–69. Philadelphia: Fortress, 1981.

Nickelsburg, George W. E., and Collins, John J. *Ideal Figures in Ancient Judaism: Profiles and Paradigms.* Septuagint and Cognate Studies 12. Chico, Cal.:Scholars Press, 1980.

Nilsson, Martin P. *Die hellenistische Schule.* Munich: Beck, 1955.

Noack, Bent. *Spätjudentum und Heilsgeschichte.* Stuttgart: Kohlhammer, 1971.

Patteson, Roy Kinneer. "A Study of the Hebrew Text of Sirach 39:27–41:24." Ph.D. diss., Duke University, Durham, N.C., 1967.

Pautrel, Raymond. "Ben Sira et le stoicisme." *Recherches de science religieuse 51* (1963): 535–49.

Pepin, Jean. *Mythe et allegorie: Les origines Grecques et les contestations Judéo-Chrétiennes.* 1958. Rev. ed. Paris: Études Augustiniennes, 1976.

Perdue, Leo G. *Wisdom and Cult.* SBL Dissertation Series 30. Missoula, Mont.: Scholars Press, 1977.

Perelman, Chaim, and Albrechts-Tyteca, L. *The New Rhetoric: A Trea-*

tise on Argumentation, translated from the 1958 French edition by John Wilkinson and Purcell Weaver. Notre Dame: Notre Dame University Press, 1971.

Pfeiffer, Robert H. *A History of New Testament Times with an Introduction to the Apocrypha.* New York: Harper and Row, 1949.

Priest, John. "Ben Sira 45:25 in the Light of the Qumran Literature." *Revue de Qumran* 5 (1964): 111–18.

Rabe, Hugo. *Aphthonii Progymnasmata.* Rhetores Graeci 10. Leipzig: Teubner, 1926.

——. *Hermogenis Opera.* Rhetores Graeci 6. Leipzig: Teubner, 1913.

Rickenbacher, Otto. *Weisheitsperikopen bei Ben Sira.* Orbis Biblicus et Orientalis 1. Göttingen: Vandenhoeck und Ruprecht, 1973.

Rist, J. M. *Stoic Philosophy.* 1969. Reprint. Cambridge: Cambridge University Press, 1977.

Roth, Wolfgang. "On the Gnomic-Discursive Wisdom of Jesus ben Sirach." *Semeia* 17 (1980): 59–79.

Rüger, Hans Peter. *Text und Textform im Hebräischen Sirach.* BZAW 112. Berlin: de Gruyter, 1970.

Rylaarsdam, J. Coert. *Revelation in Jewish Wisdom Literature.* Chicago: University of Chicago Press, 1946.

Sanders, James A. "Comparative Wisdom: L'oeuvre Terrien." In *Israelite Wisdom: Theological and Literary Essays in honor of Samuel Terrien,* edited by John G. Gammie et al., 3–14. Missoula, Mont.: Scholars Press, 1978.

——. "Hermeneutics in True and False Prophecy." In *Canon and Authority,* edited by G. W. Coats and B. O. Long, 21–41. Philadelphia: Fortress, 1977.

Schmid, H. H. *Gerechtigkeit als Weltordnung.* BhTh 40. Tübingen: Mohr, 1968.

——. *Wesen und Geschichte der Weisheit.* BZAW 101. Berlin: Töpelmann, 1966.

Schökel, Luis Alonso. *Proverbios y Eclesiastico.* Madrid: Ediciones Cristiandad, 1968.

Segal, Moshe Zevi. *Sepēr Ben Sîra' Hašālēm.* 2d ed. Jerusalem: Bialik Foundation, 1972.

Sheppard, Gerald T. *Wisdom as a Hermeneutical Construct.* BZAW 151. Berlin: de Gruyter, 1980.

Siebeneck, Robert T. "May Their Bones Return to Life! Sirach's Praise of the Fathers." *CBQ* 21 (1959): 411–28.

Skehan, Patrick W. "Staves and Nails, and Scribal Slips (Ben Sira 44:2–5)." *BASOR* 200 (1970): 66–71.

———. "Structures in Poems on Wisdom: Proverbs 8 and Sirach 24." *CBQ* 41 (1979):365–79.

Smend, Rudolph. *Die Weisheit des Jesus Sirach: Kommentar.* Berlin: Reimer, 1906.

Smith, Jonathan Z. "A Pearl of Great Price and a Cargo of Yams: A Study in Situational Incongruity." *HR* 16 (1976):1–19. Reprinted in *Imagining Religion: From Babylon to Jonestown*, 90–101. Chicago Studies in the History of Judaism. Chicago: University of Chicago Press, 1983.

Snaith, John G. "Biblical Quotations in the Hebrew of Ecclesiasticus." *JTS*, n.s. 18 (1967):1–12.

———. *Ecclesiasticus, or the Wisdom of Jesus Son of Sirach.* Cambridge Bible Commentary. London: Cambridge University Press, 1974.

Spicq, Ceslaus. "L'Ecclésiastique." In *La Sainte Bible*, edited by L. Pirot and A. Clamer, 6:529–841. Paris: Letouzey, 1951.

Stanislav, Segert. "Vorarbeiten zur Hebräischen Metrik." *Archiv Orientalni* 21 (1953): 481–524.

Steck, Odil Hannes. *Israel und das gewaltsame Geschick der Propheten.* WMANT 23. Leiden: Brill, 1967.

Te Stroete, G. "Van Henoch tot Simon: Israels geschiedenis in de 'Lof der vaderen' van Sirach 44.1–50.24." *Vruchten van de uithof: Festschrift H. A. Brongers*, edited by A. R. Hulst, 120–33. Utrecht: Theologisch Institut, 1974.

Terrien, Samuel. *The Elusive Presence: Toward a New Biblical Theology.* New York: Harper and Row, 1978.

Vattioni, Francesco. *Ecclesiastico: Testo ebraico con apparato critico e versioni greca, latina, e siriaca.* Naples: Instituto Orientale di Napoli, 1968.

Volkmann, Richard. *Die Rhetorik der Griechen und Römer in systematischer Übersicht.* 1885. Reprint. Darmstadt: Wissenschaftliche Buchgesellschaft, 1963.

Von Rad, Gerhard. "Job 38 and Ancient Egyptian Wisdom." *The Problem of the Hexateuch and Other Essays*, 281–91. New York: McGraw-Hill, 1966.

_____. *Wisdom in Israel*, translated from the 1970 German edition. Nashville: Abingdon, 1978.

Walz, Christianus, ed. *Rhetores Graeci*. Vol. 1. Stuttgart: Cottage, 1832.

Whybray, R. N. *The Intellectual Tradition in the Old Testament*. ZAW Beiheft 135. New York: de Gruyter, 1974.

Yadin, Yigael. *The Ben Sira Scroll from Masada with Introduction, Emendations and Commentary*. Jerusalem: Israel Exploration Society, 1965.

Ziebarth, Erich. *Aus der Antiken Schule: Sammlung griechischer Texte auf Papyrus, Holztafeln, Ostraka*. Lietzmann's Kleine Texte 65. Bonn: Marcus and Weber, 1910.

Ziegler, Joseph, ed. *Septuaginta, 12/2: Sapientia Iesu Filii Sirach*. Vetus Testamentum Graecum Auctoritate Societatis Litterarum Gottingensis editum. Göttingen: Vandenhoeck und Ruprecht, 1965.

Zimmerli, Walther. "The Place and Limit of Wisdom in the Framework of Old Testament Theology." *SJT* 17 (1964):146–58. Reprinted in *Ancient Israelite Wisdom*, edited by J. L. Crenshaw, 314–26. New York: KTAV, 1976.

_____. "Zur Struktur der alttestamentlichen Weisheit." *ZAW* 51 (1933):177–204.

Subject Index

Index to
Biblical Texts
Cited